The Improvisational Cook

**OTHER BOOKS BY SALLY SCHNEIDER**

*A New Way to Cook*
*The Art of Low-Calorie Cooking*

PHOTOGRAPHS BY MARIA ROBLEDO

# The Improvisational Cook

## Sally Schneider

WILLIAM MORROW
An Imprint of HarperCollins Publishers

for David

# Contents

Using different cheeses and seasonings in a basic formula for Cheese Crisps (page 84) leads to a variety of different flavors, textures, and uses.

# Introduction

Once you understand how a basic technique or recipe works, you can start to improvise on it.

Improvising on a basic brownie batter yields
Chocolate Wonders (page 332), Chocolate Planets
(page 334), and Bittersweet Black Pepper Brownie
Cake (page 334).

Improvisational cooking is thrilling. It's the key to ease and pleasure in cooking, freedom from recipes and set lists of ingredients, and liberation from other less tangible constraints: perfectionism, the voices of "I can't," fear of what will happen and maybe go wrong. Improvisation, by its very nature, is so unstructured, so vast in its possibility, and seemingly so dependent on an explorer's brand of courage that the notion stops many cooks in their tracks. It is the way I hear most people would like to cook, yet they find the process daunting and overwhelming. I suppose this is why it has been largely ignored by cookbooks, why a book on improvisation might seem to be a contradiction in terms. Improvisation runs contrary to any sort of codification; it springs out of a moment in a process that remains, mostly, mysterious.

How, then, do you teach a creative process that is by definition amorphous, undefined?

My approach—the approach of *The Improvisational Cook*—is to point *a way in* to improvising, using examples of the kinds of thought processes, formulas, and associations that cooks regularly employ. Doing so encourages once-intimidated cooks to set out on their own path of discovery and pleasure. It's how most of the creative cooks I know started, and it's the approach that I've found to be most popular in my classes: part demystification of what improvisation actually is, part deconstruction of false notions that can hold a cook back, part insight into ways to think about cooking and ingredients.

Most people who are afraid to improvise are simply stymied by their lack of understanding of how things work—how ingredients interact with one another to create the magic of taste. Once you understand how a basic technique or recipe works, you can start to improvise on it. This process is ongoing and lasts a lifetime, but you can start anywhere. And that is the premise of this book: Understanding the underlying principles and logic of a recipe and the possibilities for changing it gives you the tools and insights you need to find your own voice and cook improvisationally.

Improvisation is a way the busy everyday cook can cook with what is on hand, and with pleasure.

## How to Use This Book and Begin Improvising

*The Improvisational Cook* is a collection of appealing, easy recipes; each is a lesson in improvisation, generating other appealing, easy recipes, one cascading from another. Each main recipe is a worthy addition to a home cook's repertoire, as well as a perfect jumping-off point from which to improvise. Then you'll find a section called "Understanding," an analysis of the recipe's internal structure and logic that teaches exactly how it works, along with some suggested elements that you can play with, alter, adapt, embellish, improvise. The main recipe is followed by a handful of improvisations I've created using the basic approach—examples, really— to illustrate some of the possibilities outlined in the "Understanding" section and a bit of the associative process that occurs when improvising. Hopefully it will inspire your own improvisations.

Use a recipe as a jumping-off point for improvisation.

The recipes and improvisations are intentionally simple and made with readily available ingredients. They are meant to show that cooking and improvising are not solely the realm of driven chefs and wildly creative cooks; improvisation is a way the busy everyday cook can quickly get dinner on the table with what is on hand, and with pleasure. You can follow the recipes and notated improvisations as written, use them as a foundation to which you add your own flavorings and embellishments, or set out on your own to improvise whatever new idea they've spurred, and see what happens.

In addition, you'll find a lot of resource material in *The Improvisational Cook*: an exploration of The Creative Mind-Set, a section titled Where Does Inspiration Come From? and ways of dealing with Accidents and the Unexpected; how to learn about flavor and "what goes with what," including A Guide to Classic Flavor Affinities; and tips on organizing your kitchen to make improvising easier with Long-Keeping Staples for Pantry, Refrigerator, and Freezer and (Almost) Essential Equipment.

Using *The Improvisational Cook*, you'll learn a way of cooking that's fun, unfussy, fluid, and truly pleasurable. Everyday cooking—once routine— becomes a creative endeavor.

Leftover Caramelized Onions (page 143) transmute into a Real Onion Dip (page 143) to serve with potato chips.

Magic Peppers (page 89) chopped with herbs, olives, pine nuts, and other embellishments become a bruschetta (page 91) and a free-form tart (page 90).

# How Improvising Works

Creativity involves relinquishing total control and allowing an idea to develop organically.

## The Creative Mind-Set

Much of the process of improvising involves cultivating a mind-set—open, associative, resourceful—that spurs ideas and lets them flow. It's being willing to ask: What would happen if? What would happen if I seasoned the pork roast with Moroccan spices instead of Italian-inspired garlic and sage? What would happen if I paired prosciutto with roasted apricots? Then *you just go ahead and try out your idea*, experiment with an open mind and without fear of the outcome, the mess you make, and the possibly imperfect results. This flies in the face of our notions of what cooking is "supposed" to be and look like—a stylish setting, an orderly series of events, one following the other, an in-control, perfectly composed chef.

Improvising is being willing to ask: What would happen if? and Why not? What would happen if I flavored popcorn with a sage and garlic oil, rosemary, caramelized shallots, or smoky bacon instead of the usual butter?

Improvisational cooking demands that you shift your thinking, or at least temporarily put rigid notions and fears aside. This is true learning: gaining information and, more often than not, successes from being willing to make mistakes and a mess or two. Often what inhibits people from doing this is that they worry about what everyone else—their guests or family members or the omnipresent ghosts of stylish media cooks—will think of them if what they serve is not "perfect" or deviates from some other unrealistic standard.

Asking yourself What would happen if? and the attendant Why not? can challenge the fiercest inhibition: fear of listening to your own senses and of expressing your unique sensibility, or "voice." Ultimately, cooking is about taste, about what you think tastes good and like to eat. Recipes, including the ones in this book, are really just guides, one cook's notes about how to cook something.

Cooking creatively is about "listening" to what your senses are telling you about your ingredients and acting on your intuition. Tasting a summer apricot, you detect the faintest flavor of herbs—and decide to roast the apricots with some thyme leaves and lemon zest to bring out those inherent flavors. The flavors of a chicken in red wine you've made seem muted after you roll a taste on your tongue, "listening" to the way it hits each part, you add some cherry-infused balsamic vinegar—a previous improvisation—to lift the flavors. Or, noting the dried-fruit quality of an olive paste you are making, you add some dried currants to accentuate the fruitiness and offset the olives' saltiness.

Creativity involves relinquishing total control and allowing an idea to develop organically. Often this means that you start out with one thing in mind but, as you cook, the idea shifts and evolves until you find yourself on a different path than the one you started on. If you don't demand that you, or your food, be "perfect," you'll learn from experience, gradually absorbing what you need to know and gaining greater control over flavors, textures, and deliciousness.

Recipes, including the ones in this book, are really just guides, one cook's notes about how to cook something. Ultimately cooking is about what you think tastes good and like to eat.

9

## Accidents and the Unexpected

Like life, cooking is a dynamic, imperfect, often messy process in which unexpected events come into play. Accidents happen. We reach for vanilla yogurt instead of plain to make a savory basil-scented sauce. We inadvertently roast something at a slow 300°F instead of a searing 500°F. Or we were sure that an improvisation would go in one direction, and it veered off into another. Although we tend to view accidents as things to avoid, they often bring unexpectedly delicious results, forcing the question What would happen if? by giving us the answer before we ask it and, with it, knowledge. So, the result of my leaving a pot of sweet pepper and onion stew on a low flame much longer than intended was a dense, rich pepper jam with deliciously caramelized flavors—a lesson in the slow evaporation

of liquid producing concentrated flavors and the possibilities for using peppers like fruit in a dessert or sweet. Inadvertently pouring roasted hazelnut oil on steamed asparagus instead of my usual extra virgin olive oil taught me a new flavor affinity. One of the most illustrious accidents-turned-into-gold is the molten chocolate cake so popular in restaurants. It is said to have been "discovered" when a chef cut into an undercooked chocolate cake that had been taken out of the oven before its center had set. The warm molten chocolate batter that spilled onto the plate was a revelation in texture and flavor.

Although sometimes accidents and errant improvisations don't yield dazzling results, chances are they will be pretty good. Most of the time our notion of "failure" is much worse than the dish itself—and has nothing to do with what our guests are enjoying. People are generally so happy to be cooked for that they are much less judgmental than you think. I find that telling my guests what I was trying to do, the thinking behind it and the challenge, and enlisting their ideas and feedback makes them part of the process and engages them in a completely different way. The not-so-dazzling dish suddenly becomes much more interesting.

However, if the possibility of a chancy outcome is too much to bear, a dinner party where you really want to dazzle your guests might not be the place to improvise. It's probably better to cook a dish you feel comfortable with to ensure success. A good strategy is to gauge the riskiness of an improvisation—that is, how unsure you are of how it will turn out, or, perhaps, how in control you feel of the process—against the certainty you need in the outcome.

Improvising is not something you have to do all the time, but it is a wonderful practice to build into your life. What you will have gained from an unexpected outcome is another chunk of understanding about how things work that you'll find yourself applying down the line in another dish, or in refining one that wasn't an immediate success. Through this process you'll gradually accumulate a body of knowledge that allows you to improvise freely and easily.

Although we tend to view accidents as something to avoid, they often bring unexpectedly delicious results. Overcooking Sweet or Savory Quinces in White Wine and Honey (page 72) yields an Impromptu Jam (page 311).

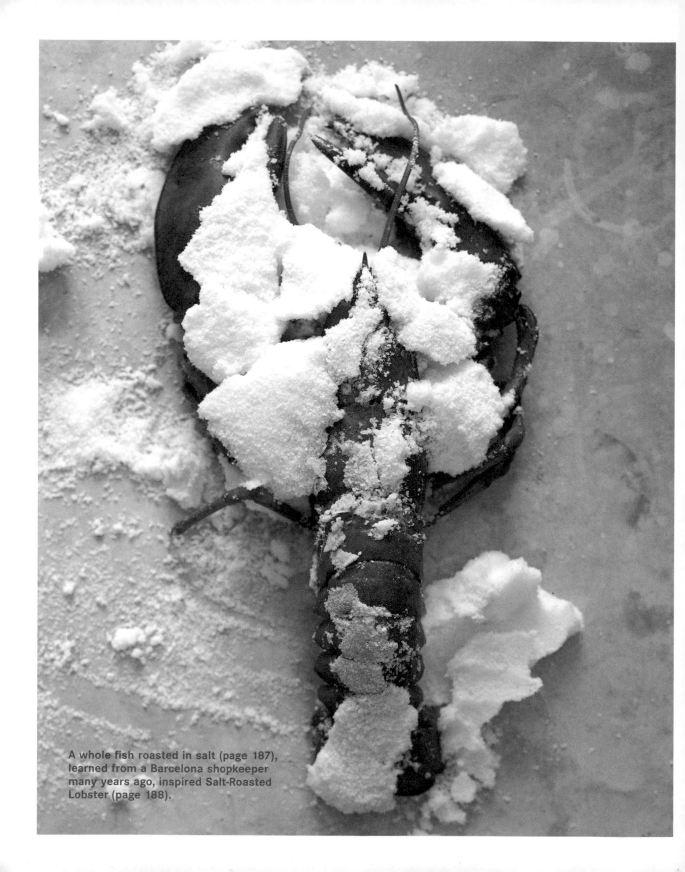

A whole fish roasted in salt (page 187), learned from a Barcelona shopkeeper many years ago, inspired Salt-Roasted Lobster (page 188).

# Where Does Inspiration Come From?

Creative cooks are by nature foragers; they forage for ideas as they do for great ingredients. And the ideas come from many places: from dishes that they've tasted in restaurants or at another cook's table, that they've seen on television cooking shows or in their travels, or that flow up from memories. Creative cooks routinely cannibalize other cooks' recipes, extracting a kernel of an idea or a combination of flavorings or a technique to use in their own improvisations. If you could track the thought processes that went into an inventive cook's dish, you'd find an assemblage of ideas taken from many sources, unified and made artful by the cook's own sensibility. This is because inspiration is largely a process of association. Something sparks an idea, and that idea sparks another, and another, and so on until a basic concept is formed. It's rarely a straight course, but, rather, a zigzagging flux of ideas, memories, snippets of recipes, and hungers that ends up inspiring a dish.

Many cooks get inspiration from walking though a market and seeing what looks freshest and most appealing, what "speaks" to them. Memory almost always comes into play. A cook might see some blackberries in the late August farmers' market. Tasting one, she remembers her grandmother's wild blackberry jam with a faintly herbal flavor. She's been hankering for pie for days, and these associations inspire her to make a blackberry tart; she tries scenting the blackberries with a sprig of thyme to impart the wild flavor she remembered so vividly. The tart indeed has the flavors of her wild blackberry memories, and she has discovered in the course of her improvisation how to turn "tame" berries into wild.

Other ideas spark from what's in front of you or in your field of vision. My friend Anne Disrude, who has more fantastic inspirations than just about any cook I know, got the idea to smoke olives one evening as she stood by her new grill-smoker drinking a glass of wine, waiting for the wood fire to burn to coals. A bowl of olives sat on the small table nearby, in her field of vision with grill and wood smoke. "What would happen if I smoked some olives?" she asked herself. She poured olive oil over the

Inspiration comes from many places, through a mysterious process that is open to all of us.

Creative cooks routinely cannibalize other cooks' recipes, extracting a kernel of an idea or a combination of flavorings or a technique to use in their own improvisations. Mario Batali's Lemon Oregano Jam becomes the jumping-off point for numerous improvisations (pages 76 to 80).

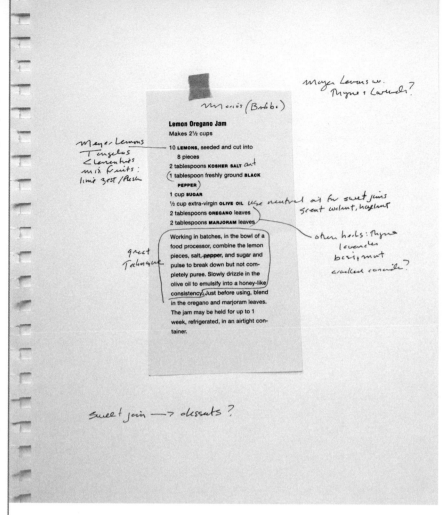

olives and put them in the smoker then and there to produce something completely original: divine smoke-scented olives and an even more divine smoke-scented olive oil, which she used to flavor and sauce all manner of foods in further improvisations.

Fueled by the hunger for something delicious, necessity or limitation often kindles an inspired idea when you have no choice but to cook with what you have. In a dreary winter mini-mart in a small town, the only fresh vegetables I found were yellow onions. What could I do with them in the spartan kitchen of the house I was renting? My thinking went something like this: The best and simplest thing to do with onions is slice them and sauté them in butter.… I began to imagine sautéing onions and then the ways I had eaten them: as pissaladière, Provençal France's delectable onion-anchovy-and-olive pizza … as a Southern-style embellishment for pan-seared pork chops … cooked long and slowly with vinegar to make a savory jam to eat on sandwiches. Sautéed onions reminded me of sautéed shallots, which I'd once used to fill an omelet, served with a simple sauce of butter and white wine vinegar splashed together in a hot pan until they emulsified (an idea I'd read in a cookbook and mentally filed years before I tried it). I'd just been given some beautiful eggs from a friend's farm … and butter and some homemade cider vinegar were among the few ingredients in my minimal larder…. What if I plugged onions into the shallot omelet idea and made a caramelized onion omelet with a brown butter–cider vinegar sauce?

These sparking memories and ideas took no more than a few moments and resulted in a perfect, simple dinner out of limited raw materials.

One of the most exciting sources of inspiration is collaboration with another cook. You bring your mutual sensibilities to bear in a kind of spontaneous free association that starts with a simple conversation. Ideas build and spark each other, one dropped for a better refinement, another added, until gradually the concept for a dish emerges.

"What shall we do with these beautiful artichokes?" one cook asks. His friend thinks…. "Remember those deep-fried artichokes?"

"Oh yeah, I love those, but I don't want to deal with deep-frying. I don't have enough oil anyway. Maybe we can panfry some."

"What if we pare the artichokes way down and slice them, braise them in olive oil, then panfry them to give them a crispy edge?"

"That's a great idea. Let's fry sage leaves and thin slices of garlic in the oil first; they'll flavor the oil and become a crispy garnish."

"I'll warm this little goat cheese in the oven while we're doing it. It'll be perfect with the artichokes."

And often ideas seem simply to come out of nowhere. Three-star Provençal chef Roger Vergé said that many of his ideas came to him while he was flying airplanes. Another chef I know routinely dreamed the dishes he served in his restaurant. I've figured out recipes walking down the street, swimming, in the shower, even napping. Inspiration comes about from a mostly unchartable confluence of associations, hungers, and memories, a mysterious process that is open to us all.

A summer market's offerings illustrate the flavor principle: What grows together, goes together.

# Understanding Flavor

As infinite as the
world's ingredients
and flavors may seem,
a great starting point
for learning about
them is a simple
principle:
What grows together,
goes together.

## Learning What Goes with What

Every culture's cuisine has its own unique flavor combinations—marriages of herbs, spices, or aromatics with local meats, poultry, seafood, vegetables, fruit. They make up the palette of everyday cooking and are the easiest way to improvise on a dish or technique: Change the flavorings to change the dish. Cooks learn how to use these combinations through experience: through their own cooking and experimenting, eating in restaurants or at other cooks' tables, traveling, reading cookbooks. A cook

Olive oil, garlic, white wine, and peperoncino, the flavor base of the Tuscan Island–Style Shellfish Stew (page 174), can be used to improvise all kinds of fish and shellfish dishes.

learns, for example, what ginger, garlic, and chile pepper do for a dish by eating Chinese food; that sage and garlic have an affinity from tasting Italian-style pork roasts or ravioli scented with those seasonings; that vanilla goes with lobster from reading that it does so in a cookbook by the chef Alain Senderens. And just by trying out different combinations, cooks gradually create their own unique palette of flavors, which defines their cooking.

As infinite as the world's ingredients and flavors may seem, a great starting point for learning about them is a simple principle: *What grows together, goes together*. Strawberries and rhubarb, which arrive together in spring are a classic combination for tarts, pies, and cobblers. The tender herbs that grow in spring and summer, such as basil, chives, tarragon, and mint, have affinities with one another and, used singly or in combination, with just about every vegetable that grows at that time, such as asparagus, peas, and artichokes. Tomatoes go with basil and garlic as well as with the eggplant and peaches that appear at the same time in summer. The traditional Thanksgiving dinner brings together the bounty of the fall market: winter squashes in side dishes, cranberries in sauce for the turkey, apples in pie, chestnuts in stuffing.

"What grows together, goes together" also applies to the mainstay foods that have been grown in a region for generations, often reflecting the different populations who have settled there. Dishes made with cornmeal, smoked ham, and beans are endlessly improvised year-round in the American South, where they were traditionally grown. The rich, spicy cuisine of Louisiana reflects the French and Creole influences on local ingredients, such as crayfish, shrimp, and oysters. The cuisine of France's Normandy region is defined by its apples and rich dairy products, Provençal cooking by the herbs that grow abundantly there—thyme, rosemary, basil, lavender—as well as fish, lamb, rabbit, and chicken, and the local wines.

Combining foods of a growing region and/or season is a principle you can rely on when you want to improvise (as well as the great joy of shopping in a seasonal farmers' market). You will rarely go wrong. Many people nowadays have only had the experience of shopping in a supermarket, where foods, such as tasteless berries in January and year-round asparagus, are trucked in and shipped from other growing seasons. They aren't familiar with what a season's foods and flavors are. It takes con-

> Combining foods of a growing region and/or season is a principle you can rely on when you want to improvise. You will rarely go wrong.

Coffee, vanilla, and cognac all have affinities with chocolate and intensify its flavor in desserts such as Chocolate Planets (page 334).

scious, and usually pleasurable, effort to find ways to become aware of them—for example, by seeking out farmers' markets that sell local, in-season foods or by reading food magazines that focus on the seasons. Just being open to the idea of seasonal foods tends to bring them into awareness; it's as though a whole world of possibilities were suddenly made visible.

Similarly, lack of familiarity with common flavor affinities keeps many willing cooks, especially novices, from improvising. They simply have not had enough experience with herbs, spices, and aromatics to be able to draw on them easily. A good way to learn is to copy flavoring combinations you've tasted or read about in cookbooks and try them out with different foods. Gradually, you'll get a sense of what works with what. Most cooks eventually develop a repertoire of flavorings that they apply in various

The sweet spicy flavors of root vegetables prompted the unorthodox addition of vanilla bean in Root Vegetable Puree with Vanilla (page 101).

ways to different foods, toward different ends. For example, you'll find the combination of garlic and sage used in this book to flavor beans, popcorn, and olive oil. Vanilla beans, brown sugar, and butter find their way into many cakes and cookies.

A Guide to Classic Flavor Affinities on page 348 illustrates a fragment of the possibilities from classic flavor combinations from around the world. Comparing the essential flavorings from different countries, you'll see that many of the same ingredients are used, but in different balances. Use the guide as a place to start learning about flavoring affinities, as a reminder of ones you know and have forgotten, and/or as an inspiration for creating new ones. As you become familiar with them, they'll become part of you, ready to call upon when improvising.

# Some Classic Flavor Affinities

(To learn more, see A Guide to Classic Flavor Affinities, page 348)

Lime, Chile, Shallot, Ginger, and Basil

**BOTTOM LEFT**
Ginger, Cilantro, Garlic, and Star Anise

**BOTTOM RIGHT**
Tarragon, Chives, Parsley, and Lemon Zest

TOP LEFT
**Olive Oil, Garlic, Peperoncino, and Sage**

TOP RIGHT
**Tomato, Saffron, Orange Zest, and
Fennel Seed**

**Ancho Chile, Ground Chile, Cinnamon,
Cumin, Cocoa, and Oregano**

## Making Flavors Come to Life:
## Salt and Other Absolutely Essential Seasonings

Salt is the universal key to unlocking inherent flavor. Often a less-than-dazzling improvisation is simply lacking enough salt.

Many people are fearful of salting because for years salt was vilified as a health risk. Like most things, salt can pose problems if you eat too much of it, which invariably results from eating lots of processed and fast foods. Exclude these high-sodium foods from your diet, and the uninhibited salting of home-cooked foods generally falls within reasonable limits.

I recommend two kinds of salt. For everyday, all-purpose cooking, use *kosher salt*, an inexpensive, additive-free salt with a coarse, uniform texture. (Regular iodized table salt has a rather muddy flavor and fine grain that is difficult to sprinkle accurately.) After a dish is cooked, sprinkling a few grains of a *medium-coarse sea salt* will bring out nuances of flavor in the dish and add a charming visual element. There is a vast range of sea salts available, from the delicate *fleur de sel* of Brittany to Hawaii's pink *Alaea salt*. Tasting different salts will reveal their subtle differences. *Maldon salt* from England is excellent, readily available, and has an appealing flaky texture.

Salt can come from other ingredients in a dish as well, such as dry-cured ham or salt-cured anchovies. Soy sauce and fermented fish sauce provide the salt in Asian dishes.

Sometimes a dish just needs a little acidity to make all its flavors come to life. A *few drops of lemon juice* or *a mellow vinegar such as Banyuls vinegar* from Banyuls-sur-Mer in southern France—my favorite all-purpose vinegar—will brighten and clarify flavors and increase the perceived saltiness of a food.

A *pinch of sugar or other sweetener* can help to round out flavors and bring forward the natural sweetness in ingredients, especially useful for vegetables with less than peak flavor. It will balance acidity, soften any bitterness, and reduce the intensity of saltiness.

How do you know the right amount of salt to use? The best answer I've

Coarse kosher salt, sea salt, and a homemade herb salt (page 46) are essential seasonings in the improvisational kitchen.

heard comes from Thomas Keller, chef of The French Laundry and Per Se: "If you taste salt in a dish, it's too salty." This goes for any of the other essential flavor enhancers as well. Season lightly, tasting as you go, until you've found the right level of salt, acid, or sweetener that makes flavors bloom without your being conscious of them.

Beyond these essential seasonings, there are endless numbers of ingredients that can bring out the flavor of food. For example, a smidgeon of cayenne or a bit of hot chile pepper (not enough to actually taste spicy) will sharpen the flavors in a dish and intensify its saltiness; a few drops of kirschwasser, the clear cherry brandy, will heighten the flavors of tomatoes and apricots. A few drops of orange flower water will illuminate

25

the flavor of citrus fruits and, curiously, the flavor of butter in butter cookies and plain cakes. You'll discover them through experience.

I'm often asked how to tell when something is "missing" in a dish. Tasting is a kind of "listening," where you focus your senses to perceive the balance of flavors in a dish. If it tastes a little flat or muted, and your response isn't an immediate Yes, this is good! it needs seasoning.

If you are unsure how to season a dish, mix a pinch of the flavoring you are thinking of adding into a spoonful or a small bowl of the mixture, then taste it. You'll get a rough idea of whether your approach is viable or not. Taste as many samples as you need to guide you.

To get a rough idea of whether a flavoring is viable, mix up a tiny taste and sample it, as in this sweet potato puree improvisation in progress.

26

Desserts also rely on a few critical seasonings to bring out their best flavor. *Sugar, in its various forms from white to dark brown, and other sweeteners such as honey and maple syrup* are the essential flavor enhancers, unlocking the potential in many dessert ingredients, including several that would be inedible without it, such as chocolate, quinces, and sour cherries. *Vanilla bean* heightens the sweetness and perfume of fruits, chocolate, and dairy products, giving them a rich, haunting flavor. Almost all fruits are enhanced by a teaspoon or two of *lemon juice;* the acidity balances the sweetness and makes a fruit's perfume more vivid.

Desserts also rely on a few critical seasonings to bring out their best flavor. Lemon juice, sugar, and vanilla bean bring out the flavors of Roasted Pears (page 86).

# The Improvisational Kitchen

The beauty of improvisation is its willing reliance on what is available for inspiration. It liberates the cook from being bound by set lists of ingredients and equipment. But it becomes a whole lot easier to cook creatively and freely if you have some basic tools and ingredients on hand.

# The Essential Pantry:
# Long-Keeping Ingredients as Opportunity

Most good cooks stock their kitchen with an array of staple ingredients they can fall back on without having to run to the market at the last minute. These are ingredients that keep a long time so they only have to be replenished once in a while. They include not only shelf staples such as pasta, dried herbs and spices, and canned plum tomatoes, but also foods that keep for weeks in the refrigerator, such as root vegetables, eggs, aged cheeses, even some fresh herbs. (You'll find a list of Long-Keeping Staples for Pantry, Refrigerator, and Freezer on page 358.) You can improvise marvelous dishes from this essential pantry alone, or use elements of it to transform fresh items you've picked up at the market, the meats, poultry, vegetables, or fruits that you feel like cooking or that are in season. You won't have to shop to cook unless you feel like it, and then you'll only need to pick up a few things.

> With a well-stocked pantry, you'll be able to apply the key strategy that good cooks live by.

With a well-stocked pantry, you'll be able to apply the key strategy that good cooks live by: *Gear your cooking to what looks best in the market that day* —without having to do an extensive shopping. For example, you have all the staples needed to make a basic pasta dish: pasta, olive oil, garlic, Parmesan cheese. You go to the market to purchase some eggplants, but find that their skin is marked with soft, brown spots, indicating that they're over the hill. Instead, you browse the produce section for other vegetables to improvise with and find some beautiful escarole. Then an unplanned stop in your fish market on the way home yields some vibrantly fresh red snapper fillets and you switch gears altogether. Knowing that the staples you need to embellish the fish are on hand, you make a quick plan to slow-roast it and serve it with a brown butter and balsamic sauce, jazzed up with thin slivers of lemon zest; you'll serve escarole sautéed in garlic on the side, and save the pasta idea for another night.

This is one of the great pleasures of cooking: to be in the moment, cooking with what the season and nature is offering at that moment.

Elemental Carbonara (Pasta with a Fried Egg and Parmigiano, page 135), improvised from long-keeping staples.

## Equipment: What You Really Need to Cook

You don't need a lot of equipment, a stylish kitchen, or the latest gadgets to cook well, though it helps a lot to have the basics. The truth is, most cooks use the same array of equipment over and over: a couple of knives, skillets, pots, bowls, tongs, and so on. (For a bottom-line, no-frills list of equipment, see (Almost) Essential Equipment, page 360.) If you lack a piece of equipment, there is almost always a way to improvise what you need by using what you have in a new way.

"Makeshift" is a wonderfully expressive term for making a shift, shifting your thinking to come up with a creative solution that accomplishes

A makeshift pestle can be crafted from a smooth heavy stone, doorknob, heavy jar, or can.

the task at hand in an unexpected way. When you find you don't have a particular piece of equipment you need, you improvise a substitute, tailoring the recipe as necessary to accommodate it.

When it comes to equipment, makeshift is an antidote to the inhibiting, very modern reliance on matching sets of pots and a stylish kitchen outfitted like a kitchen supply store. It cuts to the heart of the matter: Rather than letting a piece of equipment stand in the way, you come up with a makeshift solution, as resourceful people have for eons, so you can still make the delicious dish you were planning. For example, if you want to make the Crisp Brick-Fried Chicken with Rosemary and Whole Garlic Cloves on page 212, and you don't have an iron skillet to weight the bird; you could use a flat-bottomed pot filled with cans or a rock from your backyard. Use a wine bottle for a rolling pin or a coffee cup for a ladle. You can get by just fine with one good sharp knife. Once I heard of a woman who pulled out her ironing board when she needed more counter space.

Because I often find myself cooking in sparsely equipped kitchens when I travel, I've come up with an array of makeshift solutions over the years. These examples will give you a sense of possibility for devising your own makeshift equipment when you need it. There's only one rule: whatever works.

**citrus juicer** A dinner fork. Halve a lemon or lime and hold over a bowl; press the tines of the fork into a half and rotate the fruit to ream it.

**cookie/biscuit cutter** A clean glass with a thin lip or a clean can (with the label removed).

**double boiler/bain-marie** Fit a medium saucepan with a bowl just large enough to be suspended over, not in, water in the pan. Cover with a lid. (Alternatively, use ramekins or 1-inch balls compressed out of foil as "feet" to elevate the bowl.)

**Flame Tamer/heat diffuser** Use an iron skillet set on a burner. Place the saucepan inside it.

**meat pounder** A flat rock, the side of a cleaver, or a flat-bottomed iron skillet.

**mortar** Stainless steel bowl. You can also mash and crush foods right on the work surface.

**pestle** Smooth heavy stone, doorknob, heavy jar, or can.

Makeshift is a wonderfully expressive term for "making a shift," shifting your thinking to come up with a creative solution that accomplishes the task at hand in an unexpected way. There's only one rule: whatever works.

# Some Strategies for Improvising

**Substitute one set of flavors in a recipe for another.**
Change the flavorings in Ethereal Brown Sugar Butter Cookies
(page 302) to create other interesting cookies using vanilla
bean, Earl Grey tea, coffee, citrus zest, or maple sugar.

Creative cooks often
rely on simple strategies
to come up with
improvisations. These
strategies are second
nature, part of a natural,
often unconscious,
thought process; several
might be combined
to make one dish.
For the novice, they are
a great way to begin
cooking improvisationally.

**Change the traditional presentation of a recipe.** In Deconstructed Caesar Salad (page 58), romaine leaves are left whole rather than sliced; Parmesan cheese is shaved rather than grated; and garlic-rubbed toasts replace the traditional croutons.

**Learn some versatile "basic" preparations you can use for many dishes.** Slow-Roasted Tomatoes (page 95) quickly morph into an instant Slow-Roasted Tomato Sauce (page 96) for pasta, as well as a tart (page 97), a soup (page 96), or jam (page 97).

**Exchange similar ingredients in a recipe.** Green soybeans, instead of the usual lima or fava beans, make an unusual sauté with asparagus and sugar snap peas (page 138).

38

**Improvise dishes using separately made elements.**
This fish sandwich (page 207) is the sum of several
simple parts: Crisp Panfried Fish Fillets (page 204),
Bacon Mayonnaise (page 67), and Shallot (or Garlic)
Toasts (page 274).

**Know a few basic formulas into which you can plug different ingredients.** Impromptu Watercress Salad-Soup with Smoked Duck Breast and Ginger (page 105) is a play on a basic soup-making formula: broth + vegetable + protein + flavoring element.

**View leftovers as raw materials for improvising.** Crackling Cornmeal Cakes with Sour Cream and Shredded Close-Roasted Meat (page 241) improvised from leftover Cornmeal Cake batter (page 264) and shredded leftover Close-Roasted Pork with Ancho, Cinnamon, and Cocoa (page 235).

40

Recipes

# SAUCES, CONDIMENTS, AND SEASONINGS

# Fragrant Herb Salt

- Real Garlic Salt
- Moroccan-Style Seasoning with Cinnamon, Coriander, and Cumin
- Mole-Inspired Seasoning with Ancho, Cinnamon, and Cocoa
- Fragrant Szechuan Pepper Seasoning
- Duck, Rabbit, Game, and Charcuterie Seasoning
- All-Purpose Aromatic Pepper

Years ago, a fragment of a recipe–a vibrantly flavored salt used to flavor a pork roast–became the model for an approach to seasoning that has informed everything I've cooked since. The salt, which had been minced with garlic, rosemary, and sage and rubbed into a pork loin several hours before roasting, yielded an astonishingly flavorful roast that was gently perfumed to its core with herbs. It offered some essential lessons, a eureka moment about salt.

I learned that you could flavor salt and count on it to carry that flavor into the flesh, like a wick in an oil lamp. I also learned the wisdom of salting certain foods ahead, which flew in the face of the widely accepted rationale that since salt draws moisture out of foods, salting should only be done at the last minute to keep food from drying out and ensure a dry surface to sear and caramelize properly. In fact, salting meat and poultry ahead not only adds flavor, it slightly cures and tenderizes the flesh, making it more succulent.

After using this seasoning many times on pork, chicken, quail, and guinea hen, I began to vary the herbs and then gradually to flavor the salt with other elements, as my improvisations here illustrate. (For recipes with seasoning salts, see Herb-Scented Roast Leg of Lamb, Venison Style, page 253, and the improvisations on pages 254 to 256, notably Double Pork Tenderloin Roast with Rosemary-Sage Salt.)

Salt is the most essential of seasonings and the prime mover in just about every recipe. When used far enough in advance of cooking, its penetrating nature becomes the vehicle that carries flavors into the food, a catalyst that harmonizes them. The flavorings you can add to salt are limited only by your imagination: fresh or dried herbs such as rosemary, sage, thyme, savory, tarragon, basil, chives; aromatics such as garlic, shallots, chile peppers; zests such as orange, lemon, yuzu, Meyer lemon; spices such as fennel seed, coriander, sweet spices, peppercorns; and spice mixtures, from curry powder and cinnamon-scented Moroccan-inspired spice mixes to Mexican-inspired mixtures that blend chiles and cocoa. These flavorings can be used singly or, best and most creatively, in combination. Salt curiously removes the edge and ferocity of seasonings such as garlic, shallot, and chiles, leaving their sweet selves intact, allowing them to be rolled inside a roast as well as sprinkled or rubbed on the outside.

I've figured out some very rough proportions of flavorings to salt to help you gauge amounts when seasoning meats or poultry; ultimately you need to go with your instincts. Allow a scant ¾ teaspoon of salt per pound of meat or poultry. To figure the amount of salt, weigh the meat and multiply the number of pounds by ½ to ¾ teaspoon. Then add the amount of seasonings you need: approximately ¼ to ½ cup fresh herbs or 1 tablespoon ground spices per tablespoon of salt by feel or by eye.

Meat and poultry benefit most from these fragrant salts. The amount of time to salt them ahead should be determined by the size and density of the food you are salting. Roasts at least 2 inches thick can be salted 24 to 48 hours ahead. Thinner cuts such as steaks need 1 to 4 hours; small game birds such as quail, an hour or two. Because fish has a very delicate flesh, it is easily overwhelmed by prolonged salting and flavoring. Salt fish within a half hour of cooking and add the seasoning separately.

You can also use seasoning mixes, such as the improvisations that follow, without salt, to flavor soups, stews, braises, oils, and so on.

. . . . . .

## Fragrant Herb Salt  Makes about ¼ cup, enough for about 4 pounds meat

> 1 garlic clove, peeled
> 1 tablespoon kosher salt
> About ½ cup loosely packed pungent fresh herbs, such as sage,
>   rosemary, thyme, or savory (for a Tuscan flavor, about 30 sage leaves
>   and about ¼ cup fresh rosemary leaves)

**Mince the garlic with the salt.** Mound the salt and garlic on a cutting board. Use a chef's knife to mince the garlic, blending it with the salt as you work. Alternatively, grate the garlic finely, then mix with the salt.

**Add the herbs or spices to the salt and blend together.** Place the herbs in a mound and coarsely chop them. Add the herbs to the garlic salt and chop them together to the texture of fine sand.

**Note:** Although it's best when fresh, let any leftover herb salt dry out in an uncovered bowl to use as a seasoning. It is an excellent instant flavoring for vegetables. Store in a clean, dry jar.

## Improvisations

### Real Garlic Salt  Makes 3 to 4 tablespoons

*It dawned on me that I could use this seasoned-salt method to make a real garlic salt without the acrid flavor of the commercial products.*

Mince a small garlic clove as fine as possible with a few tablespoons kosher salt or sea salt. Add more salt to taste until the garlic intensity is just how you like it. Put the fresh garlic salt in a bowl to dry out, uncovered, for a day or two; the salt preserves the garlic's pure flavor. Store it in a jar and use it the way you would garlic salt. It's great on popcorn.

### Moroccan-Style Seasoning with Cinnamon, Coriander, and Cumin
Makes about ¼ cup

*This salt was inspired by the flavors used in Moroccan-style tagines. Use it to season roast chicken, lamb, and pork. Without salt, this seasoning is an excellent flavoring for beans, potatoes, peppers, and tomato-based dishes.*

In a small bowl, combine 1 tablespoon each ground coriander, cinnamon, and sweet paprika, 1 teaspoon ground cumin, and 1 teaspoon freshly ground black pepper.

For each pound of meat, combine ¾ teaspoon kosher salt, ¼ to ½ teaspoon grated garlic, ¼ teaspoon sugar, and 1 to 2 teaspoons spice mixture.

### Mole-Inspired Seasoning with Ancho, Cinnamon, and Cocoa    Makes about ⅓ cup

*This mix evokes the flavors of moles, the complex chile-based Mexican sauces. It is especially delicious on pork—roasts, chops, or tenderloin—and the Close-Roasted Pork on page 235.*

In a small bowl, combine 3 tablespoons ancho chile powder and/or pimentón de la Vera (sweet, not hot), 1 tablespoon dark brown sugar, 1½ teaspoons ground cinnamon, 1½ teaspoons cocoa powder, 1 teaspoon ground cumin, and 1 teaspoon dried oregano.

For each pound of meat, combine ¾ teaspoon kosher salt, ¼ to ½ teaspoon grated garlic, and 1 to 2 teaspoons spice mixture.

### Fragrant Szechuan Pepper Seasoning    Makes about 2 tablespoons

*Szechuan peppercorns are berries from the prickly ash tree; they have a lovely slightly floral, anisey flavor that is essential in many Chinese dishes. Try this salt on roast duck or pork, shrimp, and sea scallops and in place of the classic cracked pepper on beef steaks and roasts.*

In a small heavy skillet, toast 1 tablespoon Szechuan peppercorns, 1½ teaspoons each white and black peppercorns, and ¼ teaspoon allspice berries over moderate heat, shaking the pan occasionally, until they are fragrant, about 3 minutes. Transfer to a mortar and coarsely crush with the pestle, or coarsely grind in a spice grinder.

For each pound of meat, combine ¾ teaspoon kosher salt, 2 teaspoons grated ginger (or more to taste), and 2 teaspoons of the Szechuan pepper mixture or to taste. Crush with a pestle or the back of a spoon until the texture of coarse sand.

### Duck, Rabbit, Game, and Charcuterie Seasoning    Makes enough for 3 pounds of meat

*I've used variations on this mix to cure duck legs for confit and to season pâtés and rillettes. It is a great seasoning for somewhat gamey meats, such as duck, quail, pork, and venison.*

Combine 1½ teaspoons kosher salt and a pinch of sugar on a cutting board. Nestle 20 coriander seeds and 2 allspice berries into the salt. Crush the spices using the side of a chef's knife. Then pile on ½ imported bay leaf, crumbled, and 1 teaspoon fresh thyme leaves; chop the mixture fine. Stir in ¼ teaspoon freshly ground black pepper.

Alternatively, combine the salt, sugar, spices, and herbs in a mortar. Pound and crush to a coarse "sand" with a pestle.

### All-Purpose Aromatic Pepper    Makes ⅓ cup

*I keep a pepper mill filled with this mixture and use it often in place of freshly ground pepper; it is a great instant seasoning for just about any food. To make an instant rub for meats and poultry, blend with kosher salt.*

Combine 2 tablespoons white peppercorns, 2 tablespoons black peppercorns, 2 tablespoons pink peppercorns, 1 tablespoon coriander seed, and 1 tablespoon allspice berries. Fill a pepper mill with the mixture to coarsely grind as needed.

# Basil, Lemon, and Tomato Oil

- Parsley, Thyme, Rosemary, and Bay Leaf Oil
- Chinese Many-Flavor Oil
- Sage and Garlic Oil with Fried Sage Leaves
- Infused Oil for Grilled Meats (La Bagna Fredda)
- Ramp, Garlic, and Other Oniony Confits with Their Flavored Olive Oils
- Simple Flavored Oil Improvisations

This intensely flavored oil is the essence of summer. It is one of the many oils I make using my farmers' market–inspired offerings, such as Thai basil, lemon verbena, thyme, rosemary, or young garlic, by heating them with extra virgin olive oil. This oil is the perfect instant sauce or finish for a dish: grilled or roasted fish, poultry, steaks, or lamb; fresh cheeses, such as mozzarella, goat cheese, or ricotta salata; grilled polenta; steamed new potatoes; pasta; roasted eggplant or peppers. In winter, this oil is a welcome reminder of summer.

Although there are many flavored oils commercially available, I rarely buy them; processing leaves them with but a shade of the nuance and flavor of a homemade oil, which is easy to make and lasts a long time. Flavored oils—and the concept of flavored fats—hold endless possibilities for improvising, both in making and in using them.

The first thing to understand when making any flavored oil is that fat–whether oil, butter, or goose fat–carries flavor. It incorporates flavors easily, "captures" them, making them instantly available in cooking. The transmission of flavor into a fat is one of the essential processes of improvisational cooking, and flavored oils play a big part. The classic sautéed-garlic-peperoncino-and-olive-oil sauce for pasta is essentially a flavored oil.

The most effective way to flavor oils is to heat them gently with the flavorings; the heat activates the volatile oils and also mellows any rough flavors, making them sweeter and rounder. The method is simple: Combine flavorings such as herbs or spices and oil in a heavy pan and place over very low heat to keep the oil under a bare simmer for a few minutes; tiny bubbles should just rise up here or there from the bottom. Remove from the heat and let steep, then strain into a clean jar. The oil will keep refrigerated for at least a month.

For small batches–less than ½ cup–and a direct, less mellow flavor, crush and bruise herbs and garlic directly in the oil by mashing them in a bowl or mortar. Remove the herbs when the oil has the desired strength. Refrigerate.

Make these oils with whatever flavorings, singly or in combination, inspire you: aromatics such as sliced garlic, shallot, leeks, ginger; strips of citrus zest; and, of course, fresh herbs. For 1 cup of oil, figure about ½ cup coarsely chopped fibrous, strongly flavored herbs, such as tarragon, rosemary, savory, thyme, or sage, or about 1½ cups coarsely chopped tender mild herbs, such as basil and cilantro. To steep ground spices and other dry flavorings, such as fennel seed, curry powder, ground wild mushrooms, or saffron, soak the flavoring for 10 minutes in just enough boiling water to make a paste, then whisk it into hot oil and let steep.

Make confits of vegetables such as whole garlic cloves, roasted peppers, or artichoke hearts by cooking them in a bath of olive oil over a low flame until they are tender. The oil becomes flavored while preserving the simmered foods, refrigerated, for two to three weeks.

Vary the base oil to suit specific flavoring combinations. Roasted sesame seed oil and roasted peanut oil are great vehicles for Asian flavorings, such as ginger, hot chiles, star anise, cilantro; neutral oils such as grapeseed or canola are best with warm spices such as curry and garam masala; olive oil complements a Mediterranean palette of flavors: garlic, shallot, basil, thyme, rosemary, saffron.

## Basil, Lemon, and Tomato Oil   Makes about 1 cup

½ pound ripe tomatoes

1½ cups extra virgin olive oil

¾ cup packed fresh basil leaves, coarsely chopped

2 garlic cloves, thinly sliced

¼ teaspoon hot red pepper flakes

Two 2 × 1-inch strips lemon zest

**Prep the tomatoes or other flavoring ingredients.** Slice the tomatoes in half crosswise (through the equator) and gently squeeze out the seeds; discard them. Working in a large bowl, rub the cut sides of the tomatoes across the large holes of a metal grater so that the flesh is coarsely grated but the skin remains intact in your hand. Discard the skin.

**Heat the oil and flavorings together.** Combine the tomatoes, oil, basil, garlic, and pepper flakes in a heavy medium pan. Heat over low heat until tiny bubbles dance around the herbs. Reduce the heat to very low and cook 3 to 4 minutes longer. (Use a Flame Tamer or iron skillet to diffuse the heat if your flame can't go low enough.) Stir in the lemon zest.

**Infuse, then strain.** Remove from the heat and let infuse for at least 2 hours, or preferably overnight, before using. Strain and spoon the oil off any juices into a clean, dry jar.

**Note:** The oil will keep in a tightly sealed jar in the refrigerator for up to 1 month. Bring to room temperature about 1/2 hour before serving.

## Improvisations

### Parsley, Thyme, Rosemary, and Bay Leaf Oil   Makes 1 cup

*I improvised this oil with some herbs that were languishing in my fridge—the ones I use most often. It's a great all-purpose herb oil for instantly flavoring just about any vegetable, but especially tomatoes, dried and fresh beans, eggplants, peppers, potatoes, corn, artichokes, as well as a seasoning for lamb, chicken, and meaty fish. Vary the balance of herbs according to what you have on hand, following the principles on page 296 (Ravioli with a Handful of Herbs). A strip of lemon zest is a nice addition.*

In a small saucepan, combine 1 cup extra virgin olive oil, ½ cup coarsely chopped flat-leaf parsley, ¼ cup coarsely chopped fresh rosemary, 2 tablespoons coarsely chopped fresh thyme, 1 teaspoon finely chopped garlic, 1 bay leaf, and ½ teaspoon hot red pepper flakes. Bring to a bare simmer and cook the herbs over low heat for 4 to 5 minutes, until very fragrant and the color is beginning to fade. Turn off the heat and infuse at least 2 hours, or overnight. Strain into a clean, dry jar. Refrigerate.

## Chinese Many-Flavor Oil  Makes ¾ cup

*Classic Chinese aromatics flavor this spicy, fragrant oil. Drizzle onto brothy soups, such as Watercress Salad-Soup with Smoked Duck Breast and Ginger (page 105), or fresh tofu; toss with chilled cooked noodles or slaw-cut cabbage along with chopped cilantro; use to season vegetables, steamed shrimp or fish, and pork chops and roasts.*

With the flat side of a chef's knife, lightly smash 3 scallions, white and pale green parts only; slice into 1-inch pieces. Coarsely chop 10 quarter-sized slices fresh ginger.

In a small heavy saucepan, heat ¼ cup roasted sesame oil and ½ cup peanut oil over moderate heat until hot. Stir in ¾ teaspoon hot red pepper flakes; when the pepper flakes begin to sizzle and are surrounded by tiny bubbles, remove the pan from the heat. Stir in the scallions and ginger and 1 tablespoon Szechuan peppercorns (optional). Cover the pan and set aside to steep for at least 1 hour, or, preferably overnight, at room temperature. To further flavor the oil, if desired, add a strip of tangerine, tangelo, or clementine zest until it's flavored to your taste. Strain the oil into a clean, dry jar. Refrigerate.

## Sage and Garlic Oil with Fried Sage Leaves
### Makes a scant ½ cup oil with an abundance of crisp leaves

*Beyond its classic Tuscan flavors, the real thrill of this oil is the crispy garlic and sage leaves that result from making it. Use the oil to flavor white beans (page 168), filled pastas such as ravioli and tortelloni, polenta, mashed potatoes, bruschetta, roasted vegetables, or chicken or quail just before grilling or roasting; garnish with the crisp garlic and sage.*

In a medium heavy skillet, combine ½ cup extra virgin olive oil and 16 garlic cloves, thinly sliced; cover and cook over moderately low heat, stirring frequently, until the garlic is just barely golden, about 5 minutes. Remove the garlic with a slotted spoon and drain on paper towels. Add 60 fresh sage leaves (about 1 cup loosely packed) to the oil and heat, uncovered, until tiny bubbles surround the leaves; frizzle until the oil is fragrant and the sage has darkened somewhat and crisped. Turn off the heat. With a slotted spoon, transfer the leaves to paper towels; sprinkle with fine sea salt. Strain the oil into a clean, dry jar. Refrigerate.

### Infused Oil for Grilled Meats (La Bagna Fredda)

**Makes about 3 tablespoons, enough to bathe 4 servings of meat**

*My friend Anthony Giglio taught me his Sicilian mother-in-law Lucia LoPresti's, piquant mint, garlic, and balsamic-infused oil that she bathes meats and vegetables with as they come off a wood charcoal-fired grill. It exerts a profound effect on grilled foods, making all the flavors more vivid.*

*This oil is an example of a quick, heatless infusion: The ingredients are chopped, torn, or lightly crushed and left to steep briefly in oil. It's also a lesson in using peppermint as an herbal flavoring for savory dishes, in league with garlic or shallot. Experiment with different mints, each with subtle nuances of flavor, such as chocolate mint or black peppermint, or one of the more exotic basils.*

Prepare the sauce up to 15 minutes before you want to use it (the mint will blacken after an hour or so). In a small bowl, combine 2 tablespoons extra virgin olive oil, 1 teaspoon balsamic vinegar, red wine vinegar or fresh lemon juice, and 1 garlic clove, finely chopped. Tear up at least a dozen fresh peppermint leaves, add to the mixture, and whisk with a fork. Let sit a few minutes to infuse.

Place the just-grilled meats or vegetables on a platter and spoon the oil over them; the juices combine with the minty oil to make a warm sauce to spoon over each serving. Scatter some more torn mint leaves over the dish and serve.

### Ramp, Garlic, and Other Oniony Confits with Their Flavored Olive Oils

*Confit is a French term for "preserve," which in the hands of modern cooks can mean just about anything. One method is to simmer vegetables slowly in oil to cook and preserve them. One spring day, I tried "confiting" some ramp (wild* leeks). *A true wild food of spring, ramps have an earthy, often fiercely pungent flavor that rolls garlic, leeks, and shallots into one. Cooking them very slowly in an olive oil bath left the bulbs tender and mellowed; the oil was permeated with their heady flavor. I used the oil-preserved ramp bulbs and the oil for quick embellishments: tossed with pasta and some Parmigiano, mashed onto grilled bread for bruschetta, drizzled onto beans or mashed potatoes. Use this method for any small bulbish member of the onion family, such as whole garlic cloves, shallots, and spring onions or thinly sliced leeks (white and pale green parts only); sliced artichoke hearts and roasted peppers can be confited this way as well. (See Confited Baby Artichokes, page 199.)*

Trim the root ends and slimy skin off the ramps, rinse well, and drain; cut off the greens and reserve for another use (cook them or add to salads). Put the bulbs in a heavy saucepan and cover them completely with extra virgin olive oil. Place the pan on a heat diffuser over very low heat. Check occasionally to make sure the oil doesn't boil; it should remain on the verge of simmering the whole 45 minutes or so it takes for the ramps to become perfectly tender. Pour the ramps into a clean, dry jar and cover completely with the oil. Cool completely, cover, and refrigerate. To use, spoon as many ramps as you need and some of their oil into a small saucepan. Warm over low heat. The confit will keep 2 to 3 weeks in the refrigerator.

## Simple Flavored Oil Improvisations

*The basic method for making flavored oils is a great tool to use in improvising dishes. Here are some I used in recipes throughout this book:*

Rosemary Oil (page 68)
Shallot Oil (page 53)
Fragrant Fennel Oil (page 180)
Thyme and Shallot Oil (page 199)
Shallot Oil (with Crispy Shallots) (page 200)
Ginger Oil (with Crispy Ginger) (page 205)
Confited Baby Artichokes (page 199)

# Essential Caesar Sauce

- Bagna Cauda
- Deconstructed Caesar Salad
- Spaghetti with Garlic, Anchovy, and Hot Chile
- Warm Vegetables with Anchovies, Currants, and Pine Nuts

Throughout the Mediterranean, the combination of garlic, anchovies, and olive oil finds its way into scores of dishes, from salads, pastas, and vegetables to seafood and even veal and lamb, and comprises the classic bagna cauda, literally the "warm bath," in which raw vegetables are dipped as an hors d'oeuvre. Here in America, it is the basis for the legendary Caesar salad. With the addition of Parmigiano, the assertive flavors add up to something completely other than the sum of their parts—surprisingly mellow and satisfying. This is a far cry from the overly creamy, one-dimensional concoctions generally served in restaurants and salad bars. Since Essential Caesar Sauce seems to go with just about everything, it lends itself to improvisation.

Caesar sauce is all about balance: the balance of flavors within the sauce, and its balance with whatever food it is dressing. The primary variables in making this sauce are how much anchovy you wish to use and how much garlic. Both of these can be made milder or stronger according to your taste or that of your guests and, of course, the food you are pairing them with. Good extra virgin olive oil mellows and refines the sauce. Chopped parsley adds notes of mildly herbal sweetness. Lemon juice, essential when the sauce will be used to dress salads and some vegetables, adds necessary acidity. It should be left out for pasta dishes.

Since its flavors are assertive, Caesar sauce stands up particularly well to strongly flavored foods: bitter greens, such as dandelion, puntarelle, and radicchio, and cruciferous vegetables such as cauliflower and broccoli. However, it seems truly to go with everything: cooked vegetables of all kinds, from potatoes to eggplant to roasted peppers; cheeses, especially feta, ricotta salata, and creamy sheep and goat's milk; and dry pastas. To sauce vegetables or pasta, warm the sauce in a pan first until the garlic is fragrant and gently cooked.

Anchovy is the element that gives this sauce its indescribable flavor. It is neither fishy nor salty, rather, it adds an appealing pungency and punches up the flavors it comes into contact with, in the way salt does. I suspect that when people say, "I don't like anchovies," it's often because, when they have had them, they've been either of poor quality (which can have a distinct fishiness), or used in too great a concentration—or just because the notion of a tiny salted fish is off-putting. When anchovies are emulsified within a well-made Caesar sauce, though, nobody ever says a word.

You have two possibilities when it comes to choosing anchovies. The easiest ones to use are good-quality olive oil–packed anchovy fillets. The fillets should be plump, tender, and sweet-tasting, not fishy. Remove the anchovies from the oil, then pat dry.

The second choice is whole anchovies packed in salt. They have a much stronger, brighter flavor than oil-packed anchovies, so you'll need half as many. They must be soaked to remove their salt. Rinse off the salt and soak the anchovies in several changes of warm water until they are very pliable—from a few hours to overnight. Rinse again to remove any scales, and gently pry the fillets off the spines.

. . . . . . .

## Essential Caesar Sauce   Makes ⅓ cup, about 4 servings

1 small garlic clove, peeled
Kosher salt (optional)
4 imported anchovy fillets in oil, drained and patted dry
¼ cup extra virgin olive oil
Freshly ground black pepper
2 teaspoons fresh lemon juice, or to taste
⅛ to ¼ teaspoon sugar to taste

**Grate or mash the garlic.** Grate the garlic on a rasp grater onto a cutting board, sprinkle with a little salt, and finely chop with a chef's knife; use the side of the knife to mash the garlic to a paste (you should have about ⅓ teaspoon).

**Mash the anchovies.** Place the anchovies on the garlic puree and chop and mash them with the garlic. Transfer to a mortar or small bowl.

**Mix in the olive oil and season.** Drizzle in the olive oil, using a pestle, the back of a large spoon, or a whisk to work it into the anchovy-garlic mixture; add fresh pepper to taste. If you will be using the dressing for salads or vegetables, stir in the lemon juice and sugar. Store any unused dressing in a covered jar in the refrigerator for up to 1 week.

## Improvisations

### Bagna Cauda   Makes ⅓ cup

*Served warm, Essential Caesar Sauce could easily be mistaken for a bagna cauda, the classic Italian dipping sauce for cooked shrimp; vegetables, such as potatoes, fennel, asparagus, and sweet peppers; and grilled bread. It makes an easy, festive hors d'oeuvre, perfect with chilled rosé wine.*

Assemble the dippers on a large platter. Warm the Essential Caesar Sauce, including the lemon juice but not the sugar, in a small saucepan until hot but not boiling. Place the saucepan in the middle of the table, and let your guests dip as they please.

### Deconstructed Caesar Salad    Serves 4

*The usual method of making Caesar salad, tossing cut-up romaine lettuce with anchovy dressing and grated Parmigiano, too often makes for a gloppy, overdressed salad. I prefer to deconstruct the parts: pristine hearts of romaine leaves lined up on a plate, drizzled with the garlicky dressing and topped with shavings of Parmigiano, with toasted garlic-rubbed bread on the side. For a pretty variation, substitute whole slender Treviso radicchio leaves for the romaine.*

Discard the tough outer leaves and trim the tough ends of a 1¼- to 1½-pound head of romaine lettuce. Slice the head lengthwise through the heart into quarters, and place each quarter on a salad plate. Drizzle 2 or 3 teaspoons Essential Caesar Sauce across the leaves of each serving, followed by some chopped parsley. With a vegetable peeler or plane grater, shave long, flat strips of Parmigiano (4 to 5 ounces total) over the salad. Serve at once, with Garlic Toasts (page 274).

### Spaghetti with Garlic, Anchovy, and Hot Chile    Serves 4

*The Essential Caesar Sauce combines all the elements necessary to make this classic pasta in perfect proportion.*

Prepare the Essential Caesar Sauce without the lemon juice and sugar. Place a large pot of water on high heat to boil. Add 10 ounces spaghetti to the pot and cook until al dente. Drain the pasta, reserving about ¼ cup of the cooking water.

Pour the sauce into the same pot and add ¼ crumbled peperoncino or ⅛ teaspoon hot red pepper flakes; warm over low heat until you smell the garlic. Return the pasta to the pot with 2 tablespoons of the reserved cooking water and about ⅔ cup chopped flat-leaf parsley. Increase the heat to high and toss until the pasta is well coated and hot. Pepper generously, adjust the seasoning, and serve at once.

### Warm Vegetables with Anchovies, Currants, and Pine Nuts    Serves 4

*Use the Essential Caesar Sauce with some currants and toasted pine nuts to sauce all kinds of cooked vegetables: roasted peppers, eggplants, zucchini, pumpkin, fennel, or onions; steamed cruciferous vegetables such as cauliflower, broccoli, or brussels sprouts; and assertive greens like dandelion. It's a fast way to make a complex dish out of something simple. And it's a great way to transform leftover vegetables.*

My general approach is this: Roast, steam, or sauté 4 or 5 cups of cut-up vegetables. Then warm the Essential Caesar Sauce with an additional grated garlic clove plus a pinch of hot red pepper flakes or crumbled peperoncino in a large heavy skillet until the garlic is fragrant. Toss in the vegetables along with 2 tablespoons hot water and a few tablespoons dried currants, increase the heat to high, and cook until the liquid has evaporated, tossing frequently; then sauté the vegetables about 1 minute. Stir in ¾ cup finely chopped flat-leaf parsley, salt and pepper to taste, and a handful of toasted pine nuts, chopped medium fine. Adjust the seasoning, adding a few drops of balsamic vinegar to lift the flavors.

# Vinegar Redux

Sometimes it's an I've-got-nothing-to-lose-attitude that motivates interesting improvisations. When I discovered a couple of bottles of commercial vinegars forgotten in the back of my pantry because they were less than great, I decided to doctor them up. I plunked some almost-past-its-prime fresh tarragon I needed to use up into a slightly too aggressive vin santo vinegar I'd brought back from Italy. Within 24 hours, the tarragon had provided layers of subtle, sweet licorice flavor that balanced the wood-aged vinegar and added lovely character, yielding a complex, brightly flavored tarragon vinegar.

The tarragon improvisation reminded me of the possibilities for steeping or blending vinegars to make simple flavor resources that are better than most commercial varieties. I use my doctored vinegars to brighten or complement the flavors of stews, soups, and sauces, and to dress all kinds of salads.

The basic method for doctoring vinegars is simple: Steep a flavoring in the vinegar until the vinegar takes on as much of that flavor as you like, then strain it out. Potential for marriages between vinegars and flavorings are endless: herbs such as tarragon, basil, thyme, savory, and chive; aromatics such as shallot and garlic; citrus zest; spices. My favorite vinegar flavorings are blue and red fruits: plums, black currants, blackberries, and cherries. When exposed to the vinegar, the hard pits of cherries, peaches, and plums impart earthy, savory, fruitwood notes. I can imagine steeping sliced apples in cider vinegar to up the vinegar's apple flavor, or ripe, fragrant Comice pears in balsamic or sherry vinegar to imbue it with a pear perfume.

The better the vinegar you use, the better your flavored vinegar will be, though you can do just fine with an okay "vin ordinaire" vinegar, steeping and blending in elements until it tastes right (see below). Champagne vinegar is probably one of the most delicate and neutral, followed by white wine vinegar; these are especially good with herbs. Red wine vinegar tends to have a bit more tannin, pleasing with red fruits. Sweet, mellow, and full-bodied, balsamic vinegar is a perfect base for berries and plums and requires little aging. Sherry vinegars have a subtle wood-aged flavor that lends complexity.

There's no reason you can't blend vinegars. Add some sherry vinegar, say, to red wine or balsamic vinegar to give it more aged flavor, or some balsamic to a red wine vinegar to balance its flavor or attenuate the balsamic's sometimes cloying sweetness.

Bear in mind that it often takes time to mellow and harmonize the flavors of the vinegar you've doctored, anywhere from a day to several weeks. Set the corked bottle of vinegar aside and taste it occasionally. You'll know when it's ready. A tiny bit of brown sugar can also do wonders in mellowing a vinegar and harmonizing its flavors.

Sometimes a vinegar has a good flavor but is a bit watery. I pour it into a wide-topped vessel and leave it uncovered to evaporate some of the water for a few days, until its flavor is concentrated enough.

• • • • • •

## Vinegar Redux   Makes 1 to 2 cups

> 1 to 2 cups decent-quality vinegar, such as white wine, red wine, champagne, sherry, cider, or rice wine
>
> Flavoring: another vinegar, herbs, spices, fruit zest, or fruit (cut up or coarsely crushed, with pits)

**Combine the vinegar and flavorings.** Pour the vinegar into a clean, dry jar or large measuring cup. Add your chosen flavoring(s).

**Steep the vinegar, tasting to determine when it achieves the desired strength.** After about an hour, taste the vinegar to gauge its relative strength, that is, how quickly it is taking on flavor. (This will depend on the intensity of the flavorings you use, and how much.) Then taste the vinegar occasionally, until it achieves a pleasing intensity. This can be in as quickly as an hour, or as long as several weeks.

**Decant.** Strain the vinegar into a clean, dry jar.

## Improvisations

### Raspberry Thyme Vinegar

*Raspberry vinegar was a fine idea that became a caricature of itself when commercial vinegar makers got hold of it. Responding to its wild popularity—the clear, delicate perfume of raspberries in vinegar was a revelation—producers began to pack in the fruit, or to use potent raspberry essences, to make cloying, overbearingly raspberried vinegars that would unbalance any dish they were used in. Salads and sauces made with perfumelike raspberry vinegars were ubiquitous. I abandoned raspberry vinegar for years.*

*Then one day I found a box of fragrant raspberries in my fridge that weren't quite fresh enough to eat. So I put the raspberries in a jar with some just-okay sherry vinegar I had in my pantry. I figured the earthiness of the sherry vinegar would temper the sweetness of the raspberries; the sweet fruit would smooth out the coarseness of the vinegar. The trick was to strain the raspberries out before their flavor became too saturated, when the vinegar had only a subtle background flavor of fruit—in this case, just 24 hours. I added ¼ teaspoon brown sugar to help round out the edgy vinegar. (A sprig of thyme, bruised and left to macerate a few minutes, added a wilder quality to the vinegar that helped balance out the fruit.)*

*The result was a fragrant vinegar akin to a really good red wine vinegar with hints of berries.*

## Strawberry Balsamic Vinegar for Desserts

*In summer, I often splash ripe strawberries with balsamic vinegar and a hint of basil for dessert. One afternoon, while cutting the leafy hulls off some local, height-of-summer strawberries, I realized there was quite a bit of fragrant flesh clinging to the stems. So I threw the strawberry hulls and the too ripe and bruised berries into a bowl, poured over balsamic vinegar, and steeped them for several hours, then strained the vinegar. The balsamic had gained an extraordinary perfume and flavor of strawberry, and I used it throughout the summer to dress strawberries as well as white peaches, apricots, and muskmelon. Children love this vinegar on their salad greens and on cucumber slices. Make it with really ripe, fragrant berries.*

## Cherry Aged Cherry Vinegar

*Since vinegars are essentially alive, age effects them, even in the bottle, a lesson I learned when I tasted a cherry vinegar I'd made years before. I'd plunked smashed ripe cherries into a not-so-terrific red wine vinegar. I figured that leaving in the pits and stems might give the vinegar a lovely subtle flavor of cherrywood, as though it had been aged in a cherrywood barrel. Young, the vinegar wasn't balanced enough to love, I suspect due to the edginess of the base vinegar. But I came across the forgotten bottle a couple of years later and discovered a fabulously complex, mellow red wine vinegar. I now use the same method but with balsamic vinegar, which eliminates the need for long aging.*

Put about 2 cups smashed ripe cherries and their stems in a large jar; cover with balsamic vinegar by several inches. (You can pulse whole stem-on cherries and vinegar in a food processor.) Because cherries have a much more subtle flavor than raspberries or strawberries, and you want to draw out the woody flavor of the pits, steep the cracked cherries in the vinegar for several days or longer. Strain and decant the vinegar into a clean, dry bottle.

### Tarragon Chive, Shallot, and Other Salad Vinegars

*My homemade tarragon vinegar with a hint of fresh chive has a much brighter, truer flavor than commercial ones. Use it in salad dressings for chilled steamed spring vegetables, such as peas, fava beans, asparagus, artichokes, new potatoes, or string beans, and, of course, on green salads. Shallot-flavored vinegar is a great way to impart a subtle oniony flavor to salad dressings without actually having shallots on hand.*

Steep chopped herbs or shallots in vinegar until it has just the right subtle flavor—usually a few hours; then strain them out and decant the vinegar into a clean, dry bottle.

### Balsamic Caramel  Makes about ⅓ cup

*In Italy, the long-aged artisanal balsamic vinegars—syruplike essences really— become concentrated and mellowed through years of resting in a succession of wooden barrels. These prized and costly vinegars are drizzled over foods as a counterpoint of flavor, like a truffle in their ability to amplify the flavors of whatever they come in contact with, from young Parmigiano to prosciutto. Drizzled onto vanilla ice cream and warm fruit desserts, the piquant vinegar mellowed into a caramely syrup becomes an ethereal sauce.*

*When I used up the last of the aged balsamic I had carried back from Italy, I decided to improvise a mellow, fruity, subtly piquant amalgam of vinegar and caramel. I boiled ordinary balsamic vinegar into a concentrated syrup with some reduced Madeira wine to give it some wood-aged flavors and stirred in brown sugar to up the caramel flavor. While my Balsamic Caramel doesn't have the complexity of artisanal balsamic, it is great stuff, and especially dazzling drizzled on warm fruit-and-ice cream combinations. I also use it to give savory foods a little hit of piquant flavor, from grilled cheese sandwiches to tomato-based pasta sauces to rich stews.*

In a small heavy saucepan, boil ½ cup Rainwater or Sercial Madeira over moderate heat until it has reduced to about 1 tablespoon. Add 1 cup commercial balsamic vinegar and boil until the vinegar has reduced to about ¼ to ⅓ cup and is very syrupy with big, shiny bubbles. Watch it carefully as it approaches this point, because it can burn easily. (It is better to slightly underreduce it, as it will thicken upon cooling.) Remove from the heat and stir in 2 teaspoons dark brown sugar until dissolved. Pour into a clean, dry jar; cool completely before using.

# Almost Homemade Mayonnaise

- Bacon Mayonnaise with or without Ramps
- Garlic Mayonnaise, after Aïoli
- Saffron Garlic Sauce
- Rosemary and (Meyer) Lemon Mayonnaise
- Parmesan Mayonnaise

Mayonnaise expresses my conflicts as a too-busy, modern cook. I love the from-scratch mayonnaise of my culinary roots, made by beating fine extra virgin olive and grapeseed oils drop by drop into raw egg yolks until a creamy emulsion is formed. My problem is that I like to eat mayonnaise daily, slathered onto sandwiches and mixed into egg salad, for example, and you can't keep a homemade mayonnaise around more than 3 or 4 days due to the dangers posed by raw eggs. I'm just too busy to whip up a mayonnaise every time I want one. I need the convenience of the characterless commercial mayo with the flavor of real mayonnaise.

So I fling my notions of purity out the door and doctor commercial mayo to make a fine staple mayonnaise for everyday. I whisk extra virgin olive oil into Hellmann's/Best Foods or Kraft until it takes on the unctuous look of the real thing, with a subtle olivey flavor. This mayo will keep for weeks, is good on just about anything, and invites further improvisation. I still make from-scratch mayonnaise to serve with dishes that really need its inimitable flavor, like a cold steamed lobster or a peak-tomato-season BLT. There's a place in life for both versions.

Great oil is what gives gutsy homemade mayonnaises their character and is the secret to transforming commercial mayo into something much closer to the classic. In my doctored version, the commercial product is essentially a base for good oil, in the same way eggs are in the original. And, as with the original, you can only beat in a certain amount of oil before the creamy emulsion "breaks" and separates, though the amount is not nearly so critical. Choose a commercial mayo that is made with classic ingredients: eggs, oil, and acid in the form of lemon juice or vinegar, without fillers like cornstarch or extremes of acidity or sweetness. (Squirt-bottle mayos are too thin for this recipe.)

I doctor my mayo with extra virgin olive oil for a mayonnaise reminiscent of ones made in the south of France. If you prefer a more neutral flavor, use a good-quality peanut or grapeseed oil. A tablespoon or two of an assertively flavored oil, such as roasted sesame or peanut oil, can be blended into this neutral base as a flavoring, alone or in league with complementary flavorings such as ginger, garlic, and cilantro. Roasted walnut, hazelnut, pine nut, and pistachio oils pose interesting possibilities, as do flavored oils such as basil or rosemary; use them sparingly, to taste. To my mind, the ultimate flavoring for doctored mayo is rendered bacon fat; it makes a silky, smoky mayonnaise.

This basic doctored mayo makes an excellent base for further flavoring. The possibilities are legion: They include fresh or roasted garlic, grated horseradish, minced caramelized shallots, grated ginger, minced or grated ramps, regular or Meyer lemon zest, olive paste, and minced soft fresh herbs such as basil, mint, cilantro, and chives. Fibrous herbs, such as rosemary, thyme, savory, and sage, become gritty in a mayonnaise. Instead, warm them for several minutes in olive oil to infuse it; when cool, beat the strained infused oil into the mayo. Dried ground spices, such as ancho and other chile powders, curry powder, and garam masala, should be moistened in a few teaspoons of hot water to release their flavor before adding them to mayonnaise. Combining interesting oils and flavorings expands the possibilities manyfold. When improvising, add the flavorings a little at a time, until you get the degree of intensity you like. Heighten flavors with a pinch of salt or a few drops of fresh lemon juice or vinegar.

. . . . . .

## Almost Homemade Mayonnaise    Makes about ¾ cup

> ⅓ cup prepared mayonnaise such as Hellmann's/Best Foods or Kraft
> ½ cup extra virgin olive oil
> A few drops of fresh lemon juice (optional)
> Freshly ground white pepper to taste

**Whisk a flavorful fat into prepared mayonnaise.** Spoon the mayonnaise into a medium bowl and position the bowl on a damp tea towel to keep it from sliding around the counter. Whisk the mayo as you slowly dribble in the olive oil.

**Adjust the seasoning.** Stir in lemon juice if necessary to balance the flavors and white pepper to taste.

**Store.** Scrape into a clean, dry jar. Cover and refrigerate.

## Improvisations

### Bacon Mayonnaise with or without Ramps    Makes about ⅔ cup

*Although it seems over the top, bacon makes a sensational flavoring for mayonnaise (think BLT) that is perfect on tomato-and-Cheddar sandwiches, panfried fish sandwiches (page 207), cold roast pork, or chilled steamed shrimp and lobster, and in potato salad.*

Whisk 2 tablespoons warm strained rendered bacon fat (see page 354) into ½ cup prepared mayonnaise. Season liberally with freshly ground black pepper. In spring, ramps (wild leeks) make a wonderful garlicky addition to bacon mayonnaise. Finely grate a cleaned ramp bulb and stir in 1 to 2 teaspoons of the grated pulp, to taste.

### Garlic Mayonnaise, after Aïoli    Makes about ¾ cup

*This is a fast, unpolished version of aïoli, the classic Mediterranean sauce. It's great on sandwiches, with roasted meats and poultry, and, especially, with chilled shrimp, octopus, and salmon. The secret to a sweet, pure—not bitter—garlic flavor is twofold: First, cut a peeled garlic clove in half lengthwise and remove the green sprout, if any. Second, pound the garlic to a puree with a pinch of kosher salt; you can do it right on the work surface with a pestle. Or, using a chef's* knife, mince the garlic with the salt: Placing the flat side of the knife almost parallel to the work surface, mash the garlic a little at a time by crushing and smearing it against the cutting board until it is completely reduced to a paste.

Spoon ⅓ cup prepared mayonnaise into a medium bowl and position the bowl on a damp tea towel to keep it from sliding around the counter. Whisk the mayo as you slowly dribble in about ½ cup extra virgin olive oil. Stir in ½ teaspoon of the garlic paste to start, adding more to suit your taste; the garlic flavor will strengthen as it sits. Blend in a few drops of lemon juice if necessary to balance the flavors. Season with freshly ground black pepper to taste. Cover and refrigerate.

### Saffron Garlic Sauce    Makes about ¾ cup

*Saffron is a natural addition to Garlic Mayonnaise, as in the classic sauce rouille from the south of France, where it is stirred into fish soups. It goes with practically all seafood as well as cold roast lamb and lobster.*

Crumble a small pinch of saffron threads into a small bowl and pour over 1 teaspoon hot water; set aside to soften for 5 minutes. Whisk into the Garlic Mayonnaise; allow to infuse at least 20 minutes before serving.

### Rosemary and (Meyer) Lemon Mayonnaise    Makes ½ cup

*This herb-scented mayonnaise is made with an herb-infused oil rather than minced fresh herbs, which gives it a mellower flavor and perfectly smooth texture. It complements cold roasted or grilled meats and poultry, meaty fish, and potatoes.*

For the **rosemary oil,** in a small heavy saucepan, combine ¼ cup extra virgin olive oil and 1½ tablespoons minced fresh rosemary over very low heat. Heat until tiny bubbles just begin to dance around the rosemary, about 2 minutes, then turn off the heat. Let the oil cool completely, then strain into a small bowl.

Spoon ¼ cup prepared mayonnaise into a medium bowl and position the bowl on a damp tea towel to keep it from sliding around the counter. Whisk the mayo as you slowly dribble in the rosemary oil. Stir in ½ teaspoon finely grated lemon or Meyer lemon zest and a few drops of lemon juice if necessary to balance the flavors. Season with freshly ground black pepper. Cover and refrigerate.

## Parmesan Mayonnaise    Makes ¾ cup

*I use this thick Parmesan Mayonnaise almost exclusively on roasted or grilled vegetable sandwiches and as a dip for raw vegetables.*

Spoon ⅓ cup prepared mayonnaise into a medium bowl and position the bowl on a damp tea towel to keep it from sliding around the counter. Whisk the mayo as you slowly dribble in ½ cup extra virgin olive oil. Whisk in 6 tablespoons finely grated Parmigiano and a liberal amount of freshly ground black pepper. Stir in a few drops of lemon juice if necessary to balance the flavors. Cover and let sit at room temperature at least 1 hour before serving to allow the cheese to soften and meld.

# Sweet or Savory Quinces
# in White Wine and Honey

- Upside-Down Quince Tart
- Savory Apples with White Wine and Rosemary
- Pears in Fragrant Dessert Wine
- White Peaches in Red Wine Syrup
- Sweet-and-Sour Spiced Prunes

I often improvise with an ingredient as a way to figure out how it works. Take the quince that an Italian greengrocer friend presented me with many years ago as I passed by on my way to work in the restaurant next door. The mysterious fruit looked like a bright yellow apple and had an intoxicating scent of exotic flowers and pears, yet it proved to be full of contradictions: a charming exterior gilding a dense fibrous flesh, a taste of which made my mouth pucker and dry as though I had licked deodorant, sending a clear message that it needed to be cooked.

The quince's extraordinary fragrance spurred the idea to cook peeled slices of this fruit slowly in white wine and honey, a mixture that, I realized years later, roughly approximates a dessert wine. This cooking method urged all the fruit's floral flavors forward and gave it a lovely texture, like that of a dense, luscious, roasted apple.

That's how I stumbled on a basic quince-cooking method I use for both savory dishes and desserts. Serve them with roast pork, duck, chicken, and just about any game bird. They make a perfect dessert with heavy cream, ice cream, or Sour Cream Panna Cotta (page 339); lovely unusual tarts, as in the upside-down version (page 72); and embellishment for plain cakes like Orange Flower Cake (page 323); and as a surprising accompaniment to aged sheep's milk cheese.

Quinces are available at farmers' markets and many supermarkets from August to January or February.

The quince recipe illustrates a basic approach for cooking many kinds of fruit: simmering them in wine with sweetening and flavoring. It transforms the fruit, tenderizing its flesh and infusing it with flavor, and accentuates its natural perfume. Fruits cooked in wine can be served both as dessert and as accompaniments to savory dishes, notably roasted poultry, game, and pork.

Take this basic approach with many kinds of fruits whose flesh has some structure; apples, pears, cherries, cranberries, peaches, and plums are among the best. (Fruits that have a lot of water, like strawberries and raspberries, will fall apart before they achieve the right flavor.)

Wine is an excellent poaching liquid because it provides mild acidity and a somewhat sophisticated flavor without dominating the fruit; it helps the fruit work in both sweet and savory settings. Use wine in tandem with other flavors—like those mentioned below—or just the wine itself to provide the flavoring, as with spicy wines like Gewürztraminer or dessert wines. Sweeten to taste to make a light wine syrup. Adding wildflower honey to white wine imparts a flavor similar to a dessert wine. I find this the best universal "base" in which to cook almost any fruit. Using very fragrant, exotic honeys such as lavender or lime blossom is another way to add interesting flavor notes.

Alternatively, cook the fruit in sweet nonalcoholic liquids, such as cider or other juices, or syrups (water simmered with sugar or honey and flavorings), spiked with lemon juice for acidity.

Possible flavorings include herbs—rosemary, thyme, lavender, savory, and basil lend unusual savory notes; or sweet spices—cinnamon, cloves, nutmeg, and coriander go especially well with red wines or vinegar-laced syrups for use with rich meats like pork, game, and duck. Peppercorns and cardamom can add a subtle aromatic spiciness. Fruit zests such as lemon, orange, and Meyer lemon will lend a citrus-floral component. Vanilla bean is all you need to turn just about any fruit and wine combination into a lovely dessert.

If you allow the fruits to cook past the point of perfect tenderness (either intentionally or by accident), you can turn them into a fine chunky jam to spread on toast, breakfast breads, and pancakes or to fill a tart. Add a few tablespoons of water as needed to keep the fruit from burning while you continue cooking it until it falls apart and becomes jammy.

. . . . . .

## Sweet or Savory Quinces in White Wine and Honey   Serves 4

**1 cup dry white wine**
**¹/₂ cup plus 1 tablespoon wildflower honey**
**Juice of ¹/₂ lemon**
**2 pounds fragrant quinces (4 or 5 medium)**
**1 tablespoon unsalted butter (optional)**
**Pinch of kosher salt**

**Make the syrup.** In a medium nonstick skillet, combine the wine, honey, and lemon juice.

**Prepare the fruit and add it to the syrup.** With a vegetable peeler, peel 1 quince. With a small sharp paring knife, cut it into eighths and cut out the fibrous core. Cut each eighth in half again, to make a ¹/₄-inch slice. Place the slices in the wine mixture and toss to coat to prevent the slices from browning as you work on the others. Pare and slice the remaining quinces. Add the butter, if desired.

**Simmer the fruit in the syrup until tender.** Bring the wine to a boil, reduce the heat, and simmer until the quinces are tender and rosy but retain their shape, 25 to 40 minutes. If the wine is evaporating too quickly, add some water, ¹/₄ cup at a time.

**Fine-tune the syrup's flavor and texture.** Increase the heat to high and boil the winey juices vigorously for several minutes until the flavor is concentrated and about ¹/₂ cup of thick syrup remains.

## Improvisations

### Upside-Down Quince Tart   Makes one 10-inch tart, 6 to 8 servings

*I plugged quinces into a tarte Tatin model and baked the tender glazed fruit with pastry dough on top. Inverted at the last minute, it makes a charming and unusual tart.*

Prepare Sweet or Savory Quinces in White Wine and Honey in a 10-inch ovenproof nonstick skillet, reducing the wine until it is almost completely evaporated and very syrupy. With a fork, gently prod the quince slices to make a fairly uniform layer of fruit in the bottom of the pan.

While the quinces are cooking, roll 8 ounces of your favorite pie dough or Easy Butter Dough for Tarts, Pies, and Free-Form Pastries (page 355) on a lightly floured surface into a 10-inch circle. Prick the dough evenly with a fork. Gently roll the dough over the rolling pin and lay the pastry on a baking sheet. Cover with plastic wrap and refrigerate until ready to bake the tart.

Preheat the oven to 400°F. Just before baking the tart, slide the chilled pastry on top of the quince slices in the skillet. Prick several times with a fork. Bake until the pastry is golden brown, 25 minutes. Set aside to cool. Do not invert the tart until you are ready to serve it, or the pastry will get soggy.

To remove the tart from the skillet easily, set it over moderate heat to melt the syrup and loosen the quinces. Cover the pan with a flat serving platter and invert the tart onto the platter in one quick motion. Brush the quinces with the juices that remain in the pan. Serve warm with crème fraîche or whipped cream.

## Savory Apples with White Wine and Rosemary    Makes 1 cup

*Inspired by the famous pairing of apples and pheasant in the classic French dish faisan Vallée d'Auge, I devised this chunky, aromatic applesauce to accompany roasted pheasant. This sauce is a delicious, quick, all-purpose accompaniment for chicken, squab, guinea hen, quail, even pork. The combination of white wine and honey gives some of the effect of a fragrant dessert wine; the rosemary adds delicate herbal notes.*

In a medium saucepan, combine 2 Granny Smith apples, peeled, cored, and cut into ½-inch dice, 1 cup dry white wine, ¼ cup wildflower honey, and a sprig of fresh rosemary. Bring to a low boil and cook, stirring occasionally, until all the liquid has evaporated and the apples are tender and glazed, about 12 minutes. After about 8 minutes, taste the mixture to check the intensity of the rosemary flavor; remove the sprig when the sauce reaches a pleasing intensity. If desired, add freshly ground white pepper to taste. Serve warm.

## Pears in Fragrant Dessert Wine   Makes 1 cup

*In France many years ago, there were no cranberries to be had for the Thanksgiving dinner I was cooking. So I simmered pears in a fragrant dessert wine to make a fruit accompaniment to the turkey. This also makes a lovely dessert. Use a good inexpensive dessert wine, such as Moscato d'Alba, Barsac, or Monbazillac.*

In a medium saucepan, combine 2 large Comice pears, peeled and cut into ½-inch dice, and 1¼ cups fragrant dessert wine. Bring to a simmer and cook, stirring occasionally, until the fruit is tender, about 10 minutes. Transfer to a bowl and chill. If desired, drizzle in a few drops of Poire William (clear pear brandy).

## White Peaches in Red Wine Syrup   Serves 4

*In summer, I often splash peaches with red wine with basil leaves and a little sugar for a quick dessert. One day instead, I poached whole white peaches (which have a haunting perfume) in red wine, as I do pears, added a few drops of rose water at the end, and served them chilled. Omit the rose water and add a sprig or two of thyme to the poaching peaches, and they become the perfect accompaniment to roast duck. If only yellow-fleshed peaches are available, jazz up the syrup with whole sweet spices such as cinnamon, coriander, and clove. (If you're unsure of quantities, place the spices in a teaball and remove them when the syrup gains the intensity you like.)*

In a nonreactive saucepan large enough to hold the whole or halved fruit in one layer, combine 3½ cups (one 750-ml bottle) full-bodied red wine, 1 cup ruby port (or, if you have no port, add an additional ½ cup sugar), ½ cup sugar, and 1 strip lemon zest. Split a vanilla bean lengthwise in half and scrape out the seeds. Add the seeds and bean to the pot. Bring to a boil over moderate heat, stirring to dissolve the sugar.

Peel 4 slightly underripe white-fleshed peaches; cut in half or into slices, or leave whole with the stems intact (if they don't stand stem end up by themselves, cut a thin slice off the flower end to make a flat bottom). Arrange the peaches in the syrup. Cut a circle of parchment the diameter of the pot and place over the pears. Place a pot lid or plate slightly smaller than the saucepan on top of the parchment to hold the pears below the surface of the wine as they cook.

Return the wine to a simmer. Cook, rearranging the peaches occasionally, until a skewer passes to the core with little resistance, 10 minutes for slices, 20 minutes for halves, and 35 to 40 minutes for whole fruit. If the wine reduces to below the top of the fruit, add a little wine or water to bring the level back up. When done, gently remove the peaches with a slotted spoon to a serving bowl. Boil the wine over moderate heat until it is reduced to a syrup, about 1 cup. Add a few drops rose water, if desired (it should be barely discernible). Strain the syrup over the fruit. Serve at room temperature or chilled.

### Sweet-and-Sour Spiced Prunes    Makes about 2 cups

*In the southwest of France, prunes are often pickled and served as a sweet-tart counterpoint to rich meats like pork, duck, and all manner of charcuterie. I took the basic technique of cooking fruit in an aromatic syrup and applied it to prunes, replacing the wine with mild, sweet balsamic vinegar. In tandem with sweet spices, it makes a mellow pickle that needs no aging; the prunes can be eaten 24 hours after they are made and will keep indefinitely.*

In a medium saucepan, combine 1½ cups balsamic vinegar, ⅓ cup sugar, 3 cinnamon sticks, and 6 whole cloves. Simmer 10 minutes. Add 1 pound pitted prunes and simmer 5 minutes longer. Let cool slightly, then transfer to a clean jar. If necessary, add a little water to make a mellower syrup. Cover and refrigerate.

# Lemon Oregano Jam

I fell in love with this recipe the first time I tasted it at Babbo, Mario Batali's phenomenal Italian restaurant in New York City. It accompanied a perfectly roasted whole Italian branzino—Mediterranean sea bass—a lovely, unexpected, and deeply satisfying combination that is daring by virtue of its very simplicity: there are so few elements in the dish and each must be perfect. I never imagined how ingenious the lemon jam premise would turn out to be; the creamy texture and vivid taste are achieved by pureeing whole lemons in a food processor with some sugar, salt, herbs, and olive oil.

I've come to view the jam as an essential condiment, using it with everything from grilled veal chops to lamb chops rubbed with Moroccan-Style Seasoning with Cinnamon, Coriander, and Cumin (page 46) to roast chicken to Salt-Roasted Trout (page 187). I've folded it into mayonnaise to sauce cold meat loaf and shrimp, spread it on hazelnut-butter sandwiches for an adult peanut butter and jelly, stirred it into yogurt, spread it on feta to eat on slices of toasted peasant bread, flavored warm potato salad with it, . . .

By some magical chemistry, grinding a whole lemon in a food processor with a little sugar, salt, and oil produces a thick, light "jam." The curious addition of oil is essential: When processed into the lemon mash, it creates an emulsion without any sense of oiliness. The oil also mellows the lemon's acidity, as cream would. Just enough sugar balances the tartness of the lemons; the addition of a touch of salt and herbs turns the jam savory.

Herbs are where easy improvisations begin: Thyme, basil, chervil, lavender, and the Japanese herb shiso used sparingly provide subtle contrasting flavors. Spices should be used with restraint.

Without the herbs and pepper, and with a slight shift—more sugar, less salt, a neutral-flavored oil—the savory jam turns sweet: an ideal intensely citrus spread for toast, breakfast breads, even filling for a plain cake. A drizzle of a roasted nut oil, such as hazelnut or pistachio, in addition to the neutral oil provides interesting flavor notes.

You might imagine that you could replace the lemon with just about any citrus fruit. Bitter or tough-skinned fruits, however, such as limes and kumquats, yield a jam that is harsh and grainy. But soft-skinned aromatic citrus fruits with a sweet-rather-than-bitter peel, such as Meyer lemons and Mineola tangelos, produce marvelous, unexpected results. Because they are so juicy, Meyer lemons become like a thick, creamy sauce rather than a jam, ideal for plain cakes and ice cream. The tangelo achieves the jammy, spreadable consistency of the lemon jam. Both the tangelo and Meyer lemon purees start to thicken about a half hour after they are made, as though they contain some form of natural pectin. They can be lightened before they set with whipped cream or crème fraîche, to make mousselike desserts and fillings for cakes or cream puffs.

Using a mixture of fruits offers interesting possibilities. The zest of bitter or tough-skinned fruits such as limes or grapefruit can be finely grated and used as a flavoring. A lemon and tangelo jam with a hint of grated lime zest tastes as if it were made with yuzu, the hauntingly flavored Japanese citrus fruit.

The rule of thumb in all these improvisations is to start with less salt, sugar, and flavorings than you think you'll need, adding them to taste until you get the right balance; suit the oil to the fruit, flavorings, and use, whether savory or sweet. If the jam is too intense, blend in a little more oil.

•   •   •   •   •   •

## Lemon Oregano Jam  Makes about 1 cup

> 2 large lemons, preferably thin-skinned (4 to 5 ounces each)
> ¼ cup sugar
> ½ teaspoon kosher salt
> 3 tablespoons extra virgin olive oil, or more to taste
> ½ teaspoon freshly ground black pepper
> 2 to 4 tablespoons loosely packed fresh oregano leaves

**Slice and seed the fruit.** Cut the tough ends off the lemons and discard. Cut each lemon lengthwise into eighths, removing the seeds as you go; cut each slice in half crosswise.

**Puree the fruit with the sugar, salt, and oil.** Transfer the lemons to a food processor and add the sugar and salt. Process to a coarse puree. With the motor running, drizzle in the olive oil until creamy.

**Add the flavorings.** Add the pepper and oregano leaves, and puree until you have a thick "jam" with little flecks of green herb. Adjust the seasoning. The jam should have just enough salt to heighten the flavor without your being aware there is salt in it.

## Improvisations

### Lemon Lavender Jam  Makes about 1 cup

*This delicately scented jam goes wonderfully with grilled or roasted lamb and chicken.*

Follow the preceding recipe, replacing the oregano with ¼ teaspoon finely chopped lavender, or to taste. For a sweet jam, increase the sugar by a tablespoon or two and reduce the salt to just a pinch. A tablespoon or two of fresh thyme leaves can be added as well, for a more overtly herbal **Lemon, Thyme, and Lavender Jam.**

### Tangelo Jam  Makes about 1 cup

*Use the basic Lemon Oregano Jam method to make instant, vividly flavored jam that is great on breakfast breads, pancakes, and French toast. It is thick enough to fill plain cakes, such as the Brown Sugar Lightning Cake (page 321) or Orange*

*Flower Cake (page 323). Because the jam thickens as it sits, make it within a half hour of serving. To thin, beat in a few teaspoons of water or orange juice.*

Cut the tough ends off 2 small Mineola tangelos (about 5 ounces each) and discard. Cut each fruit lengthwise into eighths, removing any seeds as you go; cut each slice in half crosswise. Transfer to a food processor and add 5 to 6 tablespoons sugar and a pinch of salt; process to a coarse puree. With the motor running, drizzle in 3 tablespoons grapeseed, canola, or almond oil and ⅛ to ¼ teaspoon orange flower water (optional); let the motor run a minute or two, until you have a thick "jam."

Use this method to make a **Sweet Lemon Jam**, using 2 lemons instead of tangelos.

## Tangerinesicle Parfaits

*Tangelo Jam reminded me of the orange-tangerine flavors of Creamsicles, the beloved ice cream pops of my '50s childhood. So I tried serving it to a friend spooned over vanilla ice cream. "This is what I remember Creamsicles being, but they never were!" she said, scraping her bowl. For a dinner party, I turned the idea into parfaits, spooning alternating layers of ice cream and Tangelo Jam into tall narrow glasses: a huge hit. The only caveat: Because the jam congeals within an hour, make it just before serving. (If you have the fruit cut and ready to go, this takes only a couple of minutes.)*

## Meyer Lemon Dessert Sauce and Filling    Makes about 1 cup

*Intensely perfumed Meyer lemons, available from November to May, taste like an exotic lemony tangerine and have a mildly tart flesh, far sweeter than regular lemons. Because they are so juicy, when pureed by the preceding method, they make a sauce rather than a jam. It's perfect with plain cakes, berries that have been tossed with a little sugar and lemon juice, and vanilla ice cream (layered into a parfait like the Tangerinesicle Parfait).*

*Because this sauce thickens as it sits, make it just before serving. (The fruit can be prepped up to 4 hours ahead, then kept covered and refrigerated until ready to use.) If the sauce gets too thick after an hour or so, beat in a few teaspoons of water or orange juice or, even better, heavy cream to thin it. To use as a filling for the split layers of a plain cake, such as Orange Flower Cake (page 323), whisk in a few tablespoons of crème fraîche, then let the sauce firm up for 30 to 60 minutes, until spreadable, before assembling the cake.*

Cut the tough ends off 3 Meyer lemons (10 ounces total) and discard. Cut each fruit lengthwise into eighths, removing the seeds as you go; cut each slice in half crosswise. Transfer to a food processor and add 6 tablespoons sugar and a pinch of salt. Process to a coarse puree. With the motor running, drizzle in 2 tablespoons grapeseed, canola, or almond oil; let the motor run a minute or two, until you have a thick, pourable sauce. For a mellower, creamier flavor, blend in 1 to 2 tablespoons heavy cream or crème fraîche (optional).

➤ HORS D'OEUVRES, APPETIZERS, SOUPS, AND SALADS

# Cheese Crisps

I imagine that the inspired soul in Friuli, Italy, who invented fricos, the delectable crisp wafers made from fried Montasio cheese, got her idea from the crisp bits of caramelized cheese that cling to the edges of a pasta casserole. Why not forget the pasta and focus on the crispy morsels that everybody seems to crave? These lacy free-form wafers are the perfect hors d'oeuvre to serve with cocktails, wine, or champagne. Above all, they are both easy to make and very dramatic. Your guests will think you possess great skill to have made them when you've done little more than grate some cheese and sprinkle it into a hot pan.

For years, I made my frico-like cheese crisps with Parmigiano, until I decided to fool around with other cheeses. I've made crisps with sharp Cheddar, dry Jack, aged Gouda, and Manchego, to name a few, using this simple technique.

In this method, the cheese is shredded, then tossed with a little flour to provide a stabilizing starch that will make it easier to remove from the pan without breaking. The mixture is then sprinkled into a hot nonstick pan to form a thin pancake of molten, slightly caramelized cheese; as it cools, it becomes firm enough to slide onto a rack in one piece, where it hardens into a crisp, lacy wafer.

Once you get the hang of the technique—the correct heat of the pan, the thickness of the wafer, and the right degree of "set" to take the crisps out of the pan—you'll find yourself whipping up a batch in 10 minutes. As with pancakes or crepes, it is best to experiment with 1 or 2 crisps to get these variables right.

Any number of cheeses will work with this method as long they have a balanced, pungent flavor and are firm—no softer than a sharp Cheddar. (Avoid overly salty cheeses such as pecorinos; frying concentrates their saltiness.) Each cheese will cook slightly differently, due to varying moisture content. Softer cheeses like Cheddar will spread more to become a uniform sheet. Harder cheeses will produce a weblike crisp.

The possibilities for flavoring the crisps are vast. A pinch of cayenne or a coarse grating of All-Purpose Aromatic Pepper (page 48) amplifies the flavor of any cheese without being overtly spicy. For a subtly smoky flavor, use pungent sweet or hot smoky chile powder, such as pimentón de la Vera from Spain. Cumin, fennel and coriander seeds, lightly crushed, add little blasts of flavor. Dried crumbled herbs, such as rosemary or thyme, can be used singly or in combination with spices.

Uses for the crisps, beyond spectacular hors d'oeuvres, are legion. Crisps make fabulous garnishes: Just match the cheese to the dish. For example, Dry Jack Cheese Crisps are great with Mexican-style black bean soups. I use Cheddar Crisps like a pastry lid for roasted caramelized apples. Parmesan Crisps are the most universally compatible; they are wonderful with white bean soups or warm bean salads, or Tuscan-style sweet pepper stews. Broken Parmesan Crisps also make great crackerlike platforms for eggplant or sweet pepper jams, white or fava bean purees, and so on, to serve as hors d'oeuvres.

The pliable nature of the still-warm crisp means it lends itself to molding. You can drape it over a rolling pin or wine bottle to give it a curled "tile" effect. Or drape it over an overturned bowl. When cool, it becomes an edible vessel in which you can serve salad, mushroom ragùs, or other light, soft fillings.

## Cheese Crisps   Makes eight 9-inch round crisps

> 12 ounces sharp Cheddar, dry Gouda, dry Jack, or Manchego, in one piece, chilled
>
> 2 tablespoons all-purpose flour
>
> ¼ teaspoon cayenne pepper, or more to taste

**Grate the cheese.** Using a box grater (with holes about ¼ inch wide), shred the block of cheese lengthwise (longer shreds work better).

**Toss the cheese with the flour.** Place in a medium bowl and sprinkle with a teaspoon or two of flour; toss gently with a fork to coat the cheese. Then sprinkle with the cayenne and toss again.

**Sprinkle into a hot skillet.** Heat a heavy 10-inch nonstick skillet over moderately high heat until hot but not smoking. Reduce the heat slightly. Measure ½ cup of the cheese. Using your fingers, scatter it as evenly as you can over the bottom of the skillet to make a thin, lacy pancake. The cheese should sizzle when it hits the pan, but it should not smoke; adjust the heat as necessary.

**Panfry the cheese.** Cook the crisp until the strands of cheese have become molten and bubbly, about 2 minutes; if the cheese is runny, gently tip the pan in different directions to even out the cheese and fill in holes. Continue cooking until a medium golden brown shows through the molten cheese and the edges are golden.

**Allow to firm up off the heat.** Remove the pan from the heat and let sit 30 seconds to 1 minute to set. If the crisp hardens too much before you get to it, return the pan to the burner for a few seconds to warm and soften it.

**Remove from the pan and cool.** With a plastic spatula, gently peel the crisp up by one edge; if it begins to tear, let it cool a few seconds longer. Slide it onto a cake rack to cool. Let the crisp set until hardened, about 3 minutes.

**Repeat.** Wipe out the pan with a paper towel and repeat with the remaining cheese mixture. When the crisps are completely cool, they can be gently stacked and stored in a tin or box. Don't worry if the crisps break. They are charming served as free-form shards.

**Serve.** Serve the crisps whole or broken into large, irregular quarters and arranged standing in a basket.

## Improvisations

### Rough Roasted Cheese Crisps   Serves 6 to 8

*To make rough free-form crisps, spread the cheese mixture on a sheet pan and bake, breaking the crisp sheets into rough pieces when they cool. Although this method is faster and easier than panfrying the crisps, it doesn't achieve quite the same gorgeous texture. And you absolutely must use a silicone baking mat (commonly known as a Silpat) or a Teflon bakeware liner to keep the crisp from sticking to the pan.*

Preheat the oven to 375°F. Coarsely grate 12 ounces chilled firm cheese, such as Cheddar or Manchego, and toss with 2 tablespoons all-purpose flour and any seasonings you wish. Place a baking mat on a $16\frac{1}{2} \times 11\frac{1}{2}$-inch sheet pan. Scatter half the cheese evenly over the mat. Shake the pan gently to even the cheese out. Bake for 14 to 15 minutes, until the cheese is molten and golden brown. Remove from the oven and allow to cool. Break the crisp into large pieces and arrange on a platter. Wipe off the baking mat and repeat with the remaining cheese.

### Parmesan Crisps   Makes eight 9-inch crisps

*You can make beautiful thin Parmesan Crisps using the finely grated Parmigiano sold in gourmet stores and better supermarkets. This is also a good way to make use of any grated cheese languishing in the fridge. To make them adhere, you need to use a bit more flour than for the shredded ones.*

Toss 8 ounces (about 3 cups) fresh, fine, "store-grated" Parmigiano with 2 tablespoons plus 2 teaspoons all-purpose flour and 1 teaspoon freshly ground black pepper or other flavoring.

Heat a heavy 10-inch nonstick skillet over moderately high heat until hot but not smoking. Using a small flour scoop or a large pointed spoon, sprinkle a scant $\frac{1}{2}$ cup of the cheese mixture evenly over the bottom of the skillet to make a thin, lacy pancake; you should not be able to see the bottom of the skillet. Cook until the fine grains of cheese have melded together and the edges are just beginning to brown. Firm up off the heat, then remove the crisp from the pan and cool on a rack. Repeat with the remaining cheese mixture.

### Roasted Apples with Cheddar Crisps  Serves 4

*Cheese Crisps make marvelous pastrylike accompaniments for roasted fruit and for surprising and charming desserts. Pair Cheddar Crisps with roasted apples, a play on Cheddar and apple pie. You can make both the crisps and roasted fruits ahead and assemble them at the last minute.*

Prepare cheese crisps using Cheddar or aged Gouda and half the cayenne. For the Roasted Apples, peel and core 3 Golden Delicious apples; cut into eighths. Arrange in a buttered baking dish. Drizzle over ⅔ cup dry white wine and 1½ tablespoons wildflower honey. Dot with 1 tablespoon unsalted butter. Roast, basting occasionally, 30 minutes. Turn the apples over and roast 30 to 40 minutes longer, until the apples are soft and golden and almost all the liquid has evaporated.

Arrange some apple slices in each of 4 shallow dessert bowls and top each with a crisp.

### Roasted Pears with Parmesan Crisps  Serves 4

*This is a logical improvisation on Roasted Apples with Cheddar Crisps. Just substitute not-quite-ripe Comice pears for the apples, roast them the same way, and make Parmesan Crisps. Or use the small, visually charming Seckel pears, unpeeled and halved through the stem. Toss with lemon juice, dust liberally with sugar mixed with a split vanilla bean, and dot with butter. If desired, just before serving, drizzle a few drops Balsamic Caramel (page 64) or a fine aged balsamic vinegar on the pears.*

### Manchego Crisps with Greens, Figs, and Walnuts  Serves 4

*This is a play on the classic combination of salad and cheese.*

In a large bowl, combine 8 cups trimmed, cleaned, and dried peppery or mildly bitter greens (arugula, watercress, frisée, and/or Belgian endive, in any combination), 4 ripe figs, quartered, and ¼ to ½ cup coarsely chopped roasted walnuts. Toss with 2 or 3 tablespoons Essential Vinaigrette (page 355) and season liberally with pepper. Arrange on dinner plates and lean a Manchego Crisp against each salad. Pass more crisps on the side.

# Magic Peppers

- Warm Free-Form Tart of Caramelized Peppers, Olives, Pine Nuts, and Goat Cheese
- Jumbo Shells with Peppers, Pine Nuts, and Molten Mozzarella
- Pepper Bruschetta
- Roasted Romesco

These oven-roasted pepper slices are so easy, delicious, and versatile I call them Magic Peppers. I brush the pepper slices with olive oil and roast them at a high heat with whatever flavorings I feel like having, from slivers of garlic or thyme leaves to sweet, smoked chili powders. It is a revelation how something so utterly simple can become so delicious: at once tender, slightly caramelized, and chewy. They are a perfect hors d'oeuvre, because each slice is just a bite or two. (To make them easy to pick up with the fingers, and visually charming, I leave a little piece of green stem attached to each slice.) They also make a fine side dish for grilled or roasted seafood and meat. But the real reason I call them Magic Peppers is that I can do so many things with them: They are a fantastic raw material for improvising.

When you roast pepper slices at a high heat, the flesh softens and caramelizes slightly as the flavor concentrates and mellows; they are at once chewy and creamy. Spices and herbs offer simple ways to improvise on them. These seasonings could include chopped fresh thyme, rosemary, and savory leaves or fennel, cumin, or crushed coriander seeds. Ground chili powders, such as ancho powder or the fabulous smoked sweet paprikas from Spain, can give a more complex pepper flavor. In Italy, I've had divine oven-roasted peppers that were cooked with slivers of anchovy and garlic in the cavity. Magic Peppers make a fabulous bed for a fried egg, for a simple supper (see Magic Peppers and Other Recipes from This Book with a Fried Egg and Aged Grating Cheese, page 134).

But the real fun begins with all the things you can do with these oven-roasted peppers. They make a delicious little sweet, caramelly hit of flavor in soups, potato salads, or white beans. Coarsely chopped, with olives, anchovies, roasted onions, herbs, pine nuts, or walnuts and some additional olive oil, they make a flavorful rustic mash with which to top bruschetta or pizza, or to "sauce" (like an instant, hearty ragù) tossed pastas or baked pasta casseroles layered with cheese. I like to pile this pepper mash into a shallow bowl and warm it with thin slices of aged goat cheese for an unexpected appetizer. The chopped peppers could easily become a savory tart filling, bound with a drizzle of a creamy quichelike custard of eggs and cream. Roll the chopped peppers into omelets or tortillas, with a dollop of sour cream.

## Magic Peppers   Serves 4

4 large red or yellow bell peppers (2 pounds), or a combination
1½ tablespoons extra virgin olive oil
Kosher salt
Freshly ground black pepper
Seasonings, singly or in combination, such as fresh thyme or rosemary;
   fennel, cumin, or cracked coriander seeds; sweet-picante paprika or smoky
   pimentón de la Vera from Spain

**Slice the peppers.** Preheat the oven to 450°F. Quick method: If you will be chopping up the peppers for another use after they are cooked, stand a pepper, stem up, on the work surface. With a sharp knife, working from top to bottom, slice the flesh off in 4 or 5 large strips, leaving the stem and seed core intact. Cut out any white membrane clinging to the strips, and proceed with the remaining peppers.

If you will be serving the pepper slices as an hors d'oeuvre or side dish, here's how to cut them into charming uniform slices with a little bit of green stem: Halve each pepper lengthwise through the stem; if possible, keep the green stems intact. Cut each half into thirds again lengthwise, leaving the sliver of green stem intact; you will have 6 slices from each pepper. Trim away the white membrane from each slice.

**Oil the peppers.** Place the peppers in a bowl and drizzle with the olive oil; toss to coat completely. Arrange the pepper slices, skin side down, on a large baking sheet.

**Season the peppers.** Sprinkle the peppers lightly with salt, pepper to taste, and any seasoning you wish.

**Roast the peppers.** Roast for about 30 minutes, until the peppers are tender and slightly browned on the edges. Serve hot or at room temperature.

### Warm Free-Form Tart of Caramelized Peppers, Olives, Pine Nuts, and Goat Cheese    Serves 4

*I took my favorite dessert, Free-Form Fruit Tart in a Bowl (page 311), and turned it savory with a rough hash of Magic Peppers instead of fruit. It makes a perfect first course or light meal.*

Prepare the Magic Peppers. When cool enough to handle, pile them onto a cutting board, along with ½ to ⅔ cup drained, pitted Kalamata olives. Coarsely chop the olives and peppers. Chop some basil leaves and incorporate them into the mix on the cutting board. Drizzle over 2 tablespoons extra virgin olive oil and toss.

Preheat the oven to 400°F. Spoon about ½ cup of the pepper mixture onto 4 ovenproof dinner plates or shallow dessert bowls. Top each with thin shavings of aged goat cheese. Cover loosely with aluminum foil. Bake for 5 to 6 minutes, until the cheese is melted and the peppers are hot. Drizzle the cheese with a little olive oil and sprinkle each serving with toasted pine nuts. Top each with a Free-Form Pastry Lid (page 356) or nestle Shallot (or Garlic) Toasts (page 274) alongside.

### Jumbo Shells with Peppers, Pine Nuts, and Molten Mozzarella    Serves 4

*Jumbo pasta shells are really fun and satisfying to eat, but I'm not mad about having to fill each one and making a sauce to bake them in (essential to keep them from drying out). If you toss cooked shells with enough of a coarsely textured sauce, they fill up almost on their own (well, with just a little prodding with my wooden spoon). Here I use Magic Peppers, finely chopped, some pine nuts, herbs, a bit of lemon zest, and cubes of fresh mozzarella, which melts when it hits the heat. Use just about any size shell, from medium to the really huge ones, which require only 2 or 3 for a serving. Figure about 2 ounces dry pasta per person.*

Prepare a double batch of Magic Peppers. When cool enough to handle, pile them onto a cutting board and coarsely chop. Chop some basil leaves and incorporate them into the mix on the cutting board. Drizzle over 2 tablespoons extra virgin olive oil, sprinkle with some grated lemon zest, and toss. If desired, stir in 4 or 5 finely chopped anchovies or ½ to ⅔ cup drained, pitted Kalamata olives.

Cook 8 ounces large pasta shells in a large pot of boiling well-salted water. Drain, reserving some of the pasta water. Return the shells to the pot set over moderate heat, add the pepper mixture and 2 to 3 tablespoons reserved pasta water, and toss to coat. Add a few tablespoons minced fresh herbs, such as basil, chives, and/or flat-leaf parsley, in any combination, ½ cup toasted pine nuts, and freshly ground black pepper to taste and toss again. Turn off the heat and stir in 8 ounces fresh mozzarella, finely diced. When melted and stringy, serve the pasta, with grated Parmigiano on the side.

### Pepper Bruschetta

*Coarsely chopped Magic Peppers are an ideal topping for bruschetta—to my mind, a perfect simple hors d'oeuvre.*

Toss the peppers with extra virgin olive oil and any embellishments you wish, such as pitted olives, fresh herbs, pine nuts or walnuts, grated lemon zest, capers, anchovies, tiny dice of ricotta salata; even small white beans. Make this several hours ahead if you like. Close to serving time, prepare Shallot (or Garlic) Toasts (page 274) and top each toast with the pepper mixture. Drizzle with a little more olive oil and serve.

### Roasted Romesco    Makes about 1⅓ cups

*Romesco, considered Spain's greatest sauce, is a rich amalgam of garlic, tomato, roasted almonds, olive oil, and the mildly spicy Spanish nyora pepper, for which ancho is the closest equivalent. Hankering for romesco to serve with roasted fish but without any anchos on hand, I tried using oven-roasted bell peppers doctored with some sweet, spicy paprika. I prepped most of the ingredients in the oven—roasted peppers and garlic, toasted bread and almonds—then just pureed them together. I've re-created this sauce many times since. It is marvelous with all kinds of seafood, whether warm or chilled, as well as with steamed new potatoes and grilled vegetables, such as baby leeks, fennel, and peppers. It's also a great dip for potato chips. Though the recipe looks involved, it takes about 20 minutes of actual work.*

Prepare ½ recipe Magic Peppers, seasoning the peppers with a scant ½ teaspoon sweet-picante paprika or sweet pimentón de la Vera, or about ½ teaspoon sweet paprika and ¼ teaspoon hot paprika. Roast the other ingredients for the sauce while the oven is on.

Break apart 1 head of garlic into cloves and place on a piece of aluminum foil. Drizzle with some olive oil and 1 tablespoon water, and crimp the edges of the foil together to make a package. Place on the oven rack next to the peppers; remove when the peppers are cooked, after about 25 minutes. The garlic should be puree-soft.

Reduce the oven temperature to 375°F. Spread 20 blanched whole almonds in a pie tin; roast until golden and fragrant, about 10 minutes. (Alternatively, you can use Spanish Marcona almonds, which are already roasted.)

Trim the crusts from a thick slice of white peasant bread; brush with olive oil, place on a small baking sheet, and toast until dry and golden. Set aside.

In a food processor, combine the almonds and bread, broken into bits; process until finely minced. Add the oven-roasted peppers. Squeeze the soft garlic puree out of the roasted cloves directly into the work bowl. Process 1 minute.

Slice a medium ripe tomato in half through the circumference. Squeeze out the juice and seeds and discard. Working directly over the work bowl, rub the cut sides along the large holes of a metal grater so that the flesh is coarsely grated but the skin remains intact in your hand. Discard the skin. Grate or mash 1 small raw garlic clove to a paste and add to the sauce.

With the motor running, drizzle in about ⅓ cup extra virgin olive oil. Add 2 teaspoons sherry vinegar and freshly ground black pepper to taste. Let the sauce sit, refrigerated, for 1 hour, then adjust the seasoning. Stir in 2 additional tablespoons olive oil just before serving, so that it is not totally incorporated.

# Slow-Roasted Tomatoes

Slow-roasted tomatoes have become ubiquitous of late because they are so easy to make and yield such fabulous results: creamy and melting, with a concentrated, slightly caramelized tomato flavor. They make a delectable hors d'oeuvre: bite-sized, at once tart, sweet, and savory. What most recipes neglect to say is how incredibly useful they are: They can be improvised upon endlessly. In fact, a publisher who learned how to make them in a class I taught years ago suggested I write a slow-roasted tomato cookbook because they had become such an essential staple in his own improvisations.

Slow roasting is the antidote to the characterless tomatoes that are widely available in supermarkets, especially in winter. It miraculously transforms them from flavorless and woody into velvety, intensely tomato tomatoes, even in the dead of winter.

So here is my method for slow-roasting tomatoes to serve as is as an hors d'oeuvre or side dish, or to use as a base for all kinds of improvisations. You can apply the technique to any size tomato; just adjust the cooking time.

Beyond being a great hors d'oeuvre, these tomatoes are so versatile I often roast batches just to keep on hand (they freeze well). You can chop or puree them to add a concentrated hit of bright tomato flavor to recipes from soups, stews, and braises to salads and sandwiches. Or you can make them the base of your improvisations.

You could easily improvise by seasoning the tomatoes before roasting with minced fresh herbs—basil, thyme, rosemary, or savory, to name a few; minced garlic or shallot; spices such as fennel seed and cumin; or spice blends such as Moroccan-Style Seasoning with Cinnamon, Coriander, and Cumin (page 46). The tomatoes have such an intense, pure flavor just as they are that I often flavor them after they are cooked, to suit the dish I am making with them.

And what dishes you can make! Because slow roasting the tomatoes evaporates their juices, they have a lot of body. You can layer them whole onto rolled-out yeast or pastry dough to make tarts and pizzas, or use in layered casseroles—a lasagna, for example—or baked beans. Chopped or pureed, they make a thick sauce base with a creamy texture, which you can jazz up with herbs, olives, lemon zest, etc., and use for pasta and fish sauces, on risotto, and so on. They transmute easily into a soup with the addition of chicken broth or half-and-half. Unadorned, pureed slow-roasted tomatoes have a jamlike consistency. Sweetened with honey or brown sugar and flavored with lemon or other fruit zest, ginger, and sweet spices such as cinnamon or cloves, they become unusual jams (after all, tomatoes are a fruit). Or you can blend in sautéed shallots or onions, balsamic vinegar, Moroccan spice mixes with saffron and cinnamon, etc., to make a savory condiment that is great with cold meats and on sandwiches and hamburgers. Because tomatoes have an affinity for many flavorings, from chili powders to Provençal herbs and cilantro, the potential for improvisation is limitless.

Because cherry and egg or grape tomatoes cook in half the time of plum tomatoes, they can often be roasted alongside another dish in the oven to use as an interesting bed or sauce, as in Slow-Roasted Cherry Tomato, Olive, and Lemon Zest Sauce for Slow-Roasted Fish (page 182).

. . . . . .

## Slow-Roasted Tomatoes

Makes about 60 roasted tomato halves if using plum, 24–32 if using regular tomatoes, 2¼ cups mashed or pureed; 10 servings as an hors d'oeuvre

4 pounds ripe or nearly ripe tomatoes, about 30 plum tomatoes or
12 to 16 regular tomatoes
Extra virgin olive oil
About 1 teaspoon sugar
About ½ teaspoon kosher salt
Freshly ground black pepper

**Slice, oil, and season the tomatoes.** Preheat the oven to 325°F. Slice the plum tomatoes in half lengthwise through the stem; larger tomatoes should be quartered through the stem. In a medium bowl, toss the tomatoes with the olive oil to coat. Arrange the tomatoes cut side up on a large baking sheet. Sprinkle with the sugar, salt, and pepper.

**Roast the tomatoes.** Roast the tomatoes for 2½ to 3 hours, until they have lost most of their liquid and are just beginning to brown. They should look like dried apricots and hold their shape when moved. If some tomatoes are done before others, remove them with a spatula while you continue cooking the rest. Cool to room temperature.

**Serve** the tomatoes as an hors d'oeuvre or side dish, arranged in concentric circles on a round or oval platter. Drizzle with extra virgin olive oil.

**Store** the tomatoes, well covered, in the refrigerator up to 1 week, or in the freezer up to 2 months. Once refrigerated, the tomatoes will soften and lose their chewy exterior, though their flavor will be just as good.

**Note:** Roast tiny cherry, grape, and egg tomatoes in exactly the same way to make charming, chunky, tossed-together sauces. Roast egg or grape tomatoes about 1 hour, cherry tomatoes about 1½ hours.

## Improvisations

### Slow-Roasted Tomatoes with Warm Goat Cheese

*When serving Slow-Roasted Tomatoes as an hors d'oeuvre, arrange slivers of fresh goat cheese, mozzarella, or ricotta salata in the center of each tomato, and*

*season with a pinch of chopped fresh basil or thyme. Place in a hot oven or under the broiler for a few minutes to melt the cheese, then drizzle with extra virgin olive oil. They're like little crustless pizzas.*

### Slow-Roasted Tomato Sauce   Makes 2¼ cups

*This sauce—made with little more than pureed Slow-Roasted Tomatoes—has a deep caramelized flavor and a creamier texture than regular tomato sauces. It is excellent with all kinds of pasta and polenta, as a pizza sauce, or as a topping for bruschetta, as well as for grilled chicken and heartier fish such as salmon and swordfish.*

Prepare Slow-Roasted Tomatoes. Chop them coarse or finely, depending on the texture you want; you can also puree them in a food processor. Transfer to a small heavy saucepan and heat, stirring, over low heat. Thin to the desired consistency with a couple of tablespoons of chicken broth, meat or poultry juices, pasta cooking water, or heavy cream, depending on what you are serving the sauce with.

Flavor the sauce as you would any other tomato sauce: Drizzle with a good extra virgin olive oil; stir in sautéed onions and/or crisped diced bacon or pancetta; warm with a few rosemary or thyme sprigs or stir in ¼ cup minced fresh soft herbs, such as basil, cilantro, chervil, or chives, just before serving. To make a quick **Puttanesca Sauce**, warm the basic sauce with ¼ cup pitted black olives, 1 tablespoon drained small capers, and 2 teaspoons chopped fresh oregano.

### Slow-Roasted Tomato Soup   Serves 4

*When pureed, slow-roasted tomatoes make a rich, velvety soup with an intense tomato flavor that is especially welcome in winter.*

In a small skillet, combine 1 tablespoon extra virgin olive oil and 3 tablespoons finely chopped shallots; cover and cook over moderately low heat until the shallots are soft and just beginning to brown, about 7 minutes. Combine 1¾ cups Slow-Roasted Tomatoes and the sautéed shallots in a food processor or a blender. With the motor running, drizzle in 2¾ cups low-sodium chicken broth; puree. Strain, if desired, through a coarse strainer.

Pour the soup into a medium saucepan and heat over moderate heat; adjust the seasoning. Ladle the soup into 4 warm soup bowls; garnish, if desired, with a drizzle of extra virgin olive oil, a dollop of crème fraîche, or chopped fresh basil.

### Rustic Slow-Roasted Tomato Tart   Makes one 10-inch tart, 4 to 6 servings

*I threw this savory tart together one day to serve at an impromptu vegetarian luncheon with a green salad and cheese. It also makes a great hors d'oeuvre, sliced into thin wedges.*

Prepare Slow-Roasted Tomatoes; you need about 24 to 30 roasted plum tomato halves for this recipe. Preheat the oven to 400°F. On a lightly floured surface, roll out 8 ounces of your favorite flaky piecrust or Easy Butter Dough for Tarts, Pies, and Free-Form Pastries (page 355) into a rough circle 13 to 14 inches in diameter. Transfer the dough to a baking sheet and sprinkle 1 tablespoon all-purpose flour evenly over it, leaving a 1½-inch border uncovered.

Arrange the roasted tomato halves in concentric circles on top of the flour. If the tomatoes are very tart, sprinkle lightly with sugar. Slice 3 medium shallots into thin circles and toss with extra virgin olive oil and a little salt; arrange the shallot rings on top of the tomatoes in a lacy pattern. Fold the edges of the dough over the tomatoes. Moisten your fingers with water and gently press the pleats so they hold together. Bake the tart until the crust is golden brown, about 25 minutes. Let cool for 10 minutes before serving, then drizzle with a little extra virgin olive oil. Sprinkle with chopped fresh basil, if desired.

### Tomato Jam   Makes 1 cup

*My friend Eleanor Mailloux, who owns the Beekeeper Inn in the West Virginia Appalachians, served me a sweet tomato jam for breakfast my first morning there 30 years ago. I've never forgotten it, and here I have applied its subtle flavors to Slow Roasted Tomatoes.*

Prepare ½ recipe Slow-Roasted Tomatoes. Puree the tomatoes in a food processor; you should have 1 cup plus 2 tablespoons. Scrape the puree into a medium heavy saucepan. Add ¼ teaspoon ground cinnamon, ⅛ teaspoon curry powder, ¼ teaspoon grated fresh ginger, 3 tablespoons wildflower honey, 1 tablespoon water, and about 1½ teaspoons grated lemon zest. Carefully cut the rind and bitter white pith off 2 small lemons and section out the flesh (see Peeling and Sectioning Citrus Fruit, page 353); discard the membranes and rind and coarsely chop the flesh. Stir into the tomato mixture. Bring to a simmer and cook over low heat until very thick and the flavors have mellowed, about 5 minutes. Transfer to a clean, dry jar. Store in the refrigerator up to 1 month.

# Rustic Root Vegetable Soup

I love recipes I can make from whatever is on hand, like this Rustic Root Vegetable Soup. It is made from refrigerator staples: long-keeping root vegetables–leeks, potatoes, celery root, and parsnips–that retain their flavor and texture for weeks. The secret in this straightforward soup is braising the vegetables first with a little water and olive oil; it gives the soup an amazing depth of flavor and richness.

This is the ideal cold-weather soup for days when you don't want to leave the house, or to make for friends who are under the weather. It will keep about 4 days, covered, in the refrigerator, and only gets better.

This basic soup is modeled after rustic Provençal vegetable soups, which are traditionally cooked with water rather than broth and a tablespoon or two of olive oil. Simmering root vegetables in a mixture of fat and liquid suffuses them with a lovely creaminess and gives the broth body and richness for little work. When I am only using a few kinds of vegetables, as in this version, I often use chicken broth instead of water to ensure a well-flavored soup.

This basic formula can easily mutate into other creations. Because the potato provides starch to bind the other vegetables, when the soup is pureed in a blender, it becomes so creamy it can double as a velouté-style sauce for chicken pies. Replace the chicken broth with a small amount of milk or cream, and it becomes a velvety root vegetable puree as a side dish for roasted poultry and meats.

Use this basic model to fashion all kinds of rustic soups simply by playing with the essential elements. You can shift the proportions of vegetables to increase the sweet spiciness with more parsnips, or the savory onioniness with more leeks, and so on; other options include carrots, parsley root, rutabaga, and turnips, in any combination as long as the total is about 3 ½ cups sliced or chopped. For a gutsier soup, instead of olive oil or butter, render the fat from chopped smoked bacon or pancetta in the pan before adding vegetables and water. Root vegetables take well to subtle spicing, with curry powder, garam masala, nutmeg, and coriander.

Once the soup is made, you can add all kinds of embellishments: cooked dried beans or shell pasta, shredded chicken or pork (Chinese-restaurant roasted duck is marvelous), chopped raw greens, such as Swiss chard or escarole, and so on. Garnish the soup with a drizzle of extra virgin olive oil, a herb-flavored olive oil, or shavings of Parmigiano.

. . . . . .

## Rustic Root Vegetable Soup   Serves 4

1 medium yellow or red waxy potato (6 to 7 ounces), peeled, quartered, and
thinly sliced crosswise (about 1¼ cups)

1 small celery root (7 to 8 ounces), peeled, quartered, and thinly sliced
crosswise (¾ cup)

1 medium leek, white and pale green parts only, thinly sliced (½ cup)

2 medium parsnips, peeled, halved lengthwise, and thinly sliced crosswise
(½ cup)

2 garlic cloves, thinly sliced

¼ teaspoon kosher salt

¼ teaspoon sugar

1 tablespoon unsalted butter, extra virgin olive oil, or rendered bacon fat
(page 354)

¾ cup water

3 cups low-sodium chicken broth or water

Freshly ground white pepper

¼ cup coarsely chopped flat-leaf parsley

Shallot (or Garlic) Toasts (page 274), optional

**Braise the vegetables.** In a medium saucepan, combine the potato, celery root, leek, parsnips, garlic, salt, sugar, butter, and water. Bring to a simmer, cover, and cook 15 minutes, or until the water has almost evaporated.

**Add more liquid and simmer until tender.** Add the chicken broth, return to a simmer, cover, and cook an additional 15 minutes, or until the vegetables are soft.

**Season and garnish.** Adjust the seasoning and stir in the white pepper to taste. Just before serving, stir in the parsley. Pass the toasts on the side, if desired.

## Improvisations

### Creamy Root Vegetable Soup   Serves 4

*If you make the Rustic Root Vegetable Soup with butter and puree it, it becomes an exquisite "crèma," an elegant creamy soup, due to the preliminary braising of the vegetables with some fat. Additional cream only gilds the lily.*

Prepare Rustic Root Vegetable Soup. Puree the soup in batches in a blender. Or, if using a food processor, let it run at least 2 minutes. Rinse out the saucepan and strain the soup into it. Adjust the seasoning, adding a few scrapings of freshly grated nutmeg. If desired, drizzle each serving with a swirl of heavy cream or stirred crème fraîche or a few drops of white truffle oil.

### Root Vegetable Puree with Vanilla    Serves 4

*I came up with this unusual side dish one evening when I was cooking dinner for friends. I set out to make a root vegetable puree based roughly on the Rustic Root Vegetable Soup approach, using milk for creaminess instead of chicken broth. On a whim, I threw the husks of a vanilla pod, whose seeds I had used for the dessert, into the cooking water for the root vegetables. The result was quite surprising: The subtle presence of vanilla brought out the sweetness and spicy perfume of the parsnips and celery root. This is a great way to use up split vanilla pods, called for in many dessert recipes in this book, since you need only a hint of vanilla. Or you can just use a piece of vanilla bean, split, for this recipe.*

In a medium saucepan, combine 1 medium yellow or red waxy potato (7 to 8 ounces), peeled, quartered, and thinly sliced crosswise (1½ cups), 1 small celery root (7 to 8 ounces), peeled, quartered, and thinly sliced crosswise (¾ cup), 1 medium leek, white and pale green parts only, thinly sliced (½ cup), 2 to 3 medium parsnips, peeled, halved lengthwise and thinly sliced crosswise (¾ cup); ¼ teaspoon each salt and sugar, 1 tablespoon unsalted butter, and ⅔ cup water. Bring to a simmer, cover, and cook 15 minutes, or until the water has almost evaporated. Add ¾ cup milk and ½ vanilla bean—split lengthwise, seeds scraped out, bean and seeds added to the pan—or use the freshly scraped pod of a vanilla bean, if you happen to have one. Bring back to a simmer, cover, and cook an additional 15 minutes, or until the vegetables are soft.

Place a strainer over a bowl and drain the vegetables, reserving the cooking liquid. Discard the vanilla pod. Puree the vegetables in a food processor 3 minutes, using a tablespoon or two of the cooking liquid if necessary to thin the puree. Alternatively, you can pass the vegetables through a food mill. Return to the saucepan, stir in up to ¼ cup half-and-half and an additional teaspoon or two of butter, and adjust the seasoning.

### Creamy Root Vegetable Velouté for Chicken Stews and Potpies    Makes 3 cups

*While trying to make a leaner version of the delicious chicken potpie I remembered from my childhood, I used the Creamy Root Vegetable Soup, with a slightly different balance of root vegetables, in place of the usual rich cream sauce. It had subtle root-vegetable-and-leek flavors but was so smooth it tasted as if it were full of cream. The potpie was a big hit, and I've used this sauce ever since for any kind of chicken-in-cream-sauce dish, like the Free-Form Chicken Potpie.*

Follow the recipe for Creamy Root Vegetable Soup, using ⅔ cup each sliced celery root and parsnip, and enrich with a few tablespoons of heavy cream or crème fraîche, if desired.

### Free-Form Chicken Potpie    Serves 6

*This satisfying classic is really an assemblage of simple parts that you can make ahead: Creamy Root Vegetable Velouté for Chicken Stews and Potpies, chicken (roasted or rotisserie), vegetables (leftovers are fine), and some sort of old-fashioned top crust, such as buttermilk biscuits or thin slabs of prebaked pastry dough. Once the parts are made, the dish takes minutes to assemble.*

In a large heavy saucepan over moderate heat, warm the Creamy Root Vegetable Velouté. Enrich with a few tablespoons heavy cream or crème fraîche, if desired. Stir in 4½ cups skinless, boneless cooked chicken in bite-sized pieces and 4½ cups cooked mixed vegetables (carrots, asparagus, peas, potatoes, and/or pearl onions, in any combination). Bring to a simmer and adjust the seasoning, adding a teaspoon or two of fresh lemon juice, salt, and pepper as necessary. Stir in ¼ cup chopped flat-leaf parsley or a mixture of fresh parsley, chives, and tarragon. Serve in large, shallow soup bowls topped with Free-Form Pastry Disks (page 356).

# Watercress Salad-Soup with Smoked Duck Breast and Ginger

The inspiration for this soup came from a middle-of-the-night meal at a 24-hour soup joint in New York's Chinatown more than 30 years ago. I was served a large bowl of chicken broth with a bunch of fresh watercress barely wilted in it and an egg plunked in the center, perfectly cooked, with a runny yolk. The soup was a revelation: charming, delicious, nourishing, and inspired, a salad in a soup. It has been the jumping-off point for many impromptu using-what's-on-hand improvisations on chicken soup, like this favorite: thin slices of smoked duck breast, watercress, and slivered ginger in a garlic-scented broth. It is an informal meal-in-itself soup that can be made for one or many, the elements placed in each soup bowl and the broth poured over.

The Chinatown soup is an example of a composed soup, that is, a broth in which a variety of elements are assembled to make a complete meal. These elements can be whatever is on hand or inspires you: shredded cooked chicken, pork, duck, shrimp, tofu; roasted vegetables; noodles, dumplings, filled pasta, cubes of polenta; olives; cooked dried beans; greens (sautéed with garlic or, if mild–such as cress, arugula, or spinach–wilted right in the broth); wild mushrooms; roasted peppers; and chopped herbs, in endless combinations. The basic formula of a broth plus cooked or quick-cooking garnishes quickly becomes second nature, allowing you to improvise all manner of soups. Each garnish cooks in the broth just as long as it takes to become tender and warmed.

Good broth is essential, a factor that has kept these easy-to-make soups out of many busy cooks' repertoires. "Who's got time to make broth?" they wonder, and turn the page. By good broth I mean broth that has the limpid texture and pure flavor of homemade chicken broth. Real Broth for a Too-Busy Cook (page 106) outlines simple strategies for making flavorful broths, from a truly simple from-scratch one made with poultry, rabbit, and duck bones from past meals stockpiled in the freezer, to one based on decent low-sodium canned broth fortified with bones and other flavoring elements. Or, stockpile good "real" frozen chicken broth, available in better supermarkets.

To fortify a broth, doctor canned ones, or build in more complex layers of flavor, infuse broths with aromatic flavorings: fresh herbs, spices, smoked ham, lemongrass, saffron, dried wild mushrooms, garlic, kaffir lime leaves, ginger, chiles, lemon or orange zest, and prepared curry pastes, to name a few. Simmer these in the broth as you would an herb tea to release their flavor. For example, infuse chicken broth with fresh basil leaves for a vegetable soup.

Once you've composed the soup, there are several finishing elements that you can add, including a drizzle of fine extra virgin olive oil or a flavored oil (the beads of oil will "break" and float on the surface of the soup in a charming way); a scattering of chopped fresh herbs, chives, or slivered lemon zest; shaved or grated Parmigiano; Shallot (or Garlic) Toasts (page 274); and so on.

As for proportions, there are no exact formulas; gauge rough amounts according to how many different elements will be put in the bowl.

. . . . . .

# Watercress Salad-Soup with Smoked Duck Breast and Ginger

**Serves 4**

6 to 8 cups canned low-sodium chicken broth or Real Broth for
a Too-Busy Cook (page 106)

2 garlic cloves, grated

A 1-inch chunk fresh ginger, peeled

1 smoked duck breast (8 to 10 ounces), or 8 to 10 ounces
cooked chicken, duck, or pork, shredded

3 bunches watercress, tough stems removed, rinsed and
shaken dry

Salt and freshly ground black pepper

Roasted sesame oil or Chinese Many-Flavor Oil (page 52) for drizzling
(optional)

**Heat the broth, fortifying it with the flavorings and bones, if desired.** In a medium saucepan, combine the chicken broth and garlic. Simmer over moderate heat for 5 minutes. Meanwhile, slice the ginger lengthwise as thin as possible. Stack the slices and cut them lengthwise into thin slivers. Add the ginger and simmer 5 minutes longer.

**While the broth is heating, assemble the embellishments.** If using the duck, peel the fatty skin off the duck breast. Slice the skin into thin strips. Place it in a small heavy skillet and cook, covered, over moderately low heat until the skin is crisp and golden brown, about 5 minutes. Turn off the heat.

Meanwhile, thinly slice the breast. Cut the stems off the watercress, leaving a bunch of leaves and tender stems. (Reserve the tougher stems to stir-fry, if desired.) Divide the watercress among 4 deep soup bowls.

**Heat the duck, and any other elements that need to be cooked, in the broth.** Reduce the heat to very low. Add the duck (or other meat) and cook until it is just heated through, about 1 minute. Add salt and pepper to taste.

**Assemble the soup in the bowls.** With a slotted spoon, arrange the duck in the bowls, along with a few strips of crisp skin; pour the broth over. If desired, drizzle some sesame oil or a little of the melted duck fat over the soup. Serve at once.

## Real Broth for a Too-Busy Cook

I had almost given up making chicken broth–though not my craving for it–until I devised this effortless strategy. I freeze any bones, necks, and trimmings from raw and cooked poultry (including chicken, duck, quail, turkey, or squab) and rabbit that have come through my kitchen; bones from rotisserie chickens or roasted ducks; necks from whole chickens; rabbit and turkey carcasses from holiday feasts; and so on in a large Ziploc bag in my freezer. Every now and then, when I have a pile of bones, I make a batch of broth to stockpile in the freezer. A mix of different bones makes a particularly flavorful broth.

Put the collected bones in a pot with a halved shallot or two, a bay leaf, and a few thyme sprigs. Cover with water by 2 inches (or, if there aren't many bones, use some canned low-sodium broth to give an early flavor boost), bring to a simmer over moderate heat, and simmer–don't boil–for 45 minutes. Strain through a fine-mesh sieve, ladle into plastic containers, and allow to cool completely. Skim off the fat and refrigerate up to 4 days or freeze up to 3 months.

To fortify canned broth, braises, soups, or stewing beans in a pinch, add a few frozen bones or a couple of pieces of rind from Parmigiano and simmer 20 to 30 minutes, until the flavor is enriched; discard the bones using a pair of tongs. When you need cooked chicken for a recipe or a chicken salad, poach skinless chicken parts in homemade or canned broth to further enrich your broths.

· · · · · ·

## Improvisations

### Herb Soup with Tortellini    Serves 2

*One evening, fresh herbs became my solution to not having any obvious soup greens around, such as spinach or escarole. I gathered a handful of tender leaves from the motley collection in my fridge, which included flat-leaf parsley, basil, chives, and fennel fronds. I simmered them in broth briefly, then added cooked tortellini and a few slivers of lemon zest. Since then, I've used varying combinations of herbs depending on what is on hand, including small amounts of strong herbs, such as sage, thyme, and savory. (The Herb Salad mix on page 112 works well, or take a look at Ravioli with a Handful of Herbs, page 296.) I've even applied the strategy to a languishing mesclun salad that has enough unsalady greens like spinach, mizuna, and kale.*

Assemble about 1 loosely packed cup herb leaves. This can be any combination but should be composed predominantly of milder herbs, such as basil, flat-leaf parsley, fennel fronds, sorrel, mint, chervil, and watercress; go lighter on strongly flavored herbs, such as thyme, rosemary, sage, and chives. Coarsely chop them. (You can get a good idea of the balance of your herb mix by smelling the chopped herbs, and adjusting more accordingly, adding milder, sweeter herbs if rosemary or sage predominate and so on.) Use a vegetable peeler to remove 2 strips of zest from a lemon; cut them crosswise into fine slivers.

Boil about 6 to 8 ounces tortellini, ravioli, or other filled pasta in salted water until al dente. Meanwhile, heat 3 cups chicken broth in a medium saucepan. When the pasta is cooked, use a slotted spoon to transfer it to 2 large soup bowls. Add the herbs to the broth, stir, and add salt and pepper to taste. Ladle the herb broth over the pasta and scatter some lemon zest over the top.

### Parmesan Cream    Serves 1

*I came up with this comforting, nourishing soup one chilly day when I needed a jolt of protein and had only a bare-bones cupboard. A beaten egg whisked into hot chicken broth creates a light creamy soup without cream; grated Parmigiano and black pepper give it a pungent yet mellow flavor that can be dressed up in any number of simple ways. A drizzle of fine olive oil is the simplest and best; it forms jewel-like beads on the surface and provides little hits of flavor in each spoonful. Shallot (or Garlic) Toasts (page 274) can be placed in the bowl before the soup is poured over, or served alongside, or, diced, for croutons. Sometimes I pile garlicky sautéed greens in the center of the soup. This amount can be easily scaled up if you increase the cooking time slightly.*

Bring 1 cup chicken broth to a boil in a small saucepan. Reduce the heat to the barest simmer and whisk in 1 large egg, beaten. Whisk continuously for 30 seconds. Whisk in 3 tablespoons grated Parmigiano and continue cooking, whisking constantly, until the mixture is the consistency of cream; do not allow to boil. Remove from the heat and add salt and plenty of freshly ground black pepper. Pour into a soup bowl and drizzle in about ½ teaspoon extra virgin olive oil.

## Chicken, Corn, and Avocado in Chipotle Lime Broth  Serves 4

*This soup was inspired by a conversation with a stranger in Mexico about a chipotle chile–infused broth used to nap pumpkin ravioli he had tasted at a nouvelle Mexican restaurant in Mexico City. Chipotles give the broth a mildly smoky, spicy flavor that is balanced by a hefty squeeze of lime juice and mellow avocado slices, floated in at the last minute.*

Rinse 2 chipotle chiles in adobo; slice each in half lengthwise and remove the seeds, then slice crosswise into thin strips; reserve.

Heat 2 teaspoons vegetable oil in a large saucepan over moderate heat. Add 1 medium onion, thinly sliced, cover, and cook until the onion has softened slightly and released some liquid, about 3 minutes. Uncover, increase the heat slightly, and sauté, tossing frequently, until the onion is soft and golden brown, 6 minutes. Add 2 garlic cloves, finely chopped, and continue cooking until the garlic is soft, about 2 minutes. Add 6 cups chicken broth and bring to a simmer. Add ¾ of the reserved chipotle strips and cook 2 minutes. Add 1 to 1½ cups frozen or fresh corn kernels and simmer 5 minutes. Taste the broth; if you prefer it spicier, add the remaining chipotle. Add the juice of 1½ limes and salt to taste.

Just before serving, slice 2 ripe avocados into wedges and arrange on a plate, along with 1½ limes, sliced into wedges, and a handful of fresh cilantro sprigs. Add 1 pound cooked chicken, shredded, to the soup. Simmer 2 to 3 minutes, until the chicken is hot. Stir in 1 cup roughly chopped cilantro leaves, and serve. Instruct guests to add a slice or two of avocado and cilantro sprigs to their soup and squeeze in more lime to taste.

# Herb Salad

- Spring Salad with Pea Shoots, Tarragon, and Chives
- Cilantro Salad with Fragrant Peanut or Sesame Oil
- Salad of Cress, Pine Nuts, Pears, and Chives
- Doctored Mesclun Salad

A few years ago, mesclun salad—a mix of many greens, both mild and spicy—began to shake up our rather conservative American salad repertoire. What tends to be a standardized mix in America has its roots in the variegated lettuce-and-herb population of a French kitchen garden. There, mesclun is made up of the best of the moment—vibrant combinations of young and tender leaves in a fabulous tumble of textures and flavors. Herbs often figure in, as do flowers. Mesclun centers around the idea of salad as expression—both of the cook and of the season, garden, or market. The natural evolution of that notion is this herb salad served to me by Sondra Davidson, who cooks in America as though she were in France, where she lived for many years. The effect of this salad is very different from the sum of its parts would indicate: at once surprising, unique, refreshing, satisfying, and utterly delightful. Sondra created a wild flavor using ordinary supermarket herbs. It reminded me of the improvisational heart of salad making, and how herbs figure into that.

It makes the perfect salad course in a rich meal, or serve with warm goat cheese and peasant bread for a charming lunch.

When I asked her about her herb salad, Sondra gave no quantities. She just told me what herbs she used, her method of picking and washing the tender leaves, and how she dressed them; it was just theory really, a guide with which to forge my own. Key to combining herbs is the fact that, although individually they may taste strong, in combination they tend to balance each other and to become, surprisingly, more subtle. Also key is to taste them as you make your combination: Pinch a sampling of leaves and pop them in your mouth; you'll see if the balance pleases you or if you need to increase the amount of certain herbs, or even some milder lettuces, to create a pleasing effect.

Sondra made her unique salad in the dead of winter with what she found available in New York City supermarkets. (She left out basil, which she said throws the other flavors off.) To create this recipe, I used the herbs she named, figuring out the proportions by intuition and the taste-as-you-go method. They are only an example of the possibilities, depending on what is available to you. The list shown here gives a sense of the herbs you could include. Herb salads can also be made of one mild herb–say, pea leaves or flat-leaf parsley leaves–or just a few, as you'll see with the improvisations that follow. In the course of many herb salad improvisations, I discovered that chives, used judiciously, will give almost any green–including commercial mesclun–a wilder flavor.

Dressings are the other key element in herb salads that mellow and unify the flavors. Sondra's instructions were to use the best extra virgin olive oil possible, with just a few drops of sherry vinegar and salt and pepper. In other words, subtlety is important, a principle that holds true for every herb salad I've made. Although Sondra's dressing is an excellent all-purpose one for just about any salad, you can tailor the dressing to your herbs, using different combinations of oil and vinegars or lemon juice. Roasted walnut oil and red wine vinegar go well with many herb mixes. Roasted peanut oil and roasted sesame oil are great with cilantro.

Another strategy for making herb salads is to use prepared mesclun–mixes of young greens–as a base into which you add herbs. When including strongly flavored herbs, such as sage or thyme, in a mix of mild greens, use them judiciously, because they can easily overwhelm the salad.

anise hyssop

arugula

basil

borage

burnet

chervil

chickweed

chives

cilantro

cress

dill

fennel fronds

flat-leaf parsley

lemon balm

lovage

mâche

mint

nasturtium leaves

sage

tarragon

Herb salads are complemented by the sweetness of fruits such as pears, figs, oranges, and apples and by mild salty-savory cheeses, such as feta, goat, and ricotta salata.

When cleaning greens for salad, we often throw away leaves and stems that aren't damaged; they are just too fibrous to eat raw. Many, such as tough, outer dandelion or escarole leaves or watercress stems, need only to be cooked to be delicious; save them for braises and soups. Or sauté watercress stems with garlic and/or ginger.

. . . . . .

## Herb Salad   Serves 4

8 to 9 cups assorted fresh herb leaves; or use the following proportions:
2 cups flat-leaf parsley leaves
2 cups dill leaves
2 cups cilantro leaves
1 cup peppermint leaves
1 cup chervil sprigs (optional)
1 cup tarragon leaves
¼ cup chives cut into ½-inch lengths

Olive Oil and Sherry Vinegar Dressing
1 teaspoon sherry vinegar, preferably aged
Pinch of kosher salt
2 tablespoons fine extra virgin olive oil

Freshly ground black pepper

**Wash the leaves and spin dry.** Wash the leaves gently and dry them in a salad spinner. Place the leaves in a bowl, cover with a damp paper towel and plastic wrap, and refrigerate until you are ready to serve the salad.

**Make the dressing.** In a small bowl, combine the vinegar and salt. Whisk in the olive oil.

**Just before serving, dress the salad.** Drizzle the dressing over the salad. Toss to coat each leaf. Adjust the seasoning and add pepper to taste.

**Note:** Assembling the herb leaves can be done more quickly than you might think: Strip the leaves off by sliding your fingers backward along the stem, opposite the direction in which the leaves point. Leave out any large leaves; small and medium ones are the most tender and pleasing to eat.

## Improvisations

### Spring Salad with Pea Shoots, Tarragon, and Chives   Serves 4

*The idea for this salad came from the New York City restaurant Sumile, where chef Josh DeChellis does a very original Japanese-French fusion. My salad arrived looking like a vividly fresh though not out of the ordinary mesclun salad, but it tasted like spring, with the green flavors of peas, tarragon, and chives. Guided by my taste memory of Sumile's salad, I improvised my own version, using pea shoots as an herb. The beauty of this salad is that all these spring-flavored ingredients are available year-round, since pea shoots or snow pea sprouts, once found only in summer farmers' markets, have joined the array of sprouts sold in supermarkets.*

Place 8 cups washed and dried mesclun or mild greens, such as baby red oak leaf lettuce, Bibb, or butter lettuce in a large bowl. Add ⅔ to ¾ cup loosely packed fresh tarragon leaves, ½ cup fresh chervil sprigs (optional), ¼ cup chives cut into ½-inch lengths, and 3 to 4 cups (3 to 4 ounces) pea shoot leaves (if using snow pea sprouts, use only the top 1½ inches of the leafy stems). Dress the salad with the Olive Oil and Sherry Vinegar Dressing. Serve at once.

### Cilantro Salad with Fragrant Peanut or Sesame Oil   Serves 2

*Cilantro is another herb I didn't think to eat as a green until I was jarred out of that notion at a restaurant in New York's Chinatown, which served cilantro leaves dressed with roasted sesame oil as a foil for rich meats. So I took the idea home with me and created this salad, perfect with roast duck or pork or Asian-style shrimp and fish dishes. Sample a leaf of cilantro before you buy it; some are tough. You want soft, tender leaves for this salad. Be sure to dress the salad just before serving.*

In a small bowl, combine 1 teaspoon fresh lime juice, ⅛ teaspoon sugar, and a pinch of salt. Whisk in 1 tablespoon roasted peanut oil, or 1½ teaspoons roasted sesame oil and 1½ teaspoons canola or grapeseed oil. If you like, infuse the dressing with 2 bruised slices fresh ginger and a small strip of orange zest. Strip the leaves off an 8-ounce bunch cilantro; discard the stems. Wash and spin dry. Place in a medium bowl, drizzle the dressing over, and toss to coat.

### Salad of Cress, Pine Nuts, Pears, and Chives    Serves 4

*Watercress is just one of many kinds of cresses available these days. Some, like upland cress, are available in supermarkets. Others, like wild watercress and garden cress, can be found in summer farmers' markets. Nasturtium leaves are also a cress, with a bright, peppery flavor. I make this salad with whatever cress I find—or a mix of them. The few simple ingredients—ripe pears, chives, and roasted pine nuts—yield a satisfying play of peppery, sweet, salty, fragrant, and subtly smoky. It is also superb made with Roasted Pears (page 86).*

Cut the tough stems off 2 bunches (about 12 ounces) cress; you should have about 6 ounces tender sprigs. Wash, spin dry, and place in a large bowl. Add 1 ripe Comice or Bartlett pear, peeled, cored, and diced, ¼ cup chives cut into ½-inch lengths, ¼ cup roasted pine nuts, and a 3-inch strip of lemon zest, finely slivered. Dress the salad with the Olive Oil and Sherry Vinegar Dressing and serve.

### Doctored Mesclun Salad    Serves 4

*Mesclun salad has become ubiquitous these days, sold in plastic tubs and cello-paks in every supermarket; it is a far cry from the mix of just-picked baby greens and herbs of its French origins. In improvising herb salads, I inadvertently discovered a simple way to make ho-hum commercial salad mixes taste more like "real" greens with a slightly wild flavor: Add fresh chives.*

In a large bowl, arrange 8 cups washed and dried mesclun and about 3 tablespoons finely sliced fresh chives. Dress the salad with 2 tablespoons fine extra virgin olive oil, 1 teaspoon sherry vinegar, preferably aged, or Banyuls vinegar; add salt and pepper to taste.

# Sugar Snaps with Extra Virgin Olive Oil and Shaved Parmigiano

- Sugar Snaps, Asparagus, and Baby Artichokes with Parmigiano
- Mushroom and Squash Carpaccio with Pine Nuts, Basil, and Parmigiano
- Fennel and Parmigiano Salad with Toasted Pecans
- Botanical Sliced Pears, Apples, Figs, or Persimmons with Parmigiano and Balsamic Caramel

My favorite appetizer evolved from the classic Italian combination of raw vegetables—most commonly, arugula, thinly sliced fennel, and raw baby artichoke hearts—dressed with olive oil and lemon and thin shavings of Parmigiano. One day, when I was looking around the market, I thought, Why not try making it with sugar snap peas? I sliced them on an extreme diagonal to reveal the peas hidden within, and applied the basic Italian formula to make a surprising play on the classic hors d'oeuvre. It's a perfect recipe: at once rustic and sophisticated, easy for even the novice cook, with the bright appeal of a plate of fresh peas.

I often serve this dish as an hors d'oeuvre with drinks while getting the rest of the meal together. I put a bowl of it on the table for friends to spoon onto small plates, accompanied by good bread.

If asked to choose one cheese if they were marooned on an island, most cooks I know would say Parmigiano. It is an astonishingly versatile cheese, great alone or with almost any food, both sweet and savory. It acts like an exotic salt to illuminate the flavors of whatever it is paired with. Having a chunk of good Parmigiano on hand means you always have the makings for *à-la-minute* appetizers, hors d'oeuvres, and desserts.

This recipe is inherently improvisational, a formula really, into which you can plug just about any vegetable that looks best in your market. The list is long and traverses the seasons: celery, fennel, radishes, young brussels sprouts, peas, fava beans, fresh soybeans (see "Lazy Man's Favas" with Extra Virgin Olive Oil and Parmigiano, page 139), mushrooms of all kinds, raw baby artichokes, asparagus, zucchini and other tender summer squashes, cherry tomatoes, radicchio, arugula, escarole. . . . They must be sliced thin enough to be crisp but not too crunchy. Play with different ways of cutting to find the most visually appealing shape; for example, slicing celery thinly on an extreme diagonal produces dramatic elongated crescents. A mandoline or Benriner makes short work of slicing many vegetables.

Dressing is minimal: excellent extra virgin olive oil with lemon juice or a drizzle of fine balsamic vinegar. Stirring the dressing with a fork speared with a bruised garlic clove allows you to control the garlic's intensity. Additional elements include chopped fresh tender herbs, such as chives, basil, and flat-leaf parsley; roasted nuts, including pine nuts, walnuts, and sliced roasted hazelnuts; and slivers of lemon or orange zest.

Apply the formula to cooked vegetables: roasted mushrooms or fennel, Magic Peppers (page 89), white beans. Paper-thin slices of beef or bresaola, the delicate salt-cured air-dried beef, make a more substantial appetizer or a light lunch. Try thinly sliced ripe figs, apples, pears, and Fuyu persimmons with or without thin slices of prosciutto.

If you can only find Parmigiano that has already been plastic wrapped, press it with your fingers; it should give a little, indicating that it is still moist.

.　.　.　.　.　.

## Sugar Snaps with Extra Virgin Olive Oil and Shaved Parmigiano   Serves 4

4 cups sugar snap peas (about 12 ounces)

Lemon and Olive Oil Dressing
   1 garlic clove, bruised, then cut in half lengthwise
   2 teaspoons fresh lemon juice, or more to taste
   Pinch of kosher salt
   Pinch of sugar
   ¼ cup fruity extra virgin olive oil

One 2-inch strip lemon zest, cut into thin slivers
Freshly ground black pepper
2 to 3 ounces Parmigiano in 1 piece

**Slice the vegetables.** With a chef's knife, cut the sugar snap peas on an extreme diagonal into thirds or halves, discarding any tough stem ends. Place in a plastic bag and refrigerate until ready to serve.

**Make the dressing.** Rub the cut side of one of the garlic halves over the inside of a small bowl. Add the lemon juice, salt, and sugar. Spear both garlic halves with a dinner fork. Using this as a whisk, drizzle in the olive oil until the sauce has formed a thin emulsion with a subtle garlic flavor; discard the garlic.

**Dress the vegetables.** Up to ½ hour before serving, add the sugar snap peas and lemon zest and toss to coat; season with pepper to taste.

**Garnish with the cheese.** Just before serving, using a mandoline or Benriner or a vegetable peeler, shave the Parmigiano into paper-thin shavings. Scatter over the peas and toss gently.

## Improvisations

### Sugar Snaps, Asparagus, and Baby Artichokes with Parmigiano   Serves 4

*In spring, when asparagus and baby artichokes appear, I often replace some of the sugar snaps in the preceding recipe with one or both of these vegetables, to play on their affinity for each other. Use any proportions you wish. If using artichokes, make twice as much dressing, and add it as required to keep the salad moist.*

The key is cutting each vegetable so it is of equal crunch and weight as the sugar snaps: To prepare asparagus, break off the tough ends and discard. Grouping a few stalks at a time, slice them with a chef's knife on an extreme diagonal into ¼-inch slices.

To prepare baby artichokes: Squeeze 1 lemon into a medium bowl and fill it with cold water. Working with 1 artichoke at a time, pull off 4 or 5 layers of the tough green outer leaves from the base to reveal the pale yellow ones; they will resemble closed rosebuds. Cut off the top third of each artichoke and trim all but ¼ inch of the stem. Trim away the tough dark green bumps, where the leaves were broken off. Using a mandoline or Benriner or a thin sharp knife, slice each artichoke lengthwise through the stem into ¹⁄₁₆-inch slices. Place the slices in the lemon water as you work. (You may prepare the artichokes up to 1 hour ahead.) Drain well and blot dry with a paper towel just before mixing the salad.

## Mushroom and Squash Carpaccio with Pine Nuts, Basil, and Parmigiano    Serves 4

*When sliced paper-thin on a mandoline or Benriner and arranged like a mosaic on a plate, ordinary button mushrooms and summer squashes such as zucchini and yellow squash make a charming vegetarian carpaccio for a light, summery appetizer.*

In a small bowl, combine 1 teaspoon fresh lemon juice and a pinch each of salt and sugar. Spear a halved garlic clove with a dinner fork. Using this as a whisk, drizzle in ¼ cup extra virgin olive oil until the sauce has formed a thin emulsion with a subtle garlic flavor; discard the garlic.

Trim the ends off 4 ounces medium zucchini and/or yellow squash; using a mandoline or Benriner, cut the squash into paper-thin circles. Trim the stems off 4 ounces button or cremini mushrooms, wipe off any dirt, and slice the mushrooms paper-thin. Arrange the vegetables in slightly overlapping circles on 4 dinner plates. Drizzle each serving with dressing. Grind over black pepper and scatter thinly sliced fresh basil leaves over each serving. Using the slicer, slice 2 to 3 ounces Parmigiano into ¹⁄₁₆-inch shavings. Arrange the shavings over each plate and scatter liberally with toasted pine nuts (about ⅓ cup total).

## Fennel and Parmigiano Salad with Toasted Pecans    Serves 4

*I often mix culinary idioms—for example, adding pecans, which are very American, to a fennel and Parmigiano salad. The nuts have the perfect caramel sweetness and crunch. Cutting the fennel thin but not paper-thin prevents it from becoming wilted and watery.*

Cut the branches off 2 large fennel bulbs (about 1 pound each) and reserve; with a vegetable peeler, peel any bruised spots off the bulbs. Slice each fennel bulb into quarters through the stem and cut out the tough core. Using a mandoline or Benriner or a chef's knife, cut each quarter lengthwise into thin—but not paper-thin—$\frac{1}{16}$-inch slices (you should have about 8 cups). Place in a medium bowl and add $\frac{1}{2}$ cup coarsely chopped toasted pecans. Toss with 2 tablespoons extra virgin olive oil to coat and 2 to 3 teaspoons Banyuls or sherry vinegar. Add salt and plenty of freshly ground black pepper to taste. If desired, chop a few tablespoons of the reserved fennel fronds and add to the salad, and scatter thin shavings of Parmigiano over the top. Serve at once.

## Botanical Sliced Pears, Apples, Figs, or Persimmons with Parmigiano and Balsamic Caramel

*This is less a recipe than an assemblage of simple elements made charming by the way the fruit is cut: in thin cross sections, pits and stems intact, that look like a botanical print. It is an always-satisfying dessert. The quality of the fruit is critical: Use ripe in-season pears, apples, figs, or fuyu persimmons, singly or in combination. Figure about $\frac{1}{2}$ pear's volume of sliced fruit per person. Roasted almonds, such as Spanish Marcona almonds, make a nice accompaniment.*

Slice pears, apples, or figs in half through the stem; cut only the bottom off the persimmons. Using a mandoline or Benriner or a long thin sharp knife, beginning at the cut side, slice the fruit parallel to the cut edge to make thin $\frac{1}{8}$- to $\frac{1}{4}$-inch cross sections, with a pretty diagram of seeds. Arrange the fruit on dinner plates or on a large platter. Shave a chunk of Parmigiano into thin sheets and arrange on the plates. If desired, drizzle some Balsamic Caramel (page 64) in a pool on the plates for dipping the cheese.

# Celery Root, Parsnip, and Yellow Beet Slaw

I make a habit of stocking my fridge with sturdy vegetables, such as celery, parsley root, parsnips, beets, carrots, and cabbage, that can keep for several weeks if need be, as though in a traditional subterranean root cellar. When I've eaten my supply of salad greens, I turn these sweet, flavorful vegetables into satisfying rustic slaws like this one, made of julienned parsnips, celery root, and parsley root dressed with a roasted hazelnut oil vinaigrette. A mound of grated red or yellow beets nestled in just before serving provide a shock of color and sweet, earthy flavor. A friend said, "It makes you feel like flying," due to the energizing properties of raw vegetables.

Serve it as you would any slaw, alongside roasted chicken, pork, or lamb. By itself, it makes an excellent first course, along the lines of the classic French bistro salad. With the addition of goat cheese and paper-thin slices of prosciutto or bresaola, it makes a great light lunch.

This is a permutation of the vast universe of simply dressed, grated, or julienned raw vegetable salads that includes France's grated carrot and celery root salads and the endless variety of shredded cabbage slaws in America. They all share a purity and directness of flavor, with a pleasingly rustic, elemental look.

Crunchy vegetable slaws invite improvisation in any season; they can be as simple or as elaborate as you like. Start with whatever vegetables look best in your market or that you have on hand: root vegetables, such as celery root, parsnips, turnips, rutabagas, and carrots; cabbage (green, red, or Chinese), young brussels sprouts, and rough, somewhat bitter, greens, such as radicchio, endive, or dandelion; and fennel, celery, red or yellow peppers, cucumbers, snow peas, and radishes . . . singly or in combination. Figure on 5 to 6 cups cut-up vegetables for 4 servings.

Decide the best way to cut the vegetables—thinly sliced, finely julienned, or grated—to render them pleasingly crunchy without being tough. (A mandoline or Benriner makes quick work of julienning and shredding.) Embellish them with any elements you like, such as roasted pine nuts, chopped pecans, walnuts, or hazelnuts; finely diced crisp apple or green mango or thinly sliced kumquats; or the slivered zest or tiny bits of flesh from an orange or lemon, Meyer lemon being especially good.

The dressing will largely determine the character of your salad. Vary the fat at will, from a fragrant roasted nut oil to an herb-flavored oil to rendered bacon or pancetta fat. Extra virgin olive oil with lemon juice or a fine vinegar—cider, sherry, Banyuls—and salt and pepper enhances the flavor of just about any vegetable. Dressings based on mayonnaise, sour cream, and buttermilk evoke classic creamy American-style coleslaws. Flavorings can include chopped fresh tender herbs, such as chives, tarragon, basil, flat-leaf parsley, or cilantro; minced shallot; cracked spices, such as caraway, celery or cumin seed; and condiments, such as mustard, Worcestershire sauce, hot sauce, or grated horseradish. Ginger and lemongrass in league with lime juice, roasted sesame oil, rice vinegar, and sugar will give the vegetables a Southeast Asian spin. The key is to add enough acidity and salt to bring out their flavors.

. . . . . .

## Celery Root, Parsnip, and Yellow Beet Slaw  Serves 4

1 small celery root (about 12 ounces)
4 medium parsnips (8 ounces)
2 parsley roots (8 ounces)
1 teaspoon finely slivered Meyer lemon, lemon, or orange zest
8 ounces yellow or red beets

Fragrant Hazelnut Vinaigrette
2 tablespoons cider vinegar (preferably organic), or to taste
Kosher salt to taste
Pinch of sugar
2½ tablespoons roasted hazelnut or walnut oil, or fruity extra virgin olive oil
1 teaspoon warm water
Freshly ground black pepper

**Slice and combine the vegetables.** Peel the celery root, parsnips, and parsley root. Use a mandoline or Benriner or a box grater to julienne or coarsely grate them. Place in a large bowl and toss with the zest. Peel and grate the beets; place in a separate bowl.

**Dress the vegetables.** In a small bowl, combine the cider vinegar, salt, and sugar. Whisk in the nut oil and water. Toss the root vegetables and the beets separately with some of the dressing and salt and pepper to taste; add additional vinegar if necessary.

**Add the beets or other embellishments.** Nestle the beets in a mound slightly off center in the root vegetable slaw. Serve at once.

## Improvisations

### Creamy Cilantro Slaw  Serves 4 to 6

*I devised this slaw to accompany Close-Roasted Pork with Ancho, Cinnamon, and Cocoa (page 235) and Crackling Corn Bread (page 261), as a kind of Southern play on a Mexican dish. It is a perfect if unorthodox menu, the slaw providing a cool counterpoint to the rich meat. To shift the flavors, replace the cilantro with fresh basil and flat-leaf parsley, or a teaspoon or so of celery seed, and serve with ham, pork chops, grilled chicken, or shrimp.*

In a small bowl, whisk together ½ cup sour cream or reduced-fat sour cream, ¼ cup buttermilk, 1½ tablespoons apple cider vinegar, ½ teaspoon Worcestershire sauce, 3 to 5 dashes hot sauce, 1½ to 2 teaspoons sugar, ¾ teaspoon kosher salt, and ¾ teaspoon freshly ground black pepper. Set aside.

Remove the tough outer leaves from a small head of cabbage (1 pound); quarter the cabbage and cut out the core. With a mandoline or Benriner or a chef's knife, slice lengthwise into ¼-inch-wide shreds. In a large bowl, toss the cabbage with the dressing, ¼ cup chopped fresh chives, and ½ cup chopped fresh cilantro; correct the seasonings, adding more salt, sugar, and pepper as necessary.

## Warm Smoky Cabbage Slaw with Cracklings and Croutons    Serves 4 to 6

*I fused two salads I love, warm dandelion greens dressed with smoked-bacon dressing and coleslaw, to make this gutsy warm cabbage slaw. The cabbage wilts in the hot dressing just enough to keep its crunch, and then is tossed with bacon cracklings and fried croutons. Use an excellent bacon, smoked over sweet wood such as apple or hickory.*

Remove the tough outer leaves from a small head of green cabbage (1 pound); quarter the cabbage and cut out the core. Using a mechanical slicer such as a mandoline or Benriner or a chef's knife, slice lengthwise into thin shreds; reserve.

In a medium heavy skillet over moderately low heat, cook 4 ounces apple-wood-smoked or double-smoked bacon, cut into ⅓-inch-wide pieces, covered, until it is crisp and browned, 8 to 10 minutes. Transfer the bacon and all but about 2 teaspoons of the fat to a small bowl. Add 2 ounces coarse white peasant bread, cut into ⅓-inch dice, to the skillet and sauté, stirring occasionally, until golden brown, 4 to 5 minutes. Transfer the croutons to a plate.

Add the reserved bacon fat and bacon to the skillet. When hot, stir in 2 tablespoons apple cider vinegar, 1 tablespoon water, and ¼ teaspoon sugar and bring to a boil. Turn off the heat, add the cabbage to the pan, and toss constantly until slightly wilted, about 1 minute. Adjust the seasoning with salt, additional vinegar, and freshly ground black pepper. Transfer the cabbage to a large bowl. Just before serving, toss with the croutons.

### Dandelion, Pea Shoot, and Herb Slaw   Serves 4

*Because dandelion greens can be slightly tough and a bit bitter, I often slice them into a coarse chiffonade (from the French, literally, "made of rags") or strips, which makes them slawlike and tender, but with enough body to stand up to rough treatment without wilting. Chopped pea shoots, chives, basil, lemon zest, and pine nuts balance the slight bitterness of the dandelion greens. It makes a satisfyingly green slaw with many levels of flavor. This salad is mutable and welcomes other summer greens, including purslane, arugula, mint, and tatsoi, to name a few. Avocado and/or feta cheese or ricotta salata are fine additions. A fried egg on each serving turns it into an energizing light meal.*

Cut the tough stems off a large bunch of young, not-too-bitter dandelion greens (about 1 pound 6 ounces) at the base of the leaves and discard. With a chef's knife, cut the leaves crosswise into ¼-inch-wide slices; you should have about 6 cups. Place in a large bowl. Slice 4 ounces pea shoots the same way and add to the bowl, along with 3 tablespoons chopped fresh basil and 2 tablespoons finely chopped fresh chives. Slice a 2½ × ¾-inch strip lemon zest into fine slivers and toss with the greens.

In a small bowl, whisk together 1 teaspoon sherry, Banyuls or cider vinegar, and a large pinch each of salt and sugar. Whisk in 2 tablespoons extra virgin olive oil. Pour the dressing over the greens and toss to coat. Add 3 tablespoons toasted pine nuts, toss, and adjust the seasoning, adding salt, pepper, and/or a squeeze of lemon juice as needed.

### Impromptu Cabbage Slaws

*My formula for quick cabbage slaws relies on made-ahead flavored oils, such as Basil, Lemon, and Tomato Oil (page 51) or Chinese Many-Flavor Oil (page 52), which are powerhouses of instant flavor.*

Remove the tough outer leaves from a small head of green cabbage (1 pound); quarter the cabbage and cut out the core. With a mandoline or Benriner or a chef's knife, slice lengthwise into thin shreds. Place in a bowl. Toss with enough flavored oil to coat lightly. Season with sherry, apple cider, or Banyuls vinegar and plenty of salt and pepper. If desired, toss in a handful of coarsely chopped toasted pine nuts or walnuts.

 VEGETABLES AND BEANS

# Post-Modern Fries

My indulgence for crispy things like French fries is ruled by an idiosyncratic logic that has made them mostly off-limits. It goes something like this: Perfectly fried French fries are rare in restaurants. At home they are daunting: hours of Fryolator air lingering in my apartment, and a quart or two of hot fat to discard. Because they are deep-fried and fattening, they must be really superb to be worth eating. . . .

So I now have a way in which to enjoy their divine effect and flavor without either the mess or the dietary wallop. Even if they weren't more healthful, I'd choose these post-modern versions over most of the fries in restaurants any day.

It took me a while to figure out just how to take my oven fries beyond okay, half-too-crisp, half-limp ersatz fries that many recipes yield. Roast them hot for most of the time, then turn the oven down to dry the interiors out just enough to be truly frylike. Use the right potato. And the right fat.

Idaho, the baking potato used for classic French fries, has better flavor and texture than waxy potatoes like Red Bliss. Don't rinse the slices; blotting the moisture with paper towels leaves the right amount of surface starch to help a crust to form. (In browning, a dry exterior is essential; if wet, the vegetable will steam.) Starting them in a hot oven will "fry" the potato sticks, browning and caramelizing their surface. Leaving them in a low oven for 10 minutes after they crisp dries out their flesh enough to keep them from turning soggy.

The choice of fat offers the best and simplest way to manipulate the flavor and texture of oven fries. Olive oil, arguably the healthiest fat, produces great results without assertive flavor. Rendered double-smoked bacon fat gives a delectable smoky flavor and some of the uniquely crispy texture of lard-fried potatoes. Melted butter is always good. A true French peanut oil, or a good-quality cold-pressed one, will give a classic French-fry flavor.

Embellish the potatoes with minced fresh herbs such as rosemary and sage, sprinkled on halfway through cooking to keep them from burning. Coarsely crushed spices, like coriander, fennel or cumin seeds, offer other possibilities. For a clear, mellow garlic flavor, steep sliced raw garlic in the fat for 15 minutes before using.

Sauces or embellishments provide other opportunities for improvising. Doctor ketchup with ancho chile or dried mushroom powder (moistened first with a little hot water to release their flavor). Serve fries with Real Onion Dip (page 144) or with shavings of a hard, aged cheese, such as Parmigiano or Manchego.

Although they seem as if they would make great oven fries, turnips, carrots, and sweet potatoes contain too much water, becoming soft or mushy or overcaramelized–i.e., burned. The exception is parsnips, which roast (longer, at a lower temperature) into crispy-chewy caramelized fries.

I also applied the method to vaguely fry-shaped tubular pastas and dusted them with grated Parmigiano that caramelized in the oven to make crispy pasta fries.

. . . . . .

## Post-Modern Fries   Serves 4

> 4 large baking potatoes (about 2 pounds)
> 2 tablespoons extra virgin olive oil
> Salt, preferably fine sea salt

**Peel and slice the potatoes.** Adjust a rack to the top part of the oven; preheat the oven to 475°F. Peel the potatoes; using a knife or French-fry cutter, slice them lengthwise into ⅓-inch sticks.

**Blot dry and coat with fat.** Place the potatoes in a large bowl; roughly blot them dry with bunched-up paper toweling. Drizzle the olive oil over and toss to coat them completely. Scatter the potatoes on a large baking sheet in one layer, making sure that they don't stick together or overlap.

**Bake, rearranging periodically.** Bake the potatoes for 15 minutes. With a thin metal spatula, toss and rearrange the potatoes; shake the pan back and forth a few times to spread them out in one layer again. Reverse the pan and bake until the potatoes are golden brown and crisp, about 10 minutes longer.

**Reduce the heat and continue baking.** Remove the pan from the oven. Turn the temperature down to 325°F and leave the oven door open to cool down the oven while you toss and rearrange the potatoes again. Return the pan to the oven to let the potatoes dry out for 10 minutes.

Transfer the fries to a platter, sprinkle liberally with salt, and serve at once.


## Improvisations

### Smoky Fries   Serves 4

*Potatoes fried in lard have a uniquely crisp texture and delectable flavor. Using double-smoked bacon fat achieves a similar effect, along with an appealingly smoky flavor.*

Prepare Post-Modern Fries using 2 tablespoons rendered double-smoked bacon fat instead of olive oil. To render the fat, in a small heavy skillet, cook 3 ounces thinly sliced or finely diced double-smoked bacon (¾ cup) covered, over low heat, stirring occasionally until the fat is liquid and the bacon is crisp. Strain into a small bowl (toss the fries with the crisp bacon or use it in another recipe).

## Rosemary Fries   Serves 4

*These are delectable fries with the flavor of classic rosemary-roasted potatoes. The trick to getting intense flavor is to steep the olive oil with garlic and to toss the potatoes with minced fresh rosemary while they are roasting.*

Pour 2 tablespoons extra virgin olive oil into a small bowl and stir in 1 large garlic clove, thinly sliced. Let sit 15 minutes while you peel and slice the potatoes and blot them dry. Remove the garlic, coat the potatoes with the garlic oil, and spread on the baking sheet. Bake for 15 minutes on the top rack of the oven.

With a thin metal spatula, toss and rearrange the potatoes. Sprinkle the fries with 1 tablespoon minced fresh rosemary and toss again; shake the pan back and forth a few times to spread them out in one layer. Reverse the pan and bake until the potatoes are golden brown and crisp, 10 minutes longer.

Remove the pan from the oven; turn the temperature down to 325°F and leave the oven door open while you toss and rearrange the potatoes again. Return the pan to the oven to let the potatoes dry out for 10 minutes. Transfer the fries to a platter, sprinkle liberally with salt, and serve at once.

## Parsnip Fries   Serves 4

*Anne Disrude, one of the best cooks I know, came up with these parsnip fries, which she serves with drinks before dinner. Serve them as a side dish with roasts and grilled beef or duck steak.*

Place a rack in the upper third of the oven and preheat the oven to 375°F. Peel 3 pounds medium parsnips and cut into 4 × ⅓-inch sticks; if the core is very thick and woody, cut it out. Place the parsnip sticks in a bowl and toss to coat with 2 tablespoons extra virgin olive oil or rendered bacon fat (see Smoky Fries). Spread them in a single layer on one or two large baking sheets, making sure they don't stick together. Roast the parsnips, tossing once or twice, until tender and browned in spots, about 1 hour. Sprinkle with salt, transfer to a platter, and serve at once.

## Parmesan Fries    Serves 4

*Parmigiano proves to be a much more satisfying, Italianate embellishment for oven fries than ketchup.*

Make Post-Modern Fries. Just before serving, use a vegetable peeler to shave thin shavings of Parmigiano over them.

## Pasta "Fries"    Serves 4

*Inspired by the crispy satisfaction of oven fries, I tried using tube pasta to make something like the caramelized noodles on the top of baked casseroles like macaroni and cheese. A dusting of grated Parmigiano caramelizes on the pasta as it roasts, ensuring a crisp-chewy texture. Although you can use almost any pasta, vaguely fry–shaped tube pastas, such as trenne, penne, ziti, or strozzapreti, or long twisted pastas are the most fun.*

Preheat the oven to 475°F. In a large pot of boiling salted water, cook 12 ounces tube pasta until al dente (tender but still slightly firm to the bite). Pour into a colander to drain several minutes. Meanwhile, in a small saucepan, melt 1½ tablespoons unsalted butter over low heat. Add 1 roughly crushed but intact peeled garlic clove and swirl several times to infuse; turn off the heat. Grease a large heavy baking sheet or 2 large oven-proof skillets with a little of the butter.

Pour the pasta onto the baking sheet. Pour the remaining butter over and toss to coat completely; add salt and pepper to taste. Shake the pan to let the pasta spread out and settle. Sprinkle with ⅔ cup grated Parmigiano.

Bake the pasta until the top is golden and crisp, 25 to 30 minutes. Serve at once.

# Asparagus with a Fried Egg and Parmigiano

On nights alone, one of my favorite meals is pan-steamed asparagus tossed with Parmigiano and a soft-yolk fried egg, a dish I first ate in Italy. When broken, the runny yolk combines with the cheese to make a creamy sauce for the asparagus. The dish is fast, healthful, and supremely satisfying; it exemplifies the ingenious simplicity of so much of Italian cooking. This recipe changed my life, affording me a formula for throwing together a delicious meal when the larder is almost bare, for it relies on two long-keeping staples, hard aged grating cheeses and eggs, and can be made with equally long-keeping vegetables, such as potatoes, onions, or root vegetables. The recipe can be scaled down to feed two or even one.

The basic formula is a bed of something filling and somewhat mildly flavored, such as cooked vegetables, risotto, or, spectacularly, pasta, sprinkled with a pungent grated cheese like Parmigiano, then topped with a soft-yolk fried egg, which will make a sauce when the egg is broken. Your main elements for improvising are the bed/base and the cheese you use. The bases can be almost any cooked vegetable in your repertoire (including many of the vegetable recipes in this book), from simple steamed spinach to mashed or hashed potatoes and root vegetables to ratatouille to my favorite, which is not a vegetable at all but, surprisingly, spaghetti. Starchy bases such as Shallot (or Garlic) Toasts (page 274), soft or panfried polenta and warmed leftover risotto offer additional possibilities. Cheeses could include Manchego, aged Gouda, dry Jack, pecorino Toscano, or an aged grating goat cheese; all keep for weeks in the fridge. Sometimes I throw minced herbs such as chives or rosemary into the butter I cook the eggs in to add another layer of flavor. As you begin to improvise on the basic formula, you'll find that the dish changes dramatically with different bases; each provides its own unique pleasures.

•    •    •    •    •    •

## Asparagus with a Fried Egg and Parmigiano    Serves 4

1 large bunch asparagus (about 1 pound)
⅓ cup water
Kosher salt
1 tablespoon unsalted butter or extra virgin olive oil
4 extra-large eggs, preferably organic
Freshly ground black pepper
¾ cup grated Parmigiano

**Prepare the vegetable or starchy base.** Break the tough stems off the asparagus and discard. Arrange the asparagus in a large skillet set over high heat; add the water and salt. Cover and steam the asparagus, rearranging them occasionally, until they are crisp-tender and all but 1 tablespoon of the water has evaporated, 5 to 8 minutes. (Check the asparagus periodically; if the water is evaporating too quickly, add a few more tablespoons. Or, if there is still too much by the time the vegetables are tender, pour it off, holding the vegetables in the pan with the lid.) Remove the lid and add 1 teaspoon of the butter or olive oil; toss the asparagus well to coat them. Turn off the heat.

**Fry the eggs.** Carefully break the eggs into a bowl without breaking the yolks. Heat a 12-inch nonstick skillet over moderate heat. Add the remaining butter or oil and swirl to coat. Add the eggs, gently nudging the yolks so they are evenly spaced in the pan; sprinkle with salt and pepper. Reduce the heat, cover, and cook until the whites are set but the yolks are still runny. When the eggs are done, separate them with a spatula.

**Assemble the dish.** Arrange some of the asparagus on each of 4 dinner plates. Sprinkle each serving with some cheese and place an egg on top. Spoon some of the remaining cheese over each egg. Serve at once.

# Improvisations

### Magic Peppers and Other Recipes from This Book with a Fried Egg and Aged Grating Cheese

*Replace the asparagus in Asparagus with a Fried Egg and Parmigiano with any number of cooked vegetables, including simple steamed or garlic-and-oil tossed greens like spinach, kale, chard, or broccoli rabe; mashed potatoes; or one of these recipes:*

Magic Peppers (page 89)
Root Vegetable Hash Browns with Bacon or Pancetta (page 151)
Slow-Roasted Tomatoes (page 95)
Braise/Sauté of Asparagus, Sugar Snap Peas, and Green Soybeans
   (page 138)
Caramelized Onions (page 143)
Onion Tartines (page 144)
Warm Smoky Cabbage Slaw with Cracklings and Croutons (page 123)
Dandelion, Pea Shoot, and Herb Slaw (page 124)

### Potatoes with Rosemary-Scented Fried Egg and Parmigiano

*Almost any kind of potato dish would be good as a base for the eggs and cheese in place of the asparagus, including leftover potatoes; Potatoes with White Wine, Thyme, and Olives (page 149) or Post-Modern Fries (page 128).*

Or, just boil up new potatoes or fingerlings—about 1¼ pounds for 4 people—until they are tender. Drain them and then crush them roughly with a fork before topping them with cheese and egg. Fry the eggs, adding a sprig of rosemary to the pan while the fat is heating. Arrange the cheese and eggs on the warm potatoes.

### Roasted Caramelized Sweet Onions with Fried Egg and Manchego    Serves 4

*I was staying at a friend's country house and the summer days were so beautiful we couldn't bring ourselves to leave to go to the market, so we cooked with what was in our diminishing larder. That's how some Vidalia onions became the base for a neighboring farmer's fabulous eggs and some grated Manchego cheese, a perfect supper.*

For the Roasted Caramelized Sweet Onions, preheat the oven to 400°F. Halve 2 medium-sweet onions, such as Vidalia or Walla Walla Sweets, through the circumference. Keeping each half intact, pull off the outer skin. Brush each half lightly with extra virgin olive oil. Sprinkle with salt and scatter a few spikes of fresh or dried rosemary over the top.

Place cut side down on a baking sheet and roast 40 minutes. Turn the onions over, sprinkle with a little more salt and rosemary, and roast until the onions are tender, about 40 minutes.

Fry the eggs. Arrange 1 onion half on each of 4 dinner plates. Sprinkle some grated aged cheese such as Manchego or Parmigiano over them. Top each half with a fried egg and sprinkle with more cheese.

### Elemental Carbonara (Pasta with a Fried Egg and Parmigiano)   Serves 4

*One day when I was craving a creamy pasta dish, I made the fried egg dish with spaghetti instead of asparagus. The soft-cooked yolk and cheese melted into a satisfying sauce, a lazy person's elemental carbonara, the ultimate instant soul food. To gild the lily, cook some diced bacon, fry the eggs in the fat, and toss the crispy pieces with the pasta. Or, as a further improvisation, toss the spaghetti with a cooked vegetable, such as oven-roasted Magic Peppers (page 89), before topping it with the egg, which takes you full circle to the asparagus dish.*

In a large pot of boiling well-salted water, cook 12 to 16 ounces (depending on how hungry you are) spaghetti, linguine, or other pasta until it is slightly underdone (the pasta will keep cooking after it's drained). With a measuring cup, scoop out ½ cup of the cooking water. Drain the pasta and set the colander over a bowl while you start the eggs; set the pot aside.

Fry 4 extra-large eggs in butter or olive oil. While the eggs are cooking, return the pasta to the cooking pot. Add about ⅓ cup of the cooking water and 6 tablespoons grated Parmigiano (you'll need ¾ cup cheese altogether). Toss until the cheese has melted and the pasta is coated with a creamy sauce, adding more cooking water if necessary to keep the pasta moist. Season generously with salt and pepper.

Divide the pasta evenly among 4 warm dinner plates. Sprinkle with an additional 6 tablespoons grated cheese and arrange a fried egg in the center of each mound. Scatter coarsely chopped flat-leaf parsley over the top, if desired. Serve at once, instructing your guests to break the yolk and toss the egg with the pasta.

# Braise/Sauté of Asparagus, Sugar Snap Peas, and Green Soybeans

- Succotash of Fresh Green Soybeans, Corn, and Bacon
- "Lazy Man's Favas" with Extra Virgin Olive Oil and Parmigiano
- Ragout of Green Soybeans with Rosemary and Thyme

Every spring, I make vibrant sautés of spring vegetables whose flavors have an extraordinary affinity for each other: artichokes, asparagus, peas, fava beans, green beans, tiny new potatoes. At some point, I began to feel the constraints of this approach, due in large measure for the need to double-peel fava beans, an essential element; they take too long to prepare to make the dish more than an occasional pleasure. Inspired by the favalike possibilities of fresh green soybeans, and their availability frozen, I created this simpler sauté made with year-round "spring" vegetables—asparagus and sugar snap peas—along with tarragon, chives, and flat-leaf parsley, so I can enjoy their spring flavors in winter.

It is delicious as is, as a side dish for just about any meat, fish, or poultry, or as a light main course, with shavings of fine aged goat or sheep's milk cheese or ricotta salata and good bread. It is wonderful stirred into risotto, folded into an omelet, or tossed into pasta (with some additional olive oil and a few tablespoons of the cooking water).

The Braise/Sauté of Asparagus, Sugar Snap Peas, and Green Soybeans is less a formula than a vivid example of thinking out of the box about an ingredient. Using green soybeans, classically an Asian ingredient, in a Western culinary vocabulary became the guiding notion behind many improvisations.

Fresh green soybeans in their pods used to be found only at Japanese restaurants, where they were boiled in salty water and served as an exotic hors d'oeuvre called edamame to nibble on with sake or a beer. They've become so popular that I find them in my supermarket and at salad bars. Once I got past the Japanese associations and my old hippie notions of stodgy dried yellow soybeans (which are a different, very starchy variety), I saw them for what they are: a green shell bean and close cousin to fresh favas or limas, with a fabulous nutritional profile: high in protein and fiber. So I started plugging them into Western-style treatments with great success.

Buy fresh soybeans in their pods at farmers' markets throughout the summer (you'll need to shuck them like peas) or conveniently flash-frozen in the freezer case all year round. To make them digestible, they need to be cooked briefly, about 5 minutes, until tender. Boiling the soybeans is the simplest method, or cook them right into dishes. Braising them in a mixture of water and a flavorful fat is a great cooking method, since they need some fat to make them really delicious and give them a pleasing texture. They adore extra virgin olive oil and fatty pork products like pancetta and bacon; and brown butter is fabulous.

Since they are so similar, pair soybeans with any foods that go well with favas, limas, and peas. They also go well with spring onions, leeks, asparagus, artichokes, sugar snap peas, green beans, new potatoes, baby turnips, carrots, and ramps (wild leeks). You can take the basic braise/sauté formula and replace the asparagus and sugar snaps with other vegetables. Or instead of oil, use rendered bacon or pancetta, as in the succotash recipe on page 139. Soybeans have affinities for thyme, rosemary, mint, savory, chives, lemon zest, garlic, onions, ginger, and pine nuts. They go well with many cheeses, especially ones used in Mediterranean cooking–Parmigiano, pecorino, feta, ricotta salata–and aged sheep's milk cheeses like Manchego.

I like to make sure that the soybeans I buy are not genetically modified (non-GMO) and are organic. Packages of frozen soybeans will indicate this on the label.

·   ·   ·   ·   ·   ·

## Braise/Sauté of Asparagus, Sugar Snap Peas, and Green Soybeans   Serves 4

1 tablespoon extra virgin olive oil
1 medium leek, white and tender green parts only, thinly sliced (½ cup)
1 cup (5 to 6 ounces) frozen shelled green soybeans
¾ teaspoon salt
¼ teaspoon sugar
¼ cup water
1 pound medium asparagus, tough ends broken off and discarded, sliced on
   a diagonal into 2-inch lengths
2 cups (8 ounces) sugar snap peas, sliced on a diagonal into thirds
⅓ cup finely chopped fresh herbs, such as chervil, flat-leaf parsley, chives,
   and up to 1 tablespoon tarragon, in any combination
Freshly ground black pepper

**Sauté the leek to flavor the fat.** Combine the olive oil and leek in a large heavy skillet set over moderate heat. Cover and cook, stirring occasionally, until the leeks are softened, about 4 minutes.

**Add the soybeans and water and braise.** Add the soybeans, salt, sugar, and water; cover and cook for 2 minutes.

**Add the additional vegetables and braise until the liquid is evaporated.** Add the asparagus, cover, and cook 2 minutes longer. If the water is evaporating too quickly, add a few more tablespoons as necessary. Then stir in the snap peas, cover, and cook 2 minutes longer, or until just tender. The water should be completely evaporated; if it isn't, uncover the pan and boil vigorously until the pan is dry.

**Add the herbs and adjust the seasoning.** Stir in the herbs, pepper to taste, and more salt if necessary.

## Improvisations

### Succotash of Fresh Green Soybeans, Corn, and Bacon    Serves 4

*Most people know succotash as the simple, quintessentially American dish of cooked lima beans and corn. I replaced the traditional limas with green soybeans and found out just how well they marry with smoked bacon.*

Cut 2 thick slices bacon, preferably applewood-smoked, into ½-inch dice. Place in a large heavy skillet, cover, and cook over moderate heat, stirring occasionally, until most of the fat has rendered out and the bacon is crisp, about 6 minutes. Holding back the bacon with a slotted spoon, pour off all but about 2 teaspoons of the fat. Add 1½ cups frozen shelled green soybeans (about 8 ounces) and ⅓ cup water to the pan; toss, cover, and cook, stirring occasionally, for 3 minutes. Stir in 1½ cups corn kernels (frozen, or cut off 2 medium ears of corn); cover and cook until the soybeans and corn are just tender, 3 to 4 minutes longer. Add salt and plenty of freshly ground black pepper to taste. Stir in 1 tablespoon minced fresh chives and ½ teaspoon minced fresh pungent herbs, such as thyme, rosemary, or savory, or 1 to 2 tablespoons finely chopped milder herbs, such as basil or parsley.

### "Lazy Man's Favas" with Extra Virgin Olive Oil and Parmigiano    Serves 2

*One of the most extraordinary appetizers I've ever had was a plate of fresh fava beans drizzled with fine extra virgin olive oil and sprinkled with shavings of Parmigiano. Because favas can be hard to find and are a lot of work to prepare (they need to be peeled twice), I created this weeknight version using frozen green soybeans. It makes a perfect, healthful, utterly satisfying meal.*

Bring a large pot of water to a boil over high heat and salt liberally; stir in ½ teaspoon sugar. Stir in 3 cups (15 to 18 ounces) frozen shelled green soybeans and cook until tender but not mushy, about 3 minutes (or according to package directions). While the beans are cooking, rub 2 shallow soup bowls with a halved garlic clove. Drain the beans well and divide between the bowls. Toss each with extra virgin olive oil and season with salt and pepper. Shave Parmigiano or another hard aged cheese, such as Manchego, over the top; serve at once.

## Ragout of Green Soybeans with Rosemary and Thyme     Serves 4

*I've always loved Alice Waters's simple braise of fresh fava beans, olive oil, and rosemary, so I decided to try it using green soybeans. This is a stripped-down version of the technique of braising soybeans with a flavorful fat. Suffused with herbs and oil, green soybeans become tender and delicate, with a subtly "green" vegetal flavor. They are a meal unto themselves served with thin slabs of feta, aged goat cheese, or a fairly creamy sheep's milk cheese like Brin d'Amour. Or serve them as a base or side dish for roast lamb or robust white-fleshed fish like snapper and striped bass. The beans also make a great bruschetta topping, drained and mashed and piled onto garlic-rubbed toast. I've even spooned some of the ragout into the center of an asparagus risotto.*

Place 3 cups (15 to 18 ounces) frozen shelled green soybeans in a medium saucepan with enough water so the beans just break the surface. Pour over ½ cup extra virgin olive oil and nestle 1 large smashed garlic clove and 1 sprig each rosemary and thyme in the beans. Bring to a simmer over moderate heat and cook gently for 10 minutes. Stir in about ½ teaspoon salt and ¼ teaspoon sugar, and continue cooking until the soybeans are very tender and buttery, 5 to 10 minutes longer. Although you can serve them at once, the beans get better if left to cool a couple of hours in their liquid (reheat them in the liquid).

Before serving, pepper them generously and add a squeeze of lemon juice to lift the flavors; then adjust the salt. To serve, scoop the beans up with a large spoon and let most, but not all, of the liquid drain off before placing in a bowl or on a plate.

# Caramelized Onions

- Real Onion Dip
- Onion Tartines
- Porcini-Onion Soup with Grilled Cheese Toasts
- Savory Onion Jam

I know of few things so simple and so universally, deliciously useful as caramelized onions, cooked until deep brown with a sweet, mellow oniony flavor. They classically top pork chops and steaks, for "smothered in onions," and, of course, hamburgers. Topped with a fried egg or a slab of goat cheese warmed in the oven, they make a satisfying meal. They're also a terrific embellishment for vegetable purees, such as mashed potatoes, root vegetables, or turnips. Once you know this simple method for making them, you can use them as a base for endless improvisations. Since onions are the kitchen's staple ingredient, you always have this potential on hand.

When thinly sliced onions are cooked in a little butter in a covered nonstick or seasoned cast-iron skillet, they "sweat," that is, they release some of their juices. The juices mix with the fat to form a braising liquid to further cook the onions and mellow their flavor. When the lid is removed, all that moisture evaporates, and the onions caramelize in the residual fat.

You can use just about any kind of onion for this method, each yielding slightly different results. Sweet onions, such as Vidalias or Bermudas, have a high water content; they'll release a lot of liquid when they sweat, and the slow process of evaporating it and cooking the onions down will yield exceptionally creamy, mild-flavored onions. Yellow or white onions have less water and are more fiery; they will remain more distinct when cooked down, with a more overt oniony flavor. Shallots, with their subtle garlicky undertones, can become pleasingly crisp (see Crispy Shallots, page 200).

You can subtly vary the flavor by the choice of fat you use—butter is the ultimate; bacon fat gives a smoky spin; and so on. You can also season the onions with herbs such as thyme, rosemary, or sage . . . or spices like coriander, curry, and various peppercorns, as well as saffron.

But it is how you put the onions to use that offers immense opportunities for improvisation. Caramelized onions, the little black dress of foods, go with everything, in just about any situation. They are delicious tossed with pasta with shavings of aged goat cheese, used as a ravioli or an omelet filling, spooned on top of a risotto, used as an element in a soup or as the basis for one. I particularly like their savory flavor in hors d'oeuvres with cocktails. Since Caramelized Onions last about a week in the refrigerator, I make up big batches around the holidays, to use for impromptu entertaining.

• • • • • •

## Caramelized Onions  Makes about 1 1/2 cups, 4 servings

**2 pounds yellow onions (4 to 5 medium), peeled**
**2 tablespoons unsalted butter or extra virgin olive oil**
**1/2 teaspoon kosher salt, or to taste**
**1/2 teaspoon sugar**
**Freshly ground black pepper**

**Slice the onions.** Slice the onions in half through the stem. Using a mandoline or a Benriner or a thin sharp knife, cut into 1/8-inch lengthwise slices. You should have about 6 cups.

**Cook the onions covered to release the juices.** In a large nonstick or seasoned cast-iron skillet, melt the butter over moderately low heat. Add the onions, sprinkle with the salt, and toss to coat. Cover and cook until the onions have released their liquid, about 13 minutes.

**Caramelize the onions.** Uncover, increase the heat to moderate, and cook, stirring occasionally, until the liquid has evaporated, about 10 minutes. Sprinkle with the sugar and continue cooking, stirring frequently, until the onions are golden brown and caramelized, about 10 minutes longer. Pepper generously and adjust the seasoning. Remove from the heat. The onions can be refrigerated, covered, up to 4 days.

## Improvisations

### Real Onion Dip

*Onion soup dip, made with sour cream and dry onion soup mix, lost its chic decades ago, but I don't know anybody who didn't love it and wouldn't love it again if it were made without the ersatz flavors and intense salt of the original. Here is my revision, made with real caramelized onions stirred into sour cream for an astonishing effect. Served with excellent potato chips, this dip is the ultimate cocktail party food.*

Make Caramelized Onions using finely diced (rather than sliced) yellow onions. (Or simply chop leftover Caramelized Onions.) Let cool completely. Mix together roughly equal parts of the onions and sour cream, adjusting the balance to your taste. Add salt, freshly ground black pepper, and a squeeze of lemon juice if necessary to pick up the flavors.

## Onion Tartines    Serves 4 to 6

*Pissaladière is classically a chewy yeast dough spread with long-cooked sweet onions, anchovies, and tiny Niçoise olives—a pizza really, substantial enough to make a lunch with a green salad, and an ideal hors d'oeuvre served with chilled rosé wine or cocktails. This revisionist pissaladière was inspired by my friend Margot Wellington, who devises brilliant shortcuts to classic dishes so she can entertain frequently at home, despite being extraordinarily busy. Her improvisation is to use slabs of sourdough bread or a good Pullman loaf, both of which are yeasty and dense enough to mimic pizza dough. The trick is to cut the crusts off; the inside of the loaf melds with the onions perfectly and gets crisp on the bottom.*

Slice 2 pounds sweet onions, such as Bermudas or Vidalias, in half through the stem. Using a mandoline or a Benriner or a thin sharp knife, cut the onions into ⅛-inch lengthwise slices. In a large heavy skillet over moderately low heat, combine the onions, 2 tablespoons extra virgin olive oil, ½ teaspoon salt, and 1½ teaspoons fresh thyme leaves or ½ teaspoon dried thyme; toss to coat. Cover and cook until the onions have released their liquid, about 13 minutes. Uncover, increase the heat to moderate, and cook, stirring occasionally until the liquid has evaporated and the onions are golden and creamy, about 10 minutes. Adjust the seasoning and reserve.

Carefully slice the crust off the entire loaf of bread (discard or save for another use); or, if you prefer, slice the crusts off each slice after slicing the bread. Holding the loaf on its side, cut lengthwise in to make large, uniform slices about ½ inch thick. Brush the bread on both sides with extra virgin olive oil; arrange on a baking sheet. Spread each slice with a thick layer of the reserved onions. Bake the tartines as is, or embellish them Niçoise style: Drain some anchovies in oil and pat dry; slice in half lengthwise. Arrange the anchovies, spaced 2 or 3 inches apart, in a crisscross pattern on the onions. Then place pitted Niçoise olives in the anchovy "squares." (You can assemble these up to 3 hours ahead.)

About 15 minutes before you want to bake the tartines, preheat the oven to 375°F. Bake the tartines until the bottoms are golden and crisp, 25 minutes. Cut into 2-inch squares and drizzle with extra virgin olive oil.

## Porcini-Onion Soup with Grilled Cheese Toasts   Serves 4

*Although I adore onion soup, I rarely made it, because I usually lacked a good beef broth. Then I discovered that dried porcini mushrooms give a rich, meaty flavor to ordinary chicken stock and marry well with onions. Rather than floating a gooey blob of cheese in the soup, I serve grilled Gruyère toasts alongside.*

For the **Porcini Broth**, in a medium saucepan, combine 1 quart low-sodium chicken broth with 1 cup (1 ounce) dried porcini mushrooms and 1 cup water. Bring to a boil over high heat. Reduce the heat to a simmer and cook 20 minutes. Pour the broth through a fine-mesh strainer set over a 1-quart measuring cup or bowl, pressing the mushrooms with the back of a spoon to extract all the broth. You should have 1 quart broth; if not, add enough water to make up the difference.

Slice 2 pounds sweet onions, such as Bermudas or Vidalias, into ⅛-inch lengthwise slices as for Caramelized Onions. In a large nonstick skillet or a large heavy saucepan over moderately low heat, melt 2 tablespoons unsalted butter; stir in the onions and ½ teaspoon salt. Cover and cook until the onions have released their liquid, about 13 minutes. Uncover, increase the heat to moderate, and cook, stirring occasionally, until the liquid has evaporated, about 10 minutes. Sprinkle with ½ teaspoon sugar and continue cooking, stirring frequently, until the onions are golden brown and caramelized, about 10 minutes longer. Increase the heat to high and add ½ cup dry white wine and 1 teaspoon fresh thyme leaves; cook, stirring, until the wine completely evaporates and the onions are starting to caramelize again. Pour in the mushroom broth and bring to a boil. Reduce the heat and simmer 5 minutes. Adjust the seasoning. Keep warm.

About 10 minutes before serving the soup, prepare the Grilled Cheese Toasts. Spoon the soup into 4 shallow soup bowls. Arrange 2 Cheese Toasts on the edge of each bowl.

**Grilled Cheese Toasts**. Preheat the broiler. Slice a crusty baguette on an extreme diagonal into eight ½-inch slices; arrange on the broiler pan and broil 3 inches from the heat source until the top side is golden. Turn the slices over and sprinkle some fresh thyme leaves (about 2 teaspoons total) on each slice. Top each with shredded Gruyère (5 ounces total) and sprinkle with a little grated Parmigiano. Broil until the cheese is bubbling.

**Savory Onion Jam**   Makes 1 cup

*If you take the Caramelized Onions a step further and cook them down with a little vinegar, you end up with a marvelous sweet-and-sour onion jam that you can keep on hand in the refrigerator to embellish sandwiches or serve with pâtés and cold meats and poultry. It is also delicious served warm with grilled pork chops or steak. Improvise with different vinegars. The jam will keep about 2 weeks refrigerated.*

Prepare Caramelized Onions. Increase the heat slightly and add 1 tablespoon sherry, red wine, or apple cider vinegar and 1 teaspoon balsamic vinegar. Stir the onions to dissolve the juices that have caramelized on the pan, and cook about 3 minutes longer. Adjust the seasoning, adding freshly ground black pepper to taste.

# Potatoes with White Wine, Thyme, and Olives

- Root Vegetables with White Wine and Rosemary
- Lemon-Infused Potatoes with Thyme
- Parsnips with Roasted Sesame Oil and Cilantro
- Root Vegetable Hash Browns with Bacon or Pancetta
- Potato or Root Vegetable Hash

This is at heart a classic Provençal potato dish–potatoes braised with white wine, shallots, and olive oil–jazzed up with olives and thyme. As the liquid evaporates, the potatoes become infused with a tart, winey flavor and glazed with the olive oil, whose flavor is further punched up by the olives, because all the ingredients are combined in a skillet and simmered, so it is the easiest dish imaginable and an essential part of my repertoire. The potatoes are a perfect accompaniment to most roasts, from beef, lamb, and pork to chicken, and all kinds of fish. With thin shavings of aged goat cheese, they make a great simple supper. Because the potatoes are so saturated with flavor, this is also one of the few preparations that is delicious cold. Dice the potatoes to make a rough potato salad; just add some chopped flat-leaf parsley and a drizzle of olive oil.

This basic approach of braising potatoes in a flavorful liquid with some fat lends itself to marvelous simple improvisations, both for potato dishes and for root vegetables–parsnips, parsley root, celery root, turnips, rutabagas, carrots, Jerusalem artichokes, to name a few, which have a similarly dense texture. The secret to ensuring potatoes that are glazed and intact, rather than gluey, is to rinse the starch off them before cooking and cook them slowly; too high a heat will cause them to burst. Root vegetables do not need rinsing and can bear faster cooking.

Olive oil is the key to this dish: Without some fat, the vegetables would taste boiled, and the shallot, which is not sautéed first, would taste raw. But when fat is simmered with a liquid, it mellows both flavors and texture of all the other ingredients into a harmonious whole. Other fats offer easy possibilities: butter, brown butter, roasted nut oil, bacon or pancetta fat, or goose or duck fat.

White wine provides lovely aroma, flavor, and acidity. It can be replaced with many flavorful liquids, such as water mixed with lemon juice and broths–from chicken to game to leek to an infused broth (see "Understanding," page 104)–and hard cider. Plain water lets the individual flavors of the other ingredients shine through.

Because the potatoes simmer in liquid, any flavorings you add will infuse the liquid and thus be absorbed by the vegetables. Flavorings include herbs such as rosemary, thyme, savory, sage (used sparingly), and basil; fruit zests such as lemon, orange, or tangerine; capers, anchovy, garlic; and spices such as curry powder or garam masala, a large pinch of saffron, cracked coriander, and fennel seed.

•    •    •    •    •    •

## Potatoes with White Wine, Thyme, and Olives   Serves 4

2 pounds yellow or red potatoes, peeled and cut lengthwise into quarters or
    sixths to make 1-inch-thick wedges, rinsed well to remove their starch,
    and drained
4 to 5 medium shallots, thinly sliced
1 cup dry white wine
½ cup black olives, pitted if desired
2 tablespoons extra virgin olive oil, plus additional for drizzling if desired
1 tablespoon fresh thyme leaves or 1 teaspoon dried thyme
¾ teaspoon kosher salt
¼ teaspoon sugar

**Combine the vegetables with the wine, oil, and seasonings.** Combine the potatoes, shallots, wine, olives, olive oil, thyme, salt, and sugar in a heavy 10-inch skillet. Bring to a simmer over low heat.

**Cook the vegetables covered until tender.** Cover and cook, rearranging the potatoes occasionally, until they are tender and the liquid has almost evaporated, 40 to 45 minutes.

**Uncover and finish cooking.** Uncover the pan. If there is any liquid remaining, increase the heat slightly and cook, shaking the potatoes, until the liquid is completely evaporated and the potatoes are glazed. If desired, drizzle with a little olive oil right before serving.


## Improvisations

### Root Vegetables with White Wine and Rosemary   Serves 4

*Almost any root vegetables are delicious braised with white wine and olive oil: parsnips, carrots, parsley root, celery root (rutabagas and turnips are best in combination with sweeter ones like parsnips). Parsnips and parsley root are my favorite combination.*

Follow the recipe for Potatoes with White Wine, Thyme, and Olives, using whatever root vegetables you have on hand instead of potatoes. Cut the vegetables into ½-inch dice or, if carrot-shaped, on a diagonal ¼ inch thick. There is no need to rinse them. Use rosemary instead of thyme and leave out the olives. Before serving, toss with ⅓ cup chopped flat-leaf parsley.

### Lemon-Infused Potatoes with Thyme  Serves 4

*One of the best potato dishes I know is the lemon-and-olive oil-infused roasted potatoes my (and just about every other) Greek grandmother used to make. So, I applied the flavorings to the potato-braising technique. These appealing potatoes seem to go with everything. For saffron-scented potatoes, replace the thyme with a large pinch of saffron.*

Peel 2 pounds red or yellow potatoes and cut them lengthwise into quarters or sixths to make 1-inch-thick wedges; rinse well to remove their starch, then drain. In a heavy 10-inch skillet, combine the potatoes with 4 to 5 medium shallots, thinly sliced, ½ cup fresh lemon juice, ½ cup water, 3 tablespoons extra virgin olive oil, 1 tablespoon fresh thyme or savory, or a teaspoon or two of chopped fresh rosemary, ¾ teaspoon salt, and ¼ teaspoon sugar. If desired, add 2 to 3 tablespoons coarsely chopped fresh lemon segments (see page 353). Bring to a simmer over low heat.

Cover and cook, rearranging the potatoes occasionally, until they are tender and the liquid has almost evaporated, 40 to 45 minutes.

Uncover the pan. If there is any liquid remaining, increase the heat slightly and cook, shaking the potatoes, until the liquid is completely evaporated and the potatoes are glazed.

### Parsnips with Roasted Sesame Oil and Cilantro  Serves 4

*One evening, when I was looking for a quick side dish to serve with the Panfried Duck Steaks with Caramelized Shallots (page 227), I applied the potato-braising method to parsnips and plugged in an Asian set of flavorings: roasted sesame oil for the oil, some ginger, scallions, and cilantro. The results were delectable; the vegetables provided just the right subtly sweet, aromatic counterpoint to the rich meat.*

Combine 2 pounds peeled, diced parsnips (about 4 cups) with ½ cup water, 1 tablespoon minced fresh ginger, 2 tablespoons roasted sesame oil or fragrant roasted peanut oil, ½ teaspoon salt, ¼ teaspoon sugar, and 2 tablespoons finely chopped scallion (white and pale green parts only) or shallot in a heavy 10-inch skillet. Bring to a simmer over moderate heat.

Cover and cook, rearranging the parsnips occasionally, until they are tender and the liquid has almost evaporated, about 12 minutes.

Uncover the pan. If there is any liquid remaining, increase the heat slightly and cook, shaking the parsnips until the liquid is completely evaporated and the parsnips are glazed. Toss with freshly ground black pepper to taste and ½ cup coarsely chopped cilantro.

### Root Vegetable Hash Browns with Bacon or Pancetta   Serves 4

*I frequently make hash browns with any root vegetables I have on hand, braising them and then sautéing them in rendered bacon fat, which gives them a gutsy down-home flavor. Topped with a fried egg, they make a dandy breakfast or supper.*

In a large nonstick or seasoned cast-iron skillet, cook 2 ounces bacon or pancetta, finely diced, over moderate heat, covered, until the fat has rendered and the meat is crisp, about 6 minutes. Remove the bacon and drain on paper towels.

Add 1 medium onion or 2 or 3 shallots, finely chopped, to the skillet and cook, stirring frequently, until tender and golden brown, about 4 minutes. Add 4 cups peeled and diced root vegetables (any combination of parsnips, celery root, rutabaga, and turnips), ½ cup water, and ½ teaspoon salt; stir, cover, and cook until the vegetables are tender and the water has evaporated, about 12 minutes. If the pan seems dry, add a couple of tablespoons water.

Uncover and cook the vegetables over moderately high heat, tossing frequently, until they are glossy and golden, about 5 minutes. Continue sautéing the vegetables in the residual fat, tossing and shaking the pan frequently, until they become brown and crusty, about 5 minutes longer. Add the reserved bacon, season with freshly ground black pepper, and serve hot or at room temperature.

### Potato or Root Vegetable Hash   Serves 4

*Any of the preceding braised potato or root vegetable combinations make great foundations for meat or poultry hash, for example, roast lamb or beef with Lemon-Infused Potatoes with Thyme; shredded roast duck or pork with Parsnips with Roasted Sesame Oil and Cilantro.*

Prepare any of the braised potato or root vegetable recipes, or your own improvisation, in a large nonstick skillet. When the vegetables are cooked, sizzle them in the residual fat and toss with 2½ cups diced left-over roasted meat, such as chicken, turkey, beef, veal, venison, lamb, or pork. (If you have no leftovers, buy roasted meats by the pound.) Toss with ¼ cup chopped flat-leaf parsley and plenty of freshly ground black pepper. Serve at once.

# Leek "Noodles" with Crème Fraîche and Hazelnut Oil

- Pan-Steamed Asparagus with Butter and Hazelnut Oil
- Creamed Swiss Chard with Hazelnut Oil
- Roasted Sweet Potatoes with Butter and Hazelnut Oil
- Broken Hazelnut-Scented Dipping Sauce for Steamed Artichokes
- Hazelnut-Scented Whipped Cream

I came up with this recipe one hurried evening when I was looking for a novel way to flavor some leeks I'd simply boiled until they were tender. I drizzled over some fine roasted hazelnut oil with a little butter to mellow them out, and hit on a pretty astonishing combination. The next night I took the idea a step further for a dinner party, slicing the leeks into thin strips until they became noodlelike when cooked, and dressing them with crème fraîche barely scented with the fragrant oil. "Luxurious" is the only word to describe them, like creamy noodles with leek and hazelnut overtones. Somehow, the effect of this simple flavor combination is a great deal more than the sum of its parts.

The leeks take very little time to slice into "noodles" and just a few minutes to cook. You can do both steps ahead, and reheat them at the last minute with crème fraîche and the nut oil, making this a great dinner party side dish.

The key to both recipe and improvisations is a single ingredient: a great hazelnut oil pressed from freshly roasted nuts, which contains all the nuts' sweet, vivid flavor and aromas, like the essence of a roasted hazelnut in a bottle. The oil is one of those pricey ingredients whose virtues remain elusive–largely because, I think, many people have only tasted lackluster nut oils; they haven't experienced why good ones are worth the money.

The reason becomes apparent when you taste great nut oil, such as one made by J. LeBlanc in France, cold-pressed from carefully roasted nuts. Fine hazelnut oil inspires so many possibilities that I now view it as an essential pantry staple and a worthy investment–especially for times when I need big effect with minimal effort.

The most important thing to know is that a well-made nut oil is powerful stuff, often too concentrated to use alone. It needs a gentle foil to mellow it. For the leeks, butter or crème fraîche is the mellowing fat. In a salad dressing, say, to dress boldly flavored lettuces such as endive, radicchio, and cress, that might mean mixing it with a neutral-flavored oil, such as grapeseed or canola. The trick is just to have a subtle backdrop of hazelnut–not an obvious blast. Think of it as a flavoring rather than an oil.

The combination of butter or crème fraîche and hazelnut oil has an affinity for many vegetables: asparagus, artichokes, sweet and white potatoes, Swiss chard, and winter squashes, among others. Imagine fruits with the nut oil and butter or cream combination, particularly pears, apples, bananas.

For the adventurous cook, there are other roasted nut oils that warrant exploration: walnut, pine nut, and pecan, to name a few. Walnut oil in league with crème fraîche is terrific and surprising in a potato puree, as is pecan oil in a coleslaw. Bear in mind that nut oils are quite volatile; that is, they are more fragile than most oils. Too high a heat causes their flavor to dissipate, so they aren't good for sautéing, although the flavor comes through wonderfully in baked goods. More perishable than most oils, they will keep fine for several months in the refrigerator.

•   •   •   •   •   •

## Leek "Noodles" with Crème Fraîche and Hazelnut Oil   Serves 4

**10 medium leeks**
**Kosher salt**
**About ⅓ cup crème fraîche, or more to taste**
**1 teaspoon roasted hazelnut oil, or more to taste**
**Freshly ground black pepper**

**Trim the vegetables.** Trim the roots and tough green tops from the leeks, leaving about 1 inch of pale green. Slice each lengthwise into quarters; then slice each quarter in half again, to make thin strips. Rinse the leeks in several changes of cold water to remove any grit; drain well.

**Pan-steam the vegetables.** Place the leeks in a large heavy skillet; add enough water to come halfway up the leeks. Bring to a boil over high heat, cover, and cook, tossing occasionally, until the leeks are almost tender, about 6 minutes. Add salt to taste, uncover, and continue cooking, tossing frequently to separate the strands, until the leeks are very tender, a few minutes longer. Holding the leeks back with the lid, tilt the pan over the sink to let any remaining water drain away.

**Dress the vegetables with a mellow fat and hazelnut oil.** Place the pan of leeks back on the burner over moderate heat, tossing frequently to let any residual water evaporate, 2 to 3 minutes. Add the crème fraîche and continue simmering the leeks, tossing them frequently. At first the crème fraîche will look watery; gradually, it will thicken again to make a luxurious coating on the leeks. Stir in the hazelnut oil and adjust the seasoning, adding freshly ground pepper to taste. Serve at once.

### Pan-Steamed Asparagus with Butter and Hazelnut Oil    Serves 4

*This has become my favorite way to serve asparagus, as both side dish and first course. Use this basic approach and proportions for many simply cooked vegetables.*

Break the tough stems off 2 large bunches asparagus (1½ to 2 pounds) and discard. Arrange the asparagus in a large heavy skillet set over high heat; add salt and about ½ cup water. Cover and steam the vegetables, rearranging them occasionally, until they are crisp-tender and all but 1 tablespoon of the water has evaporated, 5 to 8 minutes. (Check the asparagus periodically; if the water is evaporating too quickly, add a few more tablespoons. Or, if there is still too much by the time the vegetables are tender, pour it off, holding the asparagus in the pan with the lid.) Remove the lid and add 1½ tablespoons unsalted butter and about 1½ teaspoons hazelnut oil, or to taste; toss the asparagus well to coat them, and add salt and freshly ground black pepper to taste. Serve at once.

### Creamed Swiss Chard with Hazelnut Oil    Serves 4

*This is my version of creamed spinach: Swiss chard, with its earthy undertones, barely glazed with crème fraîche, pepper, and the barest drizzle of hazelnut oil.*

Strip the leaves off the stems of 3 pounds Swiss chard; you should have about 1½ pounds leaves. (If desired, reserve the stems for another recipe.) Rinse the chard leaves in several changes of cold water to remove every trace of grit. Spin the leaves dry in a salad spinner and set aside.

In a large flameproof casserole, combine 2 teaspoons unsalted butter and ½ cup finely chopped shallots. Cover and cook over moderately low heat, stirring occasionally, until the shallots are softened, about 5 minutes. Uncover and continue cooking until the shallots are golden, about 2 minutes.

Add the chard leaves to the casserole. With tongs, toss the leaves so the shallots are mixed through. Cover and steam until the leaves begin to wilt, about 3 minutes, periodically rearranging the chard leaves so that the uncooked leaves are on the bottom and the wilted leaves are on top. Cover and continue cooking, turning and stirring occasionally, until the chard is completely wilted, 6 to 8 minutes longer. Uncover, increase the heat to moderately high, and boil to evaporate any water, until the greens are dry. (The chard mixture can be prepared to this point up to 3 hours ahead and refrigerated; reheat in the casserole before proceeding.)

Stir in ½ cup crème fraîche, or more to taste, ¼ teaspoon salt, and plenty of freshly ground black pepper. Simmer until the cream is thickened and glazes the chard lightly. Stir in about 1 teaspoon roasted hazelnut oil, just to give an undercurrent of hazelnut flavor. Serve at once.

### Roasted Sweet Potatoes with Butter and Hazelnut Oil    Serves 4

*When whole sweet potatoes are roasted, their flesh becomes creamy and puree-like, with a caramel sweetness that affords childlike pleasure to most of the grown-ups I know; it reminds them of pumpkin pie and marshmallow-capped sweet potato casseroles without actually being those intensely sweet dishes. The addition of butter and hazelnut oil brings out the sophisticated side of their slightly spicy flavors that go wonderfully with rich meats like pork, duck, and goose, as well as classic roast chicken.*

Preheat the oven to 400°F. With a fork, lightly prick 4 medium sweet potatoes or yams several times. Rub each one with just enough vegetable oil to coat it. Arrange on a baking pan an inch apart and roast until the centers are perfectly tender when pierced with the tip of a knife, 40 to 50 minutes. Slice each sweet potato lengthwise; using a kitchen towel to protect your fingers, press the ends toward the center to split the potatoes open and mound the flesh. Dot each with about a teaspoon of butter and drizzle over a little hazelnut oil; sprinkle with salt and freshly ground black pepper. Serve at once.

To make a **Hazelnut-Scented Sweet Potato Puree,** coarsely slice each roasted sweet potato into 4 or 5 pieces and pass them through a food mill set over a bowl. Or, alternatively, scoop out the flesh (discarding the skins) and puree in a food processor. Blend in butter, salt, freshly ground black pepper, and hazelnut oil to taste. Makes about 4 cups.

### Broken Hazelnut-Scented Dipping Sauce for Steamed Artichokes    Serves 2

*I learned of the affinity between artichokes and hazelnuts when I was working at Jim Peterson's restaurant, Le Petit Robert, in the early '80s. Just before serving a cream of artichoke soup, we'd drizzle in a little hazelnut oil. Many years later, I applied the idea to simple steamed artichokes, using the combination of butter, cream, and hazelnut oil as an over-the-top dipping sauce.*

For 2 steamed artichokes: In a small saucepan, melt 1 tablespoon unsalted butter. Add 1 tablespoon heavy cream and swirl the pan to warm the cream. Add salt and freshly ground black pepper to taste. Drizzle in ¼ to ½ teaspoon hazelnut oil and stir a couple of times; the sauce should be "broken," not uniform.

## Hazelnut-Scented Whipped Cream    Makes 1 cup

*My zealous experiments with various vegetables and fruits led me to slather a roasted sweet plantain with crème fraîche and hazelnut oil. The combination wasn't quite right, but it led to roasted bananas with whipped cream and hazelnut oil, which led in turn to this whipped cream scented with hazelnut oil, an example of a failure leading to a winner. This dessert cream is great on roasted bananas or pears or alongside chocolate cake and is the ultimate topping for chocolate sundaes and parfaits.*

Pour ½ cup heavy cream and 1 teaspoon roasted hazelnut oil into a medium chilled metal bowl. With an electric hand mixer or a balloon whisk, beat the cream until soft peaks form. Beat in 1 teaspoon granulated sugar. Refrigerate up to 1 hour before serving.

# Cauliflower and Apple Puree

Improvising is a way I get a handle on a food that I don't understand or love but want to. I just keeping following ideas, trying different combinations of flavors or cooking methods, until I find "the way in" to a recipe that is really complete and satisfying. For all its healthful virtues, cauliflower had been a vegetable whose pleasures eluded me; I avoided it for much of my life. Then, on a whim, I applied an intriguing new technique to cauliflower that I had learned from my inventive friend Margot Wellington and improvised this silky puree with a subtle cauliflower flavor. It's a fine, unexpected accompaniment to just about any roasted meat or poultry—especially duck—for an ethereal play on the classic duck with turnips.

In the Cauliflower and Apple Puree, cauliflower is cooked in milk with some pasta until it is tender enough to puree. The milk and apple mellow the cauliflower's aggressiveness. Pasta adds just enough starch to give the cauliflower—and other vegetables that are normally watery or granular when pureed—a velvety texture, creaminess, and buttery flavor.

Vegetables simmered in milk with some pasta is a formula into which you can plug a variety of root vegetables, such as celery, turnips, sunchokes (Jerusalem artichokes), and rutabagas to make interesting purees. Broccoli, asparagus, carrots, peas, and roasted bell peppers are other possibilities. Add some of the leftover cooking liquid, chicken broth, or cream to the puree, and it turns into a cream soup or, conceivably, a sauce.

When the Cauliflower and Apple Puree is diluted with some of its cooking liquid and turned into a soup, it mimics the elegant cauliflower soups served in cutting-edge restaurants. When mellowed in this way, cauliflower has an affinity with a variety of flavorings, from fennel to curry to white truffle oil.

Use the leftover puree as a ravioli filling and float the pasta in a rich duck broth; or pile it on leftover pot roast or shredded meat instead of mashed potatoes in a shepherd's pie. It makes a surprising spread for crostini.

• • • • • •

## Cauliflower and Apple Puree   Makes 3 cups, 4 servings

1 medium cauliflower (1¾ to 2 pounds), green leaves and core removed

1 small apple, peeled, cored, and chopped

1 quart 2% fat or whole milk

½ ounce angel hair pasta (about 40 strands), broken into 2-inch pieces, or other dry eggless pasta, broken into pieces if necessary

About 1¼ teaspoons kosher salt

Pinch of sugar

2 teaspoons unsalted butter

1 tablespoon crème fraîche or heavy cream

Freshly ground white pepper

**Cut up the vegetable.** Slice the cauliflower crosswise into ½-inch slices; coarsely chop. (You should have 7 to 8 cups.)

**Simmer the vegetable in milk with pasta until tender.** Transfer the cauliflower to a medium saucepan and add the apple and milk. Bring to a gentle boil over medium heat and stir in the pasta, ¾ teaspoon salt, and sugar. Cook, stirring occasionally, until the cauliflower is puree-tender, 20 to 25 minutes.

**Strain the vegetable and puree to the desired consistency.** Strain, reserving the liquid, and transfer the solids to a food processor. Puree at least 1 minute, until perfectly smooth, adding a tablespoon or two of the cooking liquid if necessary. Let the motor run for a minute or two, scraping down the sides several times, until you have a fine puree. Add the butter and crème fraîche and season with about ½ teaspoon salt, white pepper, and another pinch of sugar. (Save the remaining cooking liquid for soups or gratins, or discard.)

**Note:** You can prepare the puree several hours ahead and reheat it (or keep it warm for a shorter time), stirring occasionally, in a double boiler.

### Cauliflower Soup with Many Garnishes    Serves 4

*If you carry Cauliflower and Apple Puree one step further and add some of the reserved cooking liquid or chicken broth, you will get a velvety and very elegant soup, an excellent first course for a dinner party. It is also a good way to transform any leftover puree. The soup lends itself to an endless number of garnishes, such as crisp slivered or finely diced pancetta; diced olive oil–fried bread; a dusting of fennel pollen; Crispy Shallots (page 200); snipped fresh chives, chervil, or flat-leaf parsley; a drizzle of roasted hazelnut oil. White truffle oil, used sparingly, adds an astonishing flavor note.*

Place Cauliflower and Apple Puree in a medium saucepan, whisk in an equal amount of the reserved cooking liquid or chicken broth, and stir in a little cream. Bring to a simmer over moderate heat and adjust the seasoning. Add any of the garnishes mentioned above to each serving.

### Cauliflower Crostini on Shallot Toasts

*Remembering a cauliflower crostini I had in Tuscany, I devised this one using leftover cauliflower puree.*

In a small heavy saucepan, stir leftover Cauliflower and Apple Puree over moderately low heat until hot. Cover and keep warm.

Arrange ⅓-inch slices peasant bread on a baking sheet and toast in a preheated 450°F oven for 2 to 3 minutes until browned. (Alternatively, simply toast the bread in a toaster.) Brush both sides with extra virgin olive oil, rub each slice lightly with a halved shallot, and sprinkle salt on top. Spread some cauliflower puree on top of each toast; drizzle with extra virgin olive oil or a few drops of white truffle oil and a few grains of salt.

### Celery Root and Pear Puree    Serves 4

*Cooking celery root and other watery or fibrous root vegetables, such as turnips and rutabagas, with pasta ensures that they will be exceptionally smooth and creamy. Pear adds a gentle perfume and sweetness to the celery root.*

Follow the recipe for Cauliflower and Apple Puree, substituting 1½ pounds celery root, peeled and cut into 1-inch chunks, for the cauliflower and 1 small ripe pear for the apple.

## Pasta Cream for Sauces and Gratins     **Makes 4 cups**

*I was so intrigued with using pasta as a creamy thickener for vegetable purees, I tried cooking the pasta in milk and pureeing it to make a faux cream sauce. It was far creamier, more buttery, and lighter than traditional cream sauces. It has become the base of my Macaroni and Cheese with Extra Top (page 290). Use it whenever you need a cream sauce.*

Rinse a medium saucepan with cold water and add 1 quart whole milk, 1 cup water, ⅛ teaspoon salt, and 1 small shallot, peeled and halved. Bring the mixture to a gentle boil; add 2 ounces dry eggless pasta (such as ⅓ cup elbow macaroni) and cook, whisking frequently, until the pasta is very soft, 10 to 15 minutes longer than the package directions. Discard the shallot and ladle about ¼ cup of the mixture into a blender container. With the steam lid open to prevent the hot mixture from spurting, blend the mixture on low. With the motor running, gradually ladle in more liquid. Blend on high for 1 or 2 minutes, until the mixture is perfectly smooth.

# Rustic Bean Stew with Bacon and Caramelized Onions (Frying Pan Beans)

This is a basic, all-purpose, satisfying bean stew that I make for all kinds of occasions, from weeknight suppers to casual dinner parties. It is done on the stovetop in a skillet, with smoked bacon as the central flavoring element; it works with any cooked bean, even canned ones.

Spooned into large shallow soup bowls, the stew makes an excellent meal-in-itself. I serve different accompaniments depending on what kind of ethnic spin I want to give the beans. For example, a pan of Crackling Corn Bread (page 261) and bacony brown beans is a classic of the American South; a garnish of cilantro leaves, lime wedges, and avocado slices, accompanied by warm corn tortillas, turns the beans toward Mexico; made with white beans or flageolets, and accompanied by Shallot (or Garlic) Toasts (page 274), this dish gains a French sensibility.

If I had only one bean recipe to teach, it would be this one.

Beans are a raw material—a somewhat bland palette—that, once cooked, can be flavored in infinite ways to make satisfying and healthful dishes. Cooking dried beans from scratch may seem to some modern cooks like an unnecessary step. But it is worth the bit of effort, as these beans have much more character and flavor than canned beans. (You have only to taste canned and home-cooked beans side by side to see the vast difference.) My strategy is to cook up a batch of beans using the simplest possible method—see Basic Beans (page 167)—with whatever bean or legume I'm in the mood for. Then I scoop some out to flavor as I like; in the course of a week, I might flavor beans in several different ways. If you need to use canned beans in a pinch, look for a brand like Goya, whose beans are firm and intact; drain and rinse well, then drain again.

In this gutsy Rustic Bean Stew, onions are sautéed with bacon, two ingredients that bring out the best in any bean. Chicken broth is added to make a braising liquid that saturates the beans with smoky flavor. To shift the flavoring, change the fat: Pancetta gives that rich porkiness that beans love without the smoke; chorizo lends sweet, porky, paprika overtones; extra virgin olive oil gives a more delicate Mediterranean effect; a flavored oil, such as Sage and Garlic Oil (page 52), will carry its flavor right into the beans. Chopped herbs—rosemary, thyme, savory, or basil, for example—or ground spices and spice mixes such as fennel seed, saffron, bay leaves, chili powder, curry powder, garam masala can be stirred into hot fat to build in other layers of flavor.

Plug in other members of the onion family such as shallots, leeks, and garlic in quantities to suit your dish. For less stewlike beans, use less liquid—either broth or water—and cook them for less time.

Suit the beans to the flavorings you have in mind and vice versa. There is a world of beans—from basic cannellini to exotically named beans like Tongues of Fire and Scarlet Emperor—each with its own character and subtle differences of flavor and texture. The best way to learn about them is to cook some up. And one note: By "beans," I mean the more general category of legumes that also includes black-eyed peas and lentils.

. . . . . .

## Rustic Bean Stew with Bacon and Caramelized Onions (Frying Pan Beans) Serves 4

4 ounces thick-sliced bacon

1 pound yellow onions, sliced ⅛ inch thick

Kosher salt

4 cups cooked, drained darkish beans, such as borlotti, small red beans, or Roman beans, or black-eyed peas (or 3 cans beans, drained, rinsed well, and drained again)

2 bay leaves

1½ cups low-sodium chicken broth

1 tablespoon balsamic vinegar

1 teaspoon sugar

Freshly ground black pepper

**Cook the bacon until crisp.** Place the bacon in a large (12-inch) heavy skillet. Cover and cook over moderate heat until the fat has melted out of the bacon and the pieces are crisp and brown, about 7 minutes. With a slotted spoon, remove the bacon from the pan and reserve. Pour off all but about 1 tablespoon of the fat.

**Caramelize the onions.** Return the pan to the heat and add the onions; toss to coat. Cover and cook until the onions are wilted and have released their juices, about 5 minutes. Uncover, add about ½ teaspoon salt, and sauté until the onions are golden brown, about 20 minutes longer. Remove half the onions to a plate and reserve.

**Simmer the beans with the flavorings.** Add the beans to the pan, along with the reserved bacon, the bay leaves, chicken broth, balsamic vinegar, and sugar. Bring to a simmer, reduce the heat to low, and cook, stirring frequently, until the liquid has reduced considerably and the mixture has a stewlike consistency, about 20 minutes. Adjust the seasoning, peppering generously.

**Garnish the beans.** Spoon the beans into 4 shallow soup bowls. Top each serving with some of the reserved onions.

## Basic Beans

This method works well for any dried bean, or lentils or black-eyed peas that you wish to dress or add further flavor to once cooked, for preparations such as the Rustic Bean Stew with Bacon and Caramelized Onions, salads, or casseroles. The only variable in this recipe will be the cooking time. Lentils will take 30 to 40 minutes; navy, cannellini, and borlotti beans, from 1½ to 3 hours, depending on their age and size. For smoky-flavored beans, add a ham hock or a ½-pound chunk smoked country ham. Makes about 6 cups.

Place 1 pound dried beans in a large saucepan, cover with cool water by 1½ inches, and soak overnight. (Lentils and peas do not need to be soaked.) Discard any beans that are broken, off-colored, or floating. Add 1 small onion or shallot, halved, and a bay leaf. Bring to a boil over moderate heat, then reduce the heat to low. Simmer the beans until they are tender but not mushy and still hold their shape; do not allow the beans to boil. If necessary, replenish the water so that it stays 1 inch above the top of the beans. Halfway through the cooking time, stir in salt as desired. Let the beans cool about ½ hour in their cooking water.

Drain the beans, reserving the cooking liquid for reheating the beans or for adding to hearty soups. Discard the onion and bay leaf. (If using a ham hock, pull off the meat, shred, and add it to the beans.)

• • • • • •

## Improvisations

### White Beans with Fried Sage Leaves    Serves 4 to 6

*I tried panfrying white beans in sage and garlic oil until they were crispy and liked them, but found myself yearning for these softly cooked beans with a crispy garnish instead. (The fried bean experiment reminded me of popcorn and inspired Sage-and-Garlic Popcorn, page 285: an example of how experimenting often leads to something you don't expect.)*

*They use the basic approach of the Rustic Bean Stew with Bacon and Caramelized Onions, using the fragrant flavored oil instead of bacon. Serve the beans as an hors d'oeuvre with chilled wine or for lunch with shavings of ricotta salata or Parmigiano. Prepare the fragrant oil and crispy garnishes several hours ahead, and heat the beans at the last minute.*

For the **Sage-and-Garlic Oil,** in a large (12-inch) heavy skillet set over moderate heat, combine ¼ cup extra virgin olive oil and 10 garlic cloves, thinly sliced; cover and cook 1 minute, or until tiny bubbles dance around the garlic. Uncover, add 30 medium fresh sage leaves (½ cup loosely packed), and frizzle until the oil is fragrant, the sage has darkened and is somewhat crisped, and the garlic is barely golden, about 5 minutes. With a slotted spoon, transfer the garlic and sage leaves to paper towels to drain. Remove the pan from the heat until you are ready to reheat the beans. Pour 1 tablespoon of the oil into a small bowl and reserve.

Heat the pan with the sage oil over moderate heat. Add ¼ cup water and 4 cups cooked, drained white beans, such as cannellini, Great Northern, or baby white limas; simmer, tossing the beans, until they are heated through and most of the liquid has evaporated, 2 to 3 minutes. Add salt and pepper to taste, and the remaining oil if desired. Serve, scattering the reserved sage leaves and garlic over the beans.

## White Beans with Rosemary, Thyme, and Lavender   Serves 4 to 6

*These fragrant Provençal herb-scented beans follow the basic approach of the Rustic Bean Stew, using olive oil instead of bacon. They make a fine little meal on their own, with some shavings of Parmigiano, aged goat cheese, or ricotta salata, and Shallot (or Garlic) Toasts (page 274). They are also a classic accompaniment to grilled or roasted lamb.*

Combine 2 tablespoons extra virgin olive oil and ½ cup thinly sliced shallots in a large (12-inch) heavy skillet. Cook, covered, over moderate heat until the shallots are soft and golden, about 5 minutes. Stir in 2½ teaspoons minced fresh rosemary and thyme (and savory, if you have it), and a pinch of dried lavender. Sauté, stirring, for 1 minute.

Add 4 cups cooked, drained white beans, such as cannellini, navy, baby white limas, or flageolets, and ⅓ cup water to the pan. Bring to a simmer, reduce the heat to low, cover, and cook, stirring frequently, until the liquid has almost evaporated, about 5 minutes. Adjust the seasoning, including a teaspoon of fresh lemon juice if necessary to brighten the flavors; pepper generously. Spoon the beans into 4 shallow soup bowls. Drizzle extra virgin olive oil over each serving.

## Lentils with Caramelized Radicchio and Pancetta Cracklings    Serves 4 to 6

*Lentils are a "convenience" bean; they are quick-cooking and high in protein;
they can be eaten as a first course, side dish, or with some goat cheese as a simple meal; and they lend themselves to quick improvisations. The inspired addition of caramelized radicchio came from my assistant, Jill, when we were
improvising with pancetta and lentils. Be sure to use tiny dark green lentilles de
Puy or Beluga lentils from France, which hold their shape when cooked and have
a superb flavor.*

In a large (12-inch) heavy skillet, cook 1 cup (about 4 ounces) pancetta or
guanciale (cured pork jowl) cut into ⅛-inch dice or slivers, covered, stirring frequently, over medium-low heat until the fat is liquid and the
pancetta is golden and crisp, about 8 minutes. Transfer the cracklings to a
plate with a slotted spoon. Add 1 medium onion, thinly sliced through the
stem, to the pan, cover, and cook over moderate heat until wilted, about 3
minutes. Uncover, increase the heat, and sauté, stirring occasionally for 8
minutes.

Meanwhile, core and thinly slice 2 or 3 medium heads of radicchio (1
pound). Combine with the onions and sauté, stirring occasionally, until
well caramelized, about 5 minutes longer. Add 2 teaspoons sherry vinegar
and cook until evaporated; remove the onions and radicchio to a plate. Add
¼ cup olive oil and 1½ to 2 tablespoons sherry vinegar to the pan to warm
Add 4 cups cooked, drained lentils and toss to coat. Remove from the heat
and toss gently with the reserved onion/radicchio mixture; adjust the seasoning, adding pepper and more vinegar and salt as necessary. Scatter the
pancetta over the lentils. Serve hot or warm.

 FISH AND SHELLFISH

# Tuscan Island–Style Shellfish Stew

- Mussels and Fries
- Fish Fillets with Fennel Seed, Saffron, and Orange Zest
- Linguine with (Soft-Shell) Crab Sauce
- Clams, Mussels, or Fish Fillets in Green Curry and Coconut Milk

On the Tuscan island of Elba, I learned a profound fish-cooking lesson from Luciano Casini, chef of the renowned Il Chiasso restaurant. He used the essential combination of garlic, olive oil, and white wine to cook all manner of fish and shellfish. When cooked in this base, seafood releases briny juices into the garlicky wine to create a rich brothy sauce that can be endlessly varied. Luciano explained that this approach is the heart of the island's *cucina povera*, the traditional cooking of local people of modest means who devised cheap, delicious ways to transform the abundance of seafood into stews, soups, and pasta dishes. It was designed to be quick, he explained, because dishes were originally cooked over a wood fire, often right on the fishing boats, without elaborate ingredients or even fish broth.

This shellfish stew made with clams and mussels is a quintessential example of my Elba lesson, a model you can use for many kinds of seafood. I make it often for weeknight meals or for impromptu dinners with just one or two guests.

The basic approach is simple: Sliced garlic is cooked in olive oil until soft, then white wine is added and reduced by half. Fish or shellfish is cooked directly in this winey base, which is both fortified and mellowed by their juices. Many kinds of seafood work well: clams, mussels, and cockles; cleaned squid, cut into ¼-inch rings; crabmeat; and fish fillets and steaks.

The key to this ultraquick approach is an abundance of olive oil; it gives the wine body and richness while mellowing the acidity. Without the oil, you have to work much harder to achieve that effect and add fish broth, clam juice, or cream, ingredients I don't always have on hand. Add a bit of olive oil or butter just before serving to further enrich the broth and brighten the flavor. For a more refined effect, substitute a splash of heavy cream or crème fraîche for the enrichment.

Although you'd think this would be an overly garlicky sauce, the garlic acts as a fairly subtle and mutable base. Replace some of the garlic with finely chopped shallot or onion to give the effect of the classic moules marinière. Or add minced fresh ginger, lemongrass, or fresh fennel or spices such as fennel seed, curry powder, or saffron to the base to veer into more exotic palettes of flavor like Provençal, Southeast Asian, and Portuguese. Bolder elements include thin slices of chorizo, the spicy cured sausage; pancetta; or bacon (render the raw meat right in the pan and use the fat instead of olive oil). Peeled, seeded tomatoes; halved cherry tomatoes; or sliced pitted Kalamata or Gaeta olives add both flavor and texture. Or finish the sauce with snipped herbs, such as basil, chives, thyme, or slivered lemon or orange zest.

White wine works universally with most fish and shellfish, refining the broth into a satisfying sauce. With delicate white fish, such as sole or cod, I often use sweeter, fruitier white wines like Gewürztraminer or Riesling. Other possibilities include white vermouth and very dry hard cider with 11 to 13 percent alcohol.

Traditionally, a scrap of slightly stale or roasted rustic bread was placed in the bottom of the bowl to absorb the briny sauce and provide a satisfying and sustaining element. Push the limits on this idea by adding instead a separately cooked bed of pasta; braised fennel or leeks; potatoes of all kinds; wilted spinach; or fresh or slow-roasted tomatoes.

. . . . . .

## Tuscan Island–Style Shellfish Stew    Serves 4 as a main course, 8 as a first course

¼ cup extra virgin olive oil plus more for drizzling
4 to 5 garlic cloves, thinly sliced
Large pinch of hot red pepper flakes or ½ Serrano chile, finely sliced
1 cup dry white wine
3½ pounds shellfish, such as mussels, clams, and/or cockles, scrubbed
¼ to ½ cup chopped fresh herbs, such as flat-leaf parsley or basil
6 large slices crusty peasant bread, toasted (optional)

**Sauté the garlic in the olive oil.** In a large heavy saucepan over moderately low heat, warm 3 tablespoons of the oil. Add the garlic and hot pepper flakes and sauté, stirring frequently, until the garlic is soft and just beginning to turn golden, 3 to 4 minutes; do not allow to brown.

**Add the wine and reduce.** Add the wine, increase the heat to high, and boil until reduced by half, 6 to 7 minutes.

**Cook the shellfish in the garlic-wine mixture.** Add the shellfish, cover, and cook, shaking the pan frequently to rearrange them, until all the shells have opened, 5 to 7 minutes.

**Finish the sauce and serve.** Toss in the herbs and the remaining tablespoon of extra virgin olive oil (or butter, if you prefer). If desired, place a slice of toasted bread in each shallow soup bowl. Spoon the shellfish and sauce on top of the bread. Drizzle with a little extra virgin olive oil, if desired.

**Note:** Garlic cloves often have a green sprout in the center that can give a bitter flavor to the dish. Before slicing, halve each clove lengthwise and remove the sprout with the tip of a paring knife.

## Improvisations

### Mussels and Fries    Serves 4

*Mussels and French fries, Belgium's national dish, is less a cohesive recipe than an inspired pairing. At home, I serve bowls of white wine-steamed mussels with Post-Modern Fries (page 128). About 15 minutes before the potatoes are done, prepare Tuscan Island-Style Shellfish Stew, using only mussels; replace 3 of the garlic cloves with 2 medium shallots, minced.*

### Fish Fillets with Fennel Seed, Saffron, and Orange Zest    Serves 4

*I replaced the shellfish in Tuscan Island-Style Shellfish Stew with striped bass fillets and flavored the garlic-and-wine base with saffron, fennel seeds, and orange zest to make this classic Provençal fish dish. Use it as a model to improvise other marvelous stovetop fish dishes with their own sauce.*

*To keep skin on fillets from buckling as they cook, before cooking, lightly score the skin at 1-inch intervals in a crisscross fashion with a thin sharp knife.*

Pour 1 cup dry white wine into a measuring cup and crumble in a large pinch (about ¼ teaspoon) of saffron threads. In a large (12-inch) skillet, over moderately low heat, warm 3 tablespoons extra virgin olive oil. Add 4 to 5 garlic cloves, thinly sliced, and a large pinch of hot red pepper flakes and sauté, stirring frequently, until the garlic is soft and just beginning to turn golden, 3 to 4 minutes; do not allow to brown. Add the wine and a scant ¼ teaspoon fennel seed; increase the heat to high and boil until reduced by half, 6 to 7 minutes. Add ¼ cup water and a 2-inch strip orange zest and return to a simmer.

Arrange four 6-ounce white-flesh fish fillets, such as striped bass, red snapper, or sea bass, in the pan, cover, and turn the heat to low. Cook at a bare simmer (do not allow to boil!) until the fish is opaque and a two-pronged kitchen fork inserted in the thickest part meets with no resistance, 8 to 10 minutes. Transfer the fish to warm shallow bowls.

Taste the sauce, adjusting the seasoning and adding ¼ to ½ teaspoon honey or sugar to taste if it is too acidic. Add ¼ cup chopped flat-leaf parsley and drizzle in 1 more tablespoon extra virgin olive oil or butter, if desired. Spoon the sauce over the fish and serve.

## Linguine with (Soft-Shell) Crab Sauce    Serves 4

*The basic Tuscan Island method of cooking shellfish makes an ideal sauce for linguine or spaghetti. In this unusual improvisation, I used cut-up fresh soft-shell crabs instead of shellfish or fish. If soft-shell crabs are not in season or if you are feeling flush, use a pound of lump crabmeat; toss into the sauce at the same time as the pasta so you don't overcook it. You can also follow this basic method to sauce pasta with just about any kind of seafood cooked by the Tuscan Island method.*

Rinse 4 large or 6 small cleaned soft-shell crabs (about 1¼ pounds total); pat dry on paper towels. With a scissors or thin sharp knife, cut off the legs and claws; then cut each body into 4 pieces. Blot dry again. In a medium skillet, sauté 4 or 5 garlic cloves, thinly sliced, with a large pinch of hot red pepper flakes or half a finely sliced serrano chile in 3 tablespoons extra virgin olive oil over moderately low heat until soft and just beginning to turn golden; add 1 cup dry white wine and simmer until reduced by half. Turn off the heat.

Bring a large pot of water to a boil. Salt well and stir in 12 to 16 ounces linguine. Cook until al dente (tender but still slightly firm to the bite); drain thoroughly, reserving about ½ cup of the cooking water.

About 2 minutes before the pasta is ready, heat a large nonstick skillet over high heat. Film the pan with extra virgin olive oil; when hot, add the crab pieces. Sauté the crabs, turning once or twice, until the shells have turned orange and the flesh is opaque. Add the wine-garlic mixture and remove from the heat; toss to coat the crab well.

Add the pasta and toss, adding a tablespoon or two of the pasta water if necessary to moisten. Adjust the seasoning and stir in ½ cup chopped flat-leaf parsley.

## Clams, Mussels, or Fish Fillets in Green Curry and Coconut Milk    Serves 4

*In this improvisation, I made a Tuscan Island–Style winey base with shallots instead of garlic and flavored it with prepared Thai green curry paste, a pungent mix of cilantro, ginger, and curry spices widely available in the ethnic food section of supermarkets; coconut milk enriches the sauce and balances the extremes of the flavors. It makes a great base for clams, mussels, or fish fillets, such as striped bass or red snapper. You can use other curry pastes to flavor the sauce; add them to taste, since their intensity varies.*

In a medium saucepan, heat 1½ tablespoons extra virgin olive oil or unsalted butter over moderate heat. Add ¼ cup finely chopped shallots, cover, and cook, stirring occasionally, until soft and golden, about 5 minutes. Add ½ cup dry white wine and simmer until only 2 or 3 tablespoons are left in the pan, 5 to 6 minutes. Stir in 1 cup unsweetened coconut milk, 2 teaspoons Thai or Vietnamese fish sauce, 2 teaspoons fresh lime juice, 1½ to 2 teaspoons prepared Thai green curry paste, and 1 teaspoon sugar. Whisk until completely combined; taste and add more curry paste, if desired. Simmer 5 minutes, or until slightly thickened.

Add 3½ pounds shellfish, such as mussels or Manila clams, scrubbed. Cover and cook, shaking the pan frequently to rearrange them, until all the shells have opened, 5 to 7 minutes. Or, for fish fillets, arrange four 6-ounce white fish fillets, such as striped bass, red snapper, or sea bass, in the pan, cover, and turn the heat to low. Cook at a bare simmer (do not allow to boil!) for 8 to 10 minutes, until the fish is opaque and a two-pronged kitchen fork inserted in the thickest part meets with no resistance. Transfer the shellfish or fish to warm shallow bowls and spoon the sauce over. Sprinkle with ¼ cup chopped fresh cilantro, basil, or flat-leaf parsley.

# Slow-Roasted Fish with Fragrant Fennel Oil

When you roast fish fillets very slowly at a low temperature, the flesh becomes succulent and velvety. It is one of my favorite cooking methods, and is among the most popular ones I've taught, because it yields superb results with hardly any effort—ideal for a busy life. I serve whatever fish I've found in the market that day, slow-roasted, with a separately made sauce, such as the simple fennel oil. This method works well for just about any meaty fish: salmon, red snapper, striped bass, grouper, cod, or scallops. It is a good way to cook tuna and swordfish if you prefer them well done rather than rare, since it keeps the fish from drying out and toughening.

The first decision to make in improvising on this recipe is what fish to cook, which will depend on what looks good in the market. The technique of slow roasting yields fish with such a velvety texture and pure flavor that it can pretty much stand on its own. Your creativity comes in with ways to embellish it.

The easiest embellishment for slow-roasted fish is a separately made sauce. The possibilities are infinite: Just about any sauce designed for fish will do, from classic aïoli and beurre blanc to tomato sauce. A drizzle of fine extra virgin olive oil is the simplest. Flavor olive oil by pureeing or pounding fresh soft herbs—chives, basil, cilantro, tarragon, and so on—into it, or gently heating the oil with garlic, fennel seed, lemon zest, or minced fibrous herbs such as thyme and rosemary. (See pages 49 to 54 for more on flavored oils.) Or make olive oil–based sauces in which a chunky, slightly acidic element flavors and gives texture to the oil: the slivered zest and chopped flesh of lemons and/or oranges—sweet, mild Meyer lemons are particularly delightful in winter when they are in season—or slow-roasted cherry, egg, or grape tomatoes. Balsamic vinegar adds a sweet, mellow acidity to olive oil to make a pleasing sauce; I serve it in tandem with a garnish of crisp pancetta, playing on its almost universal affinity for all kinds of fish. Brown butter—toasted until it smells like roasted nuts—splashed with fragrant sherry vinegar is universally appealing. Other excellent sauces for Slow-Roasted Fish include Bagna Cauda (page 57) and Basil, Lemon, and Tomato Oil (page 51).

Another area of improvisation is to create beds to serve the fish on, such as mashed potatoes; Lemon-Infused Potatoes with Thyme (page 150); risottos; crushed roasted tomatoes; melting "stews" made with onions and sweet peppers or fennel; braised or creamed greens; or Confited Baby Artichokes (page 199); or sautéed wild mushrooms.

The possibilities for the simple formula—a slow-roasted fish plus a sauce and/or bed—are endless.

. . . . . .

# Slow-Roasted Fish with Fragrant Fennel Oil   Serves 4

Extra virgin olive oil
1½ pounds fish fillets: four 6-ounce salmon, striped bass, or red snapper
   fillets or one 1½-pound fillet
Kosher salt

Fragrant Fennel Oil
  2 teaspoons fennel seed
  2 tablespoons extra virgin olive oil
  One 2-inch strip lemon zest

**Prepare the fish for roasting.** Preheat the oven to 275°F. Brush an ovenproof dish lightly with olive oil. Arrange the fish fillets skin side down in the pan. Rub the top with the remaining olive oil. Sprinkle lightly with salt.

**Prepare the Fragrant Fennel Oil or another sauce or garnish, if desired.** In a small skillet, toast the fennel seed over low heat until fragrant. Add the olive oil and cook for 3 minutes. Remove from the heat, add the lemon zest, and set aside to infuse.

**Estimate the fish cooking time.** Gauge the cooking time according to the thickness of the fillets, figuring 5 to 6 minutes per ¼ inch of thickness:
  —For fillets less than ¾ inch thick, such as striped bass and red snapper, 15 to 20 minutes
  —For 1¼-inch-thick salmon or swordfish fillets, 25 to 30 minutes
If you are unsure, test the fish early, then continue cooking until done.

**Roast the fish.** Roast until a two-pronged kitchen fork inserted in the thickest part of the fish meets with no resistance and the flesh separates easily from the skin. An instant-read thermometer should read 120°F. (Don't worry if the top of the fish still has a slightly translucent raw look.)

**Assemble the dish.** Transfer the fillets to 4 warm dinner plates. Drizzle with the fennel oil or fine extra virgin olive oil. Or serve with any of the sauces in the following recipes.

# Improvisations

### Slow-Roasted Fish with Crisp Pancetta and Balsamic    Serves 4

*Pancetta, the cured unsmoked Italian bacon, has an affinity for almost any meaty, full-flavored fish, from salmon to red snapper to tuna. I often wrap fillets in it before grilling, to protect the flesh from drying out. Here the pancetta is crisped separately and used as a counterpoint of texture and flavor to the slow-roasted fillets. The delectable pancetta fat, balanced with balsamic vinegar, becomes a gutsy sauce.*

Preheat the oven to 275°F and slow-roast four 6-ounce full-flavored fish fillets such as salmon or striped bass. While the fish is roasting, arrange 8 thin slices pancetta, $1/16$ to $1/8$ inch thick, in a single layer in two large non-stick skillets (or fry the pancetta in batches in one skillet). Cook, covered, over moderately low heat, turning once, until the fat has rendered out and the pancetta is crisp, about 8 minutes. Remove the pancetta to a small baking sheet, and turn off the heat under the skillet.

A few minutes before the fish is finished cooking, place the pancetta in the oven to warm through. Heat the skillet over moderate heat, and add enough extra virgin olive oil to the fat in the pan to make about 4 tablespoons. Stir in 2 tablespoons balsamic vinegar and heat until warm. Adjust the salt and pepper to taste. Arrange 1 fillet on each of 4 warm dinner plates. Spoon some of the sauce over each fish and top with 2 slices of pancetta. Serve at once.

### Cool Meyer Lemon, Basil, and Olive Oil Sauce
### for Slow-Roasted Fish    Makes about 2/3 cup

*Meyer lemons are mildly tart, intensely perfumed citrus fruits that taste like an exotic lemony tangerine. Once a rarity outside of California, they are increasingly available in supermarkets from November to May. Here both the flesh and zest are mixed with fine extra virgin olive oil to make a vibrantly flavored sauce that seems to enhance just about any simple fish preparation. If you are unable to find Meyer lemons, substitute 3 medium navel oranges and 1 large lemon; omit the zest. Make the sauce up to 6 hours ahead; cover and refrigerate until you are ready to roast the fish.*

You'll need 2 medium Meyer lemons. With a vegetable peeler, remove the zest from 1 lemon in thin strips. Slice the zest crosswise into the thinnest possible slivers. Place in a small bowl. With a thin sharp knife, cut the stem and flower ends crosswise off the zested lemon. Place the lemon with one cut side down on the work surface. Working from top to bottom, carefully cut the skin and white pith in strips off the flesh, so that the flesh remains intact. Then, holding the peeled lemon over the bowl of zest, cut along each side of the membranes to release each lemon section into the bowl. Squeeze the membranes to extract any juices, and discard. Repeat with the remaining lemon.

Add ¼ cup fine extra virgin olive oil, ¾ to 1 teaspoon sugar, ¼ teaspoon salt, and freshly ground white pepper; toss gently. Just before serving, stir in 2 to 3 tablespoons finely chopped fresh basil.

## Slow-Roasted Cherry Tomato, Olive, and Lemon Zest Sauce for Slow-Roasted Fish    Makes about 1 cup

*One evening I decided to double up on slow roasting. I cooked small cherry tomatoes—which take only an hour to roast and caramelize—to make a quick sauce, and then I slow-roasted the fish toward the end of the tomato cooking time, along with some pitted Kalamata olives. While the fish was cooking, I tossed the roasted tomatoes with the olives, olive oil, and slivered lemon zest to make a sauce. I spooned it over each serving of cooked fish for a stunning presentation. This sauce works well with all kinds of fish. It is also a terrific topping for bruschetta (see page 274) and pasta. (If there is room in your oven, start slow roasting the fish during the last 20 minutes of the tomato cooking time; otherwise, start when the oven is available.)*

**For Slow-Roasted Cherry Tomatoes**, preheat the oven to 325°F. Stem 12 ounces (1 pint) small cherry tomatoes (under 1 inch in diameter) or grape or egg tomatoes; cut in half lengthwise through the stem. In a medium bowl, toss the tomatoes with olive oil to coat. Arrange the tomatoes cut side up on a large baking sheet. Sprinkle lightly with sugar, salt, and pepper. Roast the tomatoes until they have lost most of their liquid and are just beginning to brown, about 1 hour. They should look like tiny dried apricots.

Slice 12 pitted Kalamata olives lengthwise, place in a small ovenproof dish or skillet, and toss with 2 tablespoons extra virgin olive oil. Roast the olives for 10 minutes.

Transfer the roasted tomatoes to a medium bowl. Add the olives and olive oil. Cut two 1½-inch strips lemon zest into fine slivers. Stir them into the sauce, along with 2 additional tablespoons extra virgin olive oil; season with salt and pepper.

## Brown Butter and Vinegar Sauce for Slow-Roasted Fish   Serves 4

*White fish, such as striped bass, red snapper, and grouper, are delicious with brown butter sauce—butter that has been cooked until it gains a rich nutty flavor, made piquant with vinegar, capers, and parsley. The vinegar you choose will greatly determine the character of the sauce. I find a combination of balsamic and aged sherry vinegars produces a rich, complex nutty-flavored sauce that has a good balance of acid and sweet. Banyuls or Cava vinegars give a more delicate effect and need ½ teaspoon sugar to balance their acidity. The sauce takes only a couple of minutes to make; you can begin it when the fish comes out of the oven.*

In a small saucepan, cook 3 tablespoons unsalted butter over moderately low heat until it is golden brown and smells like roasted hazelnuts, about 4 minutes. Pour 2 tablespoons balsamic vinegar and 1 tablespoon sherry vinegar into the pan; stand back, it will sputter upon contact. When the sputtering has died down, add 2 tablespoons small capers, rinsed and drained (if using salted capers, soak them in warm water until soft and plump, about 5 minutes; rinse and drain). Boil until the sauce looks slightly creamy and thickened, about 30 seconds. Add ¼ cup finely chopped flat-leaf parsley, salt and pepper to taste, and a pinch of sugar. Spoon the sauce over the fish and serve at once.

## Cold Slow-Roasted Salmon with Creamy Curry, Lime, and Basil Sauce   Makes 1 cup

*Slow roasting is an ideal way to cook a slab of salmon you wish to serve cold: There's no unwieldy pan of poaching liquid and little danger of overcooking, the bane of poaching. To make a dramatic presentation, have the fishmonger prepare a large uncut fillet for whatever amount you need, rather than individual servings. Once slow-roasted and cooled, it slides easily onto a serving platter. Serve it with this sheep's milk yogurt sauce flavored with curry, grated lime zest, and slivered fresh basil leaves, a play on the traditional cucumber sauce, or with flavored mayonnaise (pages 65 to 69).*

Slow-roast a large slab of salmon, gauging the cooking time to the thickness of the fish (see page 186) rather than the weight. After roasting, allow the salmon to cool to room temperature, then cover with plastic wrap and refrigerate until ready to use. Slide a thin metal spatula under the fillet to loosen it, and slide it onto a platter. Garnish, if desired, with fresh chives, flat-leaf parsley, or other herbs or cucumber slices. Serve the sauce on the side.

**Creamy Curry, Lime, and Basil Sauce.** In a medium bowl, combine 1 cup sheep's milk yogurt or regular whole milk yogurt, ¾ to 1 teaspoon curry powder (warmed in a skillet until fragrant), 2 to 3 teaspoons minced fresh basil, 1 teaspoon grated lime zest, ½ teaspoon minced serrano chile or a pinch of cayenne, ¼ teaspoon sugar, a pinch of salt, and freshly ground black pepper to taste. Cover and refrigerate at least ½ hour to let the flavors marry.

# Salt-Roasted Trout and Other Whole Fish

I first learned of salt roasting in the legendary Boqueria market in Barcelona. When I stopped to admire some gray sea salt the texture of coarse sand, the stall owner raved about whole fish cooked in salt–literally buried in it–and explained the method. She promised me that this was the purest way to cook fish, to make it taste most of itself and of the sea. And in fact, it is. It yields truly succulent fish with a marvelously pure flavor. Ordinary commercial brook trout, one of the most readily available whole fish, tastes like a different, much more vividly flavored fish. And the visual effect is dramatic and primal.

The classic method for cooking fish in salt is to make a thick mud out of the salt by binding it with egg whites; in the oven, it hardens into a thick shell, as though the fish were baked in clay. While dramatic-looking, the plaster cast–like crust quickly turns problematic: You have to really work to liberate the fish, as salt flies everywhere before your waiting guests. It was enough to keep me from making this delicious treat.

I improvised this simpler approach, based on the theory that the salt mud is meant to "seal" the outside of the fish before it can seep into the flesh and oversalt it. So rather than moistening the salt, I heated it in the oven. It remained soft and free-flowing, so I could just nestle the fish into the center and pour the salt over it. The hot salt "sets" the flesh of the fish and achieves the unique penetrating heat of the original method.

The fish needs nothing more than a drizzle of a really fine extra virgin olive oil or some Lemon Oregano Jam (page 78).

The Barcelona shopkeeper taught me the secret of this method's success: Don't scale the fish. The scales protect the fish from absorbing too much salt; they pull off in a sheet when the fish is liberated from its salty encasement. This is a lesson to apply in improvising in salt roasting: Foods need to keep their skin or shell or other protection so the salt doesn't overpower the flesh. This includes whole, skin-on fish and crustaceans such as lobster and langoustines. Fish fillets end up too salty, though a center-cut portion of fish with bones and skin intact will do just fine. Whole small, unpeeled firm vegetables under 2 inches in diameter work well, such as new potatoes, sunchokes (Jerusalem artichokes), baby carrots, large whole garlic cloves and shallots. Hot salt makes a great bed on which to roast smaller shellfish, such as clams, mussels, and shell-on shrimp.

Exact quantities do not matter. You can roast as many fish as you want, of just about any size, as you can fit in one layer, and not touching, in a roasting pan. Figure 12 to 16 ounces of whole fish per person; a 3-pound fish will feed four. Use as much salt as it takes to bury the fish, roughly twice its weight. Sea salt is traditional for roasting, but it is expensive in the quantity needed; kosher salt is a fine alternative.

Gauge the cooking time according to the thickness of the fish. A 1½-inch-thick fish will take about 20 minutes to cook; a 3-inch-thick fish will require 40 minutes or more. To test for doneness, check the internal temperature with an instant-read thermometer, pushing through the salt into the thickest part of the fish; it should read 125°F. For lobster cooking times and temperature, see Salt-Roasted Lobster.

**Note:** Different brands of kosher salt have different textures and, hence, different cup yields per pound. Diamond Crystal has 10 cups per 3-pound box; Morton kosher salt has only 6 cups per box.

•   •   •   •   •   •

## Salt-Roasted Trout and Other Whole Fish   Serves 2

2 brook trout, red snapper, or striped bass, 12 ounces to 1 1/4 pounds each,
   1 1/4 to 1 1/2 inches thick, dressed (but not scaled), rinsed,
   and patted dry
Extra virgin olive oil
About 10 cups kosher salt
6 to 8 fresh thyme or rosemary sprigs
2 garlic cloves, smashed

**Season the fish.** Preheat the oven to 375°F. Rub the fish liberally inside and out with olive oil. Lightly salt each cavity and stuff with the herbs and garlic. Set aside.

**Heat the salt.** Pour half the salt into a roasting pan large enough to hold both fish side by side and smooth it out; pour the remainder of the salt into another ovenproof vessel and smooth the top. Place in the hot oven for 20 minutes.

**Bury the fish in salt.** Remove the pans of salt from the oven. Nestle the fish into the salt in the roasting pan. Pour the second pan of salt over the fish to cover completely. Make a mental note of where the thickest part of the fish is.

**Roast the fish.** Roast the fish for 20 to 25 minutes. To test for doneness, poke an instant-read thermometer right through the salt into the thickest part of the fish; it should read 125°F. Remove the fish from the oven and let stand about 5 minutes.

**Remove from the salt and serve.** Spoon the salt off the fish into a bowl. Remove the top skin and discard. Serve the fish right from its salt bed or, using two large spatulas, gently lift the fish off the salt bed and onto a platter.

To fillet the fish, using a cake server or a thin pointed spatula, cut through the skin down the back of the fish. Gently slide the spatula between the spine and the top fillet; lift up the fillet and transfer to a dinner plate. Slide the spatula under the spine and lift it off the bottom fillet; discard. Gently transfer the bottom fillet to the plate. Repeat with the remaining fish.

**Note:** Salt that is still granular and free-flowing can be used again; discard salt that is clumped together or discolored from fish juices.

### Center-Cut Salt-Roasted Salmon and Other Large Fish    Serves 8 to 10

*It is impractical to roast a whole salmon, striped bass, or other large fish in most home ovens; the head and tail alone add 9 or 10 inches to the length. However, you can roast a meaty skin-on center-cut portion with the interior bone intact. Ask your fishmonger to cut a 4- to 4½-pound head-end or center section from a whole salmon; do not fillet or scale. Any leftovers are delicious cold, served with Basil, Lemon, and Tomato Oil (page 51) or Creamy Curry, Lime, and Basil Sauce (page 184). You'll need about 20 cups (6 to 9 pounds) kosher salt.*

Preheat the oven to 375°F. Rinse the fish and pat dry. Salt lightly inside its cavity; if desired, stuff with thyme sprigs. Pour half the salt into a roasting pan large enough to hold the fish and smooth it out; pour the remainder of the salt into another ovenproof vessel and smooth the top. Heat 20 minutes in the oven.

Bury the fish completely in the salt as directed and roast until an instant-read thermometer inserted in the thickest part reads 125°F, about 40 minutes. Remove the fish from the oven and let stand 5 minutes.

Spoon the salt off the fish into a bowl. Remove the top skin and discard. Serve the fish right from its salt bed or, using two large spatulas, gently lift the fish off the salt bed and onto a platter. Fillet the fish and serve.

### Salt-Roasted Lobster    Serves 2

*Buried whole in hot salt, lobsters cook in their own juices in the shell, making them incredibly succulent; the roasted shell imparts a layer of intense, deeply lobster flavor. This method is a little more work than boiling lobster, but well worth the effort.*

*This method is easy for two 1½-pound lobsters; more than that depends on your oven size. Figure 10 cups (3 to 4 pounds) kosher salt per 1½-pound lobster. For cooking times, figure roughly 4 minutes per ¼ pound of lobster.*

Preheat the oven to 400°F. Spread 10 cups kosher salt in a roasting pan just large enough to hold two 1½-pound lobsters side by side. Spread an additional 10 cups kosher salt into another vessel. Place in the oven to heat 20 minutes.

When the salt is almost ready, kill each lobster by plunging the tip of a chef's knife straight down through the slight indentation between the head and the body that lies about 1 inch behind the eyes, severing the spinal cord.

Place 1 lobster, belly side down, on the bed of salt in the roasting pan, nestling it into the salt slightly to keep the tail from curling up. Arrange the second lobster next to the first, with its claws parallel to its tail. Pour the pan of hot salt over the lobsters to bury them completely.

Roast 25 minutes. Take the pan out of the oven and push the salt to the side of one of the lobsters. Using tongs, turn the lobster over; insert an instant-read thermometer into the thickest part of the tail—it should read 150°F. If not, rebury the lobster and continue roasting a few minutes longer. Take the pan out of the oven and let sit 3 minutes.

Push the salt aside and use a tongs or kitchen towel to pull the lobsters out of the salt. Knock off any salt that clings to the shells. To make it easier to remove the meat at the table, use a kitchen shears to cut the tails length-wise up through the center of the cartilage. Place a kitchen towel over the claws and hit them with the side of a hammer to crack them. Serve at once, with melted unsalted butter, if desired. Freeze the shells to make Lobster Essence (Rich Lobster Shell Broth) (page 193).

## Salt-Roasted New Potatoes with Crème Fraîche and Cracked Coriander     Serves 4

*As with fish, new potatoes and fingerlings roasted in salt have an extraordinarily pure flavor and creamy interior. Place the dish of potatoes buried in salt on the table (on a trivet) along with a serving spoon, allowing guests to dig the potatoes themselves; pass little bowls of unsalted butter or crème fraîche, cracked toasted coriander seeds, and snipped fresh chives on the side for guests to dress them as they like. (See page 352 for Toasting and Crushing Spices.)*

*Other whole small unpeeled vegetables under 2 inches in diameter also work well. I've tried Jerusalem artichokes (sunchokes), whole unpeeled shallots, baby carrots, and large whole garlic cloves, and imagine other possibilities— baby artichokes, parsnips, turnips, and salsify, for example. The salt can be reused several times.*

Preheat the oven to 400°F. Spread a ½-inch-thick layer of kosher salt in a large, 2 or 3-inch-deep ovenproof pan or dish. Nestle 1½ pounds new potatoes, such as Yellow Finnish or Bintje, or a mix of heirloom potatoes available at farmers' markets (no larger than 2 inches in diameter), in the salt about ½ inch apart. Cover completely with salt. Bake until tender, 35 to 40 minutes. To test for doneness, dig out one of the potatoes and press; it should split open easily. Let the dish cool for 5 minutes before serving. Place the bowls of dressings on a platter or tray to make them easy to pass.

# Lobster Essence (Rich Lobster Shell Broth)

Lobster Essence, a rich broth made from lobster shells, might sound like an extravagant preparation for a home cook—more fitting for professional kitchens. It is in reality an easy way to make pricey lobsters go twice as far. The shells left over from a lobster dinner (from Salt-Roasted Lobster, page 188, for example) are powerhouses of lobster flavor. Because the resulting essence transforms quickly into luxurious dishes, it is a perfect raw material for improvisation, as you'll discover. It's so useful I make up batches and freeze it to use as a base for luxurious soups, seafood stews, and paellas—among other improvisations—at a moment's notice.

Like bones for a stock, the lobster shells can be stockpiled in the freezer until you are ready to make Lobster Essence. (If you have a lobster dinner in a restaurant, take the shells home in a doggie bag.)

Lobster Essence combines the flavorings of Provençal fish soup–white wine, leeks, garlic, tomatoes, saffron, bay leaf, and thyme–with a classic technique for unlocking rich flavor from lobster and other crustaceans: sautéing the shells in oil. The result is a liquid flavor base that needs very little embellishment. To concentrate the flavor, boil it for a few minutes; or add water if it's too intense. (To use the Lobster Essence recipe as a model for fish broth, replace the lobster shells with fish bones, trimmings, and/or heads.)

As is, Lobster Essence makes an excellent base for soups and stews; simmer fish or shellfish such as clams, cockles, mussels, or shrimp right in it, and add pasta, wilted greens, cooked potatoes, fava beans, or peas. Wild mushrooms, especially chanterelles, and cultivated exotic ones such as shiitake and hen-of-the-woods have a particular affinity for lobster and can be cooked right in the broth. Drizzle these preparations with extra virgin olive oil, or add a bit of butter or cream to enrich and mellow the flavors, and serve with Shallot (or Garlic) Toasts (page 274).

Add crème fraîche or heavy cream to the reduced Lobster Essence to make rich lobster soups, Lobster Demitasse, and elegant sauces. Thickened lightly with arrowroot, Lobster Essence would make a marvelous creamy lobster-flavored base for a lobster potpie. Minced herbs such as tarragon, chives, flat-leaf parsley, chervil, and basil add bright flavor.

One of my favorite uses for Lobster Essence is for making paellas (see Lobster Paella, page 281); the starchy rice becomes embued with lobster flavor. Thin spaghetti can be treated in the same way, to make deeply satisfying Lobster Noodles, a play on the Catalan *fideus rossejats*. With a slight adjustment, this is the approach used in creating lobster risotto; you can add shellfish or shrimp during the last few minutes to embellish it. Cooking starchy ingredients in the rich lobster broth makes me imagine new potatoes simmered in it until tender, then mashed to make Lobster Mashed Potatoes, a savory bed, perhaps, for slow-roasted fish. . . .

. . . . . .

# Lobster Essence (Rich Lobster Shell Broth)    Makes about 6 1/2 cups

Shells (from bodies, tails, and claws) from two 1 1/2-pound lobsters
   (about 1 1/3 pounds)
5 tablespoons extra virgin olive oil
2 medium leeks, white and pale green parts only, thinly sliced crosswise
   (about 1 1/3 cups)
4 garlic cloves, crushed
2 cups dry white wine
4 fresh thyme sprigs
1 small imported bay leaf
1/4 teaspoon fennel seed
1/8 teaspoon hot red pepper flakes
Large pinch of saffron threads, crumbled (optional)
One 14-ounce can plum tomatoes, drained
About 7 cups water

**Sauté the lobster shells and aromatics.** Using kitchen shears, cut the shells into 2-inch pieces. In a very large (14-inch) straight-sided sauté pan or Dutch oven, heat 1/4 cup of the olive oil over high heat. Add the lobster shells and sauté, tossing frequently, until fragrant, 6 minutes. (If you don't have a large enough pan, sauté them in two batches.) Push the shells to one side of the pan and add the remaining tablespoon of olive oil to the empty side. Reduce the heat to medium, add the leeks to the oil, and toss with tongs; sauté until softened and golden, about 8 minutes. Add the garlic cloves and sauté for 1 minute.

**Add the wine and flavorings and simmer to extract the flavors.** Stir in the wine, thyme sprigs, bay leaf, fennel seed, pepper flakes, and saffron, if using, mixing the shells back in. Crush the tomatoes in your hands and add to the pot. Add enough cold water to cover by 1 inch. Bring to a boil, then reduce the heat. Simmer for 1 hour, adding water as necessary to keep the shells covered with liquid.

**Strain.** Pour the broth through a fine-mesh strainer, pressing to extract all the liquid from the solids. Pour into plastic containers and let cool completely before refrigerating or freezing. The broth will keep 3 days in the refrigerator and several months in the freezer.

**Note:** Scale up the Lobster Essence recipe according to how many lobster shells you have; sauté them in batches if necessary.

## Improvisations

### Lobster Demitasse with Crème Fraîche and Chives   Serves 4 to 6

*Little demitasse cups of warm lobster cream make an elegant and easy first course for a dinner party. Because it is very rich, a small serving is just the right amount, as well as charming.*

Pour 3 cups Lobster Essence into a small saucepan and simmer over medium heat until reduced to 1 cup. Just before serving, stir in 1 cup heavy cream or crème fraîche and bring back to a simmer. If desired, reduce further to intensify the flavors and richness. Adjust the seasoning. Pour into demitasse cups and garnish with minced fresh chives and tarragon or chervil leaves. Serve at once.

### Lobster Essence with Pasta and Wild Mushrooms   Serves 4

*Wild and cultivated exotic mushrooms, such as chanterelles, hen-of-the-woods, and shiitake, have an extraordinary affinity for lobster, creating a haunting, subtly earthy flavor, as in this simple, rustic soup.*

In a medium saucepan, bring 4 cups Lobster Essence to a simmer. Add 2 to 3 cups sliced mushrooms and simmer until tender, about 3 minutes. Add 2 cups cooked small pastas, such as shells or tubetti. Divide among 4 warm soup bowls and scatter over some very coarsely chopped flat-leaf parsley and snipped fresh chives; grind over a little fresh black pepper. For visual effect, float in a few enoki mushrooms, if desired. Drizzle in some fine extra virgin olive oil or stirred crème fraîche. Serve at once.

### Striped Bass or Snapper Fillets in Creamy Lobster and Wild Mushroom Broth   Serves 4

*I often use Lobster Essence as a base for impromptu fish soups and stews. Here meaty fish fillets are steamed on a rack over the broth to ensure tender, succulent, perfectly cooked fish while at the same time enriching the sauce. The fillets are served in wide shallow bowls, napped with the cream-enriched broth and wild mushrooms. Cooked sliced new potatoes or fava beans are also lovely garnishes.*

About ½ hour before serving, sprinkle four 6-ounce striped bass or red snapper fillets lightly with kosher salt; set aside.

Pour 1½ cups Lobster Essence into a 10- to 12-inch skillet or pot. Arrange a 7- to 9-inch footed round rack in the pan so it is elevated over the liquid by ½ inch (use small ramekins or wadded-up aluminum foil to create makeshift "feet" if necessary). Bring the broth to a simmer over medium heat. Blot the fish dry, arrange on the rack, and cover the pan. Steam the fish until a kitchen fork inserted in the thickest part meets with no resistance, 7 to 9 minutes. Transfer the fillets to 4 warm shallow soup bowls and cover loosely with foil. Remove the rack and add 2 cups thinly sliced flavorful mushrooms, such as chanterelles, hen-of-the-woods, and/or shiitake, to the broth and gently boil until tender, about 2 minutes. Stir in ⅓ to ½ cup crème fraîche, bring to a simmer, and adjust the seasoning. Garnish with snipped fresh herbs, such as basil, tarragon, chives, chervil, and flat-leaf parsley, in any combination. Pour the sauce around each serving.

## Lobster Noodles   Serves 4

*This recipe was inspired by* fideus rossejats, *the quintessentially Catalan dish that has haunted me since I had it many years ago in Barcelona. Thin spaghetti was toasted in a pan until golden and then simmered in fish broth until it took on a rich sea flavor. Years later, I tried simmering thin spaghetti in Lobster Essence and made silken, intensely "lobster" noodles.*

Preheat the oven to 400°F. Break 12 ounces thin spaghetti into 3-inch lengths and place on a large baking sheet. Drizzle 2 tablespoons extra virgin olive oil over the pasta and toss until it is well coated with oil. Roast for 4 minutes. Use tongs to toss and rearrange the pasta, and continue roasting, tossing frequently, until it is golden brown, about 4 minutes longer.

Meanwhile, in a large heavy skillet, combine ⅓ cup finely chopped shallots and 1 tablespoon extra virgin olive oil; cover and cook over moderate heat until soft, about 3 minutes. Uncover and cook, stirring frequently, until the shallots are golden, 5 minutes longer. Add 5 cups Lobster Essence to the pan and bring to a simmer.

Add the roasted pasta and gently rearrange to submerge it in liquid. Simmer, stirring frequently, until the pasta is tender and all of the liquid has been absorbed, 12 to 15 minutes. Serve at once, topping each serving with a dollop of crème fraîche and some snipped fresh chives.

# Shrimp in Olive Oil, Garlic, and Smoked Paprika

This recipe is a play on the most beloved appetizer in Spain: shrimp simmered in a bath of extra virgin olive oil robustly flavored with garlic. You eat the shrimp and dunk crusty bread in the delicious oil as you sip chilled bone-dry sherry. I added pungent, spicy-sweet smoked Spanish paprika and a drizzle of sherry vinegar, which gives a lively savor. Once you've prepped the few elements, the dish takes only a few minutes to cook, so it can be done at the last minute; serve it right out of the pan.

The success of this dish depends upon really fresh garlic, which is firm and unsprouted; do not use commercial minced garlic in oil. Pimentón de la Vera from Andalusia, Spain, is available in the spice section of better markets and by mail order.

The basic flavoring elements—garlic, hot pepper, and olive oil—are similar to those in Tuscan Island-Style Shellfish Stew (page 174). Here, though, the lack of white wine and its attendant brothiness makes for a very different effect: The abundance of warm garlicky oil becomes a rich sauce with a smooth, robustly garlic flavor. The just-cooked shrimp are tender and somewhat creamy.

The essential technique of this classic appetizer is seafood cooked in a bath of flavorful fat. Seafood cooked in hot simmering fat—the traditional method—should be removed when it is slightly undercooked. I often prefer cooking fish and shellfish at lower temperatures, in some cases in only warmed fat, a technique embraced by many professional chefs in dishes such as butter-poached lobster and olive oil-poached striped bass. Relatively low temperatures prevent the collagen of the fish from seizing up, making for moist, tender flesh. This cooking method works especially well with seafood that tends to be either rubbery or dry when even slightly overcooked, such as shrimp, swordfish, squid, and members of the cod family.

The key area of improvisation is in the fat. It can be any delicious fat, singly or in combination: extra virgin olive oil; butter; rendered pancetta, bacon, or guanciale fat. Most commonly, a quickly made flavored oil is used, such as extra virgin olive oil with garlic, leeks, shallots, ramps, or other members of the onion family; spicy peppers of various kinds; herbs such as thyme, savory, rosemary, basil; fennel seed or cracked spices; or curry powder or saffron (these should be moistened in hot water for a few minutes before adding to the oil). The section on flavored oils, pages 51 to 54, outlines approaches. Vegetables such as wild mushrooms, bell peppers, and sliced artichokes can also be stewed—confited—in the olive oil before the seafood is added.

· · · · · ·

## Shrimp in Olive Oil, Garlic, and Smoked Paprika   Serves 4 as an appetizer

12 ounces medium-small shrimp (about 20),
   peeled and deveined
½ teaspoon kosher salt
5 garlic cloves
½ cup extra virgin olive oil
⅛ teaspoon smoked sweet paprika (pimentón de la Vera) or scant ¼
   teaspoon hot red pepper flakes
1 teaspoon sherry, Banyuls, or white wine vinegar
¼ cup finely chopped flat-leaf parsley

**Salt the shrimp.** Pat the shrimp dry with paper towels and sprinkle with the salt. Set aside.

**Prep the flavorings.** Halve the garlic cloves lengthwise and remove the green sprout, if any. Mince or finely grate the garlic. (You will need 1 tablespoon plus 1 teaspoon.)

**Cook the shrimp in the olive oil and flavorings.** In a heavy medium skillet, heat the oil over moderate heat until hot but not smoking. Add the shrimp to the pan in one layer, along with the garlic and smoked paprika. Cook the shrimp 1 to 1½ minutes on each side, until they are pink and barely opaque, with a slight translucence (do not overcook).

**Finish with the herbs and seasonings.** Add the vinegar and parsley and shake to combine. Serve at once.

**Note:** To freshen up the flavor of frozen shrimp, soak them for 10 minutes in a brine made from 1⅓ cups water and 1 tablespoon sea salt (or 2 tablespoons kosher salt). Drain, rinse, and pat dry. Do not salt further.

# Improvisations

### Shrimp with Confited Baby Artichokes      Serves 4 as an appetizer

*I "confited" thinly sliced baby artichokes—that is, stewed them in olive oil—to make a rich, savory bath in which to cook the shrimp, in an Italianate improvisation on the Shrimp in Olive Oil, Garlic, and Smoked Paprika. Serve with crusty bread. Sometimes I use the artichoke confit without the shrimp as a saucelike accompaniment to Slow-Roasted Fish (page 180). Baby artichokes are much easier to prepare than large ones.*

Sprinkle 1 pound medium shrimp, peeled and deveined, with ½ teaspoon kosher salt and set aside. Prepare **Confited Baby Artichokes** with 1¼ pounds baby artichokes: Squeeze 1 lemon into a medium bowl and fill it with cold water. Working with 1 artichoke at a time, pull off 4 or 5 layers of the tough green outer leaves from the base to reveal the pale yellow ones; they will resemble closed rosebuds. Cut off the top third of each artichoke and trim all but ¼ inch off the stem and any tough green skin. Using a mandoline or Benriner or a thin sharp knife, slice each artichoke lengthwise through the stem into ⅛-inch slices. Place the slices in the lemon water as you work. (You may prepare the artichokes up to 1 hour ahead.)

Drain the artichokes well and add them to a heavy medium skillet, along with ¾ cup extra virgin olive oil, 4 or 5 garlic cloves, thinly sliced, ¼ teaspoon hot red pepper flakes, ¼ teaspoon salt, and 2 fresh thyme or rosemary sprigs. Cover and cook over medium-low heat, stirring occasionally, until the artichokes are tender, about 15 minutes.

Increase the heat slightly and nestle the shrimp among the artichokes in one layer; cook 1 to 1½ minutes on each side, until the shrimp have turned pink and are barely opaque (do not overcook). Add 2 to 3 teaspoons sherry or Banyuls vinegar and two 2-inch strips lemon zest, slivered, to the pan and shake to combine. Serve at once with crusty bread.

### Swordfish Poached in Thyme and Shallot Oil      Serves 4

*Cooking swordfish at a very low heat in a flavored oil renders it juicy, tender, and flavorful, a great method for people who prefer their swordfish well done rather than rare. Serve the swordfish with crushed boiled new potatoes, bathed in some of the thyme and shallot oil.*

Sprinkle four 1-inch-thick swordfish steaks (5 to 6 ounces each) lightly with kosher salt and set aside. For the **Thyme and Shallot Oil**, in a large heavy skillet, combine ⅔ cup extra virgin olive oil, 1 shallot, thinly sliced, and 2 teaspoons fresh thyme leaves. Place on a Flame Tamer over moderate heat and cook until the shallots soften and the oil is well flavored, 6 to 7 minutes. Turn the heat to low and arrange the swordfish in a single layer in the pan. Cover and cook, basting occasionally with the oil, 3½ minutes; turn and continue cooking until the swordfish is opaque and a kitchen fork meets with no resistance, about 3½ minutes longer. Arrange the fish in shallow soup bowls and spoon some of the oil over; sprinkle with a few grains sea salt.

### Shrimp in Coconut Milk with Ginger, Basil, and Crispy Shallots    Serves 4

*For a quick supper one night, I poached shrimp in creamy coconut milk infused with ginger and basil instead of garlicky olive oil, in a radical shift from the Spanish approach. Thinly sliced shallots, fried in the same pan beforehand, add a crispy, caramelized counterpoint that completes the dish. Serve as is or over thin noodles or jasmine rice.*

Sprinkle 1¼ pounds shrimp, peeled and deveined, with ½ teaspoon kosher salt and set aside. For the **Crispy Shallots**, in a medium (10-inch) heavy skillet over medium-high heat, combine ¼ cup peanut oil and 4 or 5 medium shallots, thinly sliced on a mandoline or Benriner (¾ cup). Simmer until the shallots are golden and crispy, 10 minutes. Use a slotted spoon to transfer to paper toweling. Strain the **shallot oil** into a clean, dry jar to use in other dishes and improvisations.

Pour 1½ cups unsweetened coconut milk into the skillet and add 2½ teaspoons grated fresh ginger, a scant teaspoon minced chile pepper, 1 teaspoon sugar, and 2 tablespoons fresh lime juice. Bring to a simmer over moderate heat and cook for 2 minutes. Meanwhile, stack about 40 basil leaves and cut crosswise into thin slivers to make 1½ to 1¾ loosely packed cups. Add 1 cup to the pan and cook for 1 minute. Reduce the heat to moderately low, add the shrimp, and poach at the barest simmer, rearranging frequently, until just cooked through, 3 to 4 minutes. Add additional salt and lime juice, if desired. Spoon the shrimp and sauce into bowls and scatter the crispy shallots and the remaining basil over the top.

## Squid Pasta   Serves 4

*Cut into thin strips and barely cooked in rendered pancetta fat, squid is reminiscent of pasta. So I took it a step further and tossed it with linguine to make a sensuous, earthy pasta, accentuated with bits of caramelized pancetta, with which it has a real affinity.*

You'll need 1½ pounds cleaned squid, preferably mostly bodies, not tentacles. Cut the squid bodies open with a thin sharp knife. Rinse well and pat dry. Slice lengthwise into ⅛- to ¼-inch strips. Place in a bowl, sprinkle with ½ teaspoon salt, and set aside. Bring a large pot of water to a boil.

Slice 4 ounces pancetta or guanciale into ⅛-inch strips. Place in a large heavy skillet with ¼ cup extra virgin olive oil and cook, covered, over moderately low heat until the pancetta is golden brown and chewy-crisp. Use a slotted spoon to transfer the pancetta to a plate; reserve. Turn off the heat, let the pan cool 30 seconds, and stir in 1 tablespoon plus 1 teaspoon finely chopped garlic and ¼ teaspoon hot red pepper flakes; continue stirring until the garlic is soft and golden. Set aside.

Salt the boiling water well and add 10 ounces linguine or spaghetti. Boil until slightly undercooked. Using a measuring cup, scoop out ¼ cup of the cooking water; reserve. Drain the pasta in a colander and let sit while you cook the squid.

Heat the skillet of pancetta fat over moderately low heat for about 1 minute. Reduce the heat to low. Add the squid to the pan and stir constantly for about 1½ minutes, until it is opaque with a slight translucence and has released some of its juices. Do not overcook; it should be tender and silky, not firm or rubbery. Add the pasta, 2 tablespoons of the pasta water, ⅓ cup chopped flat-leaf parsley, and the reserved pancetta; toss well. Stir in 2 teaspoons sherry or Banyuls vinegar and adjust the seasoning. Serve at once.

# Crisp Panfried Fish Fillets

- Tuna or Swordfish with Sesame Seeds, Cracked Coriander, and Crispy Ginger
- Curry-Fried Fish or Shrimp
- Trout Panfried in Dry-Cured Ham Fat or Pancetta
- Panfried Fish Sandwich with Bacon Mayonnaise

Often improvisations are fueled by memories of dishes past; they're attempts to re-create a singular set of flavors or a dish's particular pleasure. When I found myself yearning for two classic fish dishes I used to eat in France years ago, I made an amalgam of the two, to capture the crispiness of goujonettes—fillets of sole cut into strips, dusted with flour, and deep-fried, and the comforting delicate butteriness of sole meunière—whole or fillets, flour-dusted and panfried in butter.

Here I use flavorful white-fleshed fish fillets, from striped bass, red snapper, or halibut, season them, and dust them with Wondra, a finely granulated flour, or white rice flour; both flours produce much crisper crusts than all-purpose flour. I panfry the fish in butter and olive oil until it has a thin, crisp exterior shell and tender flavorful flesh. It's good as is, with just a squeeze of lemon, or with a brown butter and vinegar sauce made in the same pan. This dish is a perfect casual supper, utterly straightforward and satisfying, one I make often for myself.

The great pleasure of this dish is the delicate, crisp crust that coats the fish. To achieve this crust on fish and any other panfried food, from Crispy Panfried Risotto Cakes (page 280) to Fried Mac-and-Cheese (page 291), use Wondra, a readily available "instantized" flour that pours like fine sand, or white rice flour, available at health food stores.

Replacing a portion of the flour with a ground spice mixture or dried herbs builds flavors into the crust; curry powder is particularly appealing, and garam masala, cumin, ground coriander seed, and smoked sweet paprika such as pimentón de la Vera offer other possibilities. (These can all be used without the flour, but then won't achieve the crisp exterior.) Coarsely crushed coriander seeds, sesame seeds, wild mushroom powder, and finely ground nuts, such as pecans or almonds, also make good coatings for meaty, full-flavored fish; flour is not necessary.

Use this approach with shellfish and fish that are thin enough to panfry—under about ¾ inch thick—such as sea scallops, peeled shrimp, and just about any nonoily fish fillet or small whole fish. It's one of the best ways to cook soft-shell crabs.

Choosing a fat is the next decision. It can be any fat that can sustain a moderately high heat without breaking down and impart a nice flavor to the dish. Butter—mixed with a little olive oil to keep it from burning—gives an inimitable buttery, sweet, slightly nutty flavor. Extra virgin olive oil imparts a pleasingly olivey flavor, reminiscent of fried fish often served in Italy. Rendered bacon fat takes the fish in a smoky Southern direction. Rendered pancetta, guanciale (cured pork jowl), and prosciutto fat lend a satisfying peppery flavor of pork fat that is still mild enough to enhance the fish's own flavor. Asian sesame oil (mixed with peanut oil) moves it toward an Asian sensibility . . . and so on. Quickly flavor fat by adding sliced or chopped garlic, ginger, shallots, or herbs as it heats.

The fish needs no sauce, save perhaps brown butter finished with a touch of vinegar, which can be made in the pan after the fish comes out. Toast slivered almonds or pine nuts in the browning butter for an amandine-like effect. Or serve a cool, creamy sauce such as Roasted Romesco (page 91) or Creamy Curry, Lime, and Basil Sauce (page 184).

. . . . . .

# Crisp Panfried Fish Fillets   Serves 4

1½ pounds meaty white fish fillets, such as striped or black bass,
   red snapper, or grouper, preferably skinned
Kosher salt
Freshly ground black pepper or a scant ¼ teaspoon cayenne pepper
4 to 5 tablespoons Wondra flour or white rice flour
1½ tablespoons unsalted butter
½ tablespoon extra virgin olive oil
Lemon wedges (optional)

Brown Butter Vinegar Sauce (optional)
   2 tablespoons unsalted butter
   2 tablespoons sherry, balsamic, or Banyuls vinegar
   Kosher salt and freshly ground black pepper
   Pinch of sugar

**Prepare the fish.** To skin the fillets, if necessary: Place 1 fillet skin side down on the work surface. Starting at the thin end, slide a thin sharp knife under the skin to loosen a small flap. Hold down the flap with one hand and, with the other hand, saw the knife between the skin and flesh, angling the blade against the skin, until they are separated. Repeat with the remaining fillets.

If the fillets are thin—¾ inch or less—slice them in half lengthwise, along the center seam; then cut each half in halves or thirds on a diagonal. For thick fish fillets, use a thin sharp knife (a salmon slicer works best) to slice them on a slant from top to bottom, to make wide ½ to ¾-inch-thick slices. Alternatively, divide them along the center seam, then slice them in half horizontally.

**Season the fish.** Pat the fillets dry with paper towels. Season with salt and pepper to taste.

**Dust the fillets with the flour or another fine coating.** Pour the flour onto a dinner plate. Dredge the fillets in the flour until they are completely coated.

**Panfry the fish.** Heat a large, heavy nonstick or well-seasoned cast-iron skillet over moderately high heat. Add 1 tablespoon of the butter and the olive oil and swirl to coat the pan. When the butter has stopped bubbling and the pan is hot, tap the fish lightly to knock off any excess flour and arrange in the pan. Cook until the bottom side is golden, about 1½ minutes. Adjust the heat so that the fat bubbles and sizzles around the fish and smokes only slightly. Turn, adding the remaining 1½ teaspoons butter to the pan as you do, and cook until golden on the second side, 1 to 1½ minutes longer. Drain briefly on paper toweling and transfer to dinner plates.

**Serve with lemon wedges or make the pan sauce, if desired.** Quickly rinse the pan and wipe it out with a paper towel, return to the heat, and add the butter to the pan. When it begins to turn golden and smell like roasting nuts, add the vinegar, salt and pepper to taste, and sugar. Drizzle the sauce around—not over—the fish.

## Improvisations

### Tuna or Swordfish with Sesame Seeds, Cracked Coriander, and Crispy Ginger    Serves 4

*Meaty fish, such as tuna or swordfish, can stand up to more boldly flavored and coarsely textured coatings than simple flour, such as this mix of sesame seeds and cracked coriander. I sear the fish in ginger oil and garnish it with crispy ginger.*

To make the **Crispy Ginger** and **ginger oil**, peel a 3-inch section of fresh ginger and slice crosswise as thin as possible, to make 35 to 40 slices. Place in a small heavy saucepan with 3 tablespoons roasted peanut oil or 1½ tablespoons each roasted sesame oil and grapeseed oil. Cook over moderately low heat, tossing frequently, until the ginger is golden and crisp, 7 to 8 minutes. With a slotted spoon, transfer the ginger to paper toweling, sprinkle with salt, and set aside. Pour the ginger oil into a large heavy nonstick or well-seasoned cast-iron skillet.

Place ¼ cup sesame seeds and ¼ cup coarsely cracked coriander seed in a pie plate. Season four 6-ounce swordfish or tuna steaks with 1 teaspoon salt. Then press the steaks into the sesame mixture, turning them until completely coated.

Heat the ginger oil over moderate heat until hot. Place the steaks in the pan and cook until just golden, about 1½ minutes on each side for medium rare, 2½ minutes for well done. Transfer to a cutting board and slice the fish into ½-inch slices. Fan them out on dinner plates and scatter the crispy ginger over.

### Curry-Fried Fish or Shrimp    Serves 4

*Leafing through an Indian cookbook, I discovered that rice flour, seasoned with spices such as cumin and hot pepper, is often used in India to fry fish and shrimp. Inspired, I mixed an excellent curry powder into some rice flour and panfried the fish as usual. The result was a crisp, spicy, fragrant crust enclosing moist fish within. The Brown Butter Vinegar Sauce worked well with the flavors, in a pleasing French-Indian fusion. Or serve Creamy Curry, Lime, and Basil Sauce (page 184) or use the recipe to improvise a cool yogurt raita flavored with cilantro, chili, and lime. For "fried" shrimp, fry 1 ½ pounds large shrimp, peeled up to the tail and deveined, instead of the fish fillets.*

Prepare Crisp Panfried Fish Fillets using ¼ cup white rice flour mixed with 2 tablespoons curry powder as the coating.

### Trout Panfried in Dry-Cured Ham Fat or Pancetta    Serves 2

*When I came back from a trip to Basque Spain, I set out to duplicate one of the most memorable dishes I had there: a whole trout cooked in serrano ham fat. It was said to be an improvisation of shepherds, who used what they had during their vigils in the mountains: trout from the river, fat from the cured ham they carried with them, wild thyme. I dust the trout in Wondra or white rice flour to make the skin nice and crisp.*

*Ask the deli man for fat trimmed from dry-cured hams, such as prosciutto or Spanish serrano, or use pancetta fat. If you don't wish to use pork fat, you can fry the trout in 2 tablespoons extra virgin olive oil.*

Rinse and dry 2 dressed brook trout, 10 to 12 ounces each, head and tail removed. Season with salt and freshly ground black pepper all over and inside the cavity.

Place about ¼ cup finely diced Spanish ham fat, prosciutto fat, or pancetta fat in a small heavy skillet and cook, covered, over moderate heat until most of the fat is liquid and the remaining bits are golden, about 7 minutes. With a slotted spoon, transfer the crisp bits to a plate. Turn off the heat.

Pat the trout dry inside and out with paper toweling. Stuff each cavity with 4 or 5 fresh thyme sprigs. Pour 4 or 5 tablespoons Wondra or white rice flour onto a dinner plate and dredge the fish in it, knocking off the excess.

Pour the ham fat into a large nonstick or well-seasoned cast-iron skillet set over moderate heat. When hot, add the trout and cook, without moving the fish, until the underside is brown, about 10 minutes. Gently turn the fish over and cook until the second side is brown, about 8 minutes longer. To test for doneness, peek into the cavity of the fish; it should be opaque at the spine. Or slide the tip of a paring knife along the side of the fin to the backbone and lift up the flesh; the flesh should pull away easily from the bone. Transfer the fish to dinner plates. Scatter the crispy fat bits over them.

### Panfried Fish Sandwich with Bacon Mayonnaise    Serves 4

*This fish sandwich is the sum of several simple parts: Crisp Panfried Fish Fillets, Bacon Mayonnaise (page 67), and lettuce piled onto garlicky toasted bread. It's also great made with soft-shell crabs.*

Toast eight ½-inch slices of crusty peasant bread, either in a toaster or in the oven. When they are golden, brush each slice lightly with extra virgin olive oil and rub it with a halved garlic clove.

Spread Bacon Mayonnaise on one side of each slice. Sauté the fillets as directed above; arrange on 4 bread slices. Top with tender lettuce leaves, such as oak leaf, butter or Boston, or mesclun. Enclose the sandwiches using the remaining 4 slices of bread and serve.

➢ POULTRY, MEAT, AND GAME

# Crisp Brick-Fried Chicken with Rosemary and Whole Garlic Cloves

- Brick-Fried Birds over Salad Greens
- Brick-Fried Game Hens with Madeira and Cream
- Brick-Fried Guinea Hen with Bacon and Thyme
- Brick-Fried Squabs Marinated (or Not) in Raspberry Puree
- Herb-Rubbed Brick-Fried Quail

My favorite easy chicken dish is a whole bird, butterflied and fried in a skillet with a weight on top, Italian style. The result is succulent chicken—both white meat and dark—with a delectable crisp skin and with much more flavor than the ubiquitous boneless breast; loss of bones always means loss of flavor. In Italy, such a chicken would be cooked *al mattone*, "under a brick" of heated specially made terra-cotta. In my makeshift version, I cook the chicken in a nonstick skillet with a weight on top, such as a smaller cast-iron skillet or a saucepan with a heavy can in it. The dish takes about 5 minutes of actual work and about 25 minutes unattended cooking time, during which you can have a cocktail and put the rest of your simple meal together as your home fills with a lovely fragrance.

Bone-in birds have a bulky shape that would normally be impossible to cook in a skillet, much less achieve a crisp skin. Butterflying–cutting out the backbone with scissors–is a quick technique that flattens the bird out to a uniform thickness that will cook evenly in a pan; placing a heavy weight on top of the bird prevents it from contracting and presses the skin against the pan to crisp it.

The three variables for improvising are the birds, flavorings, and sauces. I've never seen recipes for this method made with game birds, such as quail, squab, and guinea hens, which are increasingly available in better markets but traditionally require much fussier preparations. So I tried them, hoping to find an easy way to cook them. This method produces fantastic results with these richly flavored birds, taking the theme of weeknight poultry to new heights (pheasant being the only exception; it becomes tough). Whatever bird you choose, including baby chicken (poussin) or game hen–even small ducks–it should not exceed about 3¼ pounds trimmed.

What is remarkable about this method is how delicious the birds are even with minimal flavoring. When improvising, flavorings can remain simple. Just about any you would use for a roasted bird work here: rosemary, thyme, sage, or savory; lightly smashed whole garlic cloves tossed in the pan; tarragon leaves stuffed under the skin of chicken; dry rubs; or fruit- or wine-based marinades (4 to 24 hours ahead). Salt and pepper are the only essentials; salting the bird up to 24 hours in advance ensures tender flesh that is seasoned all the way through. When salting a bird, figure about ¾ teaspoon kosher salt per pound.

This method leaves a layer of caramelized juices in the bottom of the pan, perfect for making a quick pan sauce. You can splash in a couple of tablespoons of wine, balsamic vinegar, cream, or even water to dissolve them as you stir with a wooden spoon; boil the sauce to get the consistency you want. Or you can serve the bird with a separately made sauce, such as Savory Apples with White Wine and Rosemary (page 73).

The practical adjustments to consider are cooking times and intensity of heat, which will depend on the thickness of the bird and whether you want the flesh to be medium rare, as in the case of squab and quail, or cooked through, as for chicken. For small or rare-cooked birds, you'll need fast, intense heat. For a 3-pound guinea hen or chicken, moderate heat is better.

. . . . . . .

# Crisp Brick-Fried Chicken with Rosemary and Whole Garlic Cloves  Serves 3 or 4

One 3-pound chicken, preferably organic
1 tablespoon kosher salt
Freshly ground black pepper
4 large fresh rosemary or thyme sprigs
1 tablespoon extra virgin olive oil
8 unpeeled garlic cloves, lightly smashed
¼ cup dry white wine or balsamic vinegar (optional)
Pinch of sugar (optional)

**Butterfly the bird.** Rinse the chicken and pat dry with paper toweling. Place the chicken breast side down on a work surface. With kitchen shears, cut through the bones along both sides of the backbone and remove it. Trim off any excess neck skin. Spread the bird open, skin side up, on the counter and press down firmly against the breastbone with the palms of your hands to break and flatten it. Tuck the wing tips back and under the wings so they lie flat against the breast. Or cut off the wing tips and discard.

**Season the bird.** If possible, season the bird 1 hour (unrefrigerated) or up to 24 hours (refrigerated) before cooking. Sprinkle the bird on both sides with kosher salt and pepper. Press the herbs against both sides. If it has been refrigerated, bring the bird to room temperature 1 hour before cooking.

**Panfry the bird skin side up under a weight.** Heat a large nonstick skillet over medium heat. Add the oil and swirl to coat. Blot the bird dry with paper towels and place, skin side up, in the pan. Place a heavy cast-iron skillet, about 2 inches smaller in diameter, directly on top of the chicken. If you don't have a heavy enough pan—4 to 5 pounds—use another smooth-bottomed pot, such as a saucepan. Balance it on the bird and add heavy objects to weight the pan down, such as a can or two or a meat pounder (I've even used a rock). Cook the chicken until the underside is brown, about 10 minutes.

**Turn the bird skin side down, weight, and continue cooking.** Remove the weight and turn the chicken over with a pair of tongs. Replace the weight. Nestle the garlic cloves around the chicken and continue cooking until the skin is crisp and brown, 12 minutes longer.

To test for doneness, insert an instant-read thermometer into the inside of the thigh; it should read 170°F. Alternatively, poke the thigh with a paring knife; if the juices are clear, not pink, it is done. Transfer the chicken to a cutting board and let rest 5 minutes. Discard the herbs.

**If desired, make a simple pan sauce.** Pour off all but about 1 teaspoon of the fat in the pan. Set the pan over medium-low heat and add the wine, stirring and scraping the bottom of the pan with a wooden spoon to dissolve the caramelized juices. Cook until the wine is mellow and has no trace of alcohol taste, about 1 minute. Remove the herbs and adjust the seasoning adding salt, pepper, and a pinch of sugar, if necessary.

**Serve the birds.** With a chef's knife, halve the birds down the center of the breast, and arrange one half and a few garlic cloves on each plate. Spoon a tablespoon or two of the pan sauce over each. Serve at once.

**Note:** Don't throw away the bones from your poultry dishes. They are gold mines of flavor you can use to fortify canned broths (see page 106) or to improvise soups and sauces. Collect them in a plastic bag and freeze to draw upon as you need.

## Improvisations

### Brick-Fried Birds over Salad Greens

*This dish takes very little time to put together yet is immensely satisfying to eat. Brick-fried birds—whole quail, squab, or poussin, or cut-up chicken or guinea hen—crisp out of the skillet, are placed on dressed salad greens. Their warm juices flavor the greens and wilt them slightly. The quality of the salad is critical to the success of this dish. The greens should be very fresh and crisp, with a good balance of mild and peppery greens; mesclun mixes work nicely. Frisée makes a good addition if you need more sturdy greens. Dress with your best extra virgin olive oil and a fine vinegar such as Cherry Aged Cherry Vinegar (page 63) or the mix of balsamic and sherry vinegars in Essential Vinaigrette (page 355).*

### Brick-Fried Game Hens with Madeira and Cream    Serves 2

*I wanted a rich, somewhat sophisticated sauce for the crisp birds but didn't want it to take much effort. So instead of a simple white wine sauce, I sizzled some minced shallot in the pan and then splashed in a little Madeira, a robust forti-fied, slightly sweet wine with overtones of caramel and nuts, followed by heavy cream to mellow and enrich it. Its complexity and sophistication belies its sim-*

*plicity. You can make this recipe with any size bird up to 3¼ pounds, or bone-in, skin-on chicken thighs or breasts. Small Cornish game hens or poussins (baby chickens) are the most appealing.*

Butterfly two 1-pound Cornish game hens or baby chickens. Season the birds as above, then panfry them under a 3 to 4-pound weight for about 7 minutes skin side up and 8 minutes skin side down, until the leg juices run clear when pricked with a knife.

To make a pan sauce, pour off all but about 2 teaspoons of the fat from the pan and set it over medium-low heat. (If you used 2 pans, use just one to make the sauce.) Add 1 small shallot, finely chopped (1 tablespoon), and cook, stirring frequently, until soft, about 2 minutes. Add 2 tablespoons Rainwater or Sercial Madeira, stirring and scraping the bottom of the pan with a wooden spoon to dissolve the caramelized juices. Cook until the wine is mellow and has no trace of alcohol taste, about 30 seconds. Stir in ¼ cup heavy cream or crème fraîche and cook until slightly thickened, about 1 minute longer; add salt and pepper to taste.

With a chef's knife, halve the birds down the center of the breast and arrange the halves and a few garlic cloves on each plate. Spoon a tablespoon or two of the pan sauce over each. Serve at once.

### Brick-Fried Guinea Hen with Bacon and Thyme   Serves 2 or 3

*Guinea hens are another once-exotic game bird now sold in fine supermarkets and at farmers' markets. Richer and more complexly flavored than chicken, they have both light and dark meat. Although many cookbooks warn of the difficulty of cooking these birds whole because their legs and breasts cook so differently, I found that the butterflied bird cooks perfectly in this skillet method, which I do with bacon, a play on a classic French approach. Guinea hens are usually about 3 to 3½ pounds and serve 3. Make one for two people and have the rest for leftovers. To make two for a dinner party, you need two large 12-inch skillets.*

Butterfly a 3-pound guinea hen. Slice 2 thick bacon strips, preferably applewood-smoked (about 3 ounces), into ½-inch dice and put in a 12-inch heavy nonstick skillet set over moderately low heat; cover and cook until the bacon is crisp and browned and has rendered all its fat, about 8 minutes. With a slotted spoon, remove the bacon to a small dish. In the same pan, panfry the hen under a 4 to 5-pound weight, figuring about 10 minutes skin side up and 12 minutes skin side down, until the leg juices run clear when pricked with a knife. If desired, make a pan sauce using white wine.

Cut the hen in half through the breast and then separate the thigh/leg from each breast. Arrange on a platter and scatter the bacon over the top.

## Brick-Fried Squabs Marinated (or Not) in Raspberry Puree    Serves 2

*Squabs are young pigeons with rich, dark flesh and succulent skin. Once served only in fancy restaurants, they are increasingly available in supermarkets. I discovered that they take well to this pan method, seasoned with nothing other than salt, pepper, and thyme and cooked until the skin is crisp. Marinating the birds for several hours in pureed raspberries (thawed frozen raspberries are fine) enhances the flavor of the birds and gives the skin a mahogany glaze. Squab must be cooked medium rare; any longer, and the flesh tastes livery. One 1-pound squab serves one person; you'll need two 10-inch skillets to prepare two.*

Butterfly two 1-pound squabs; season the birds with salt and freshly ground black pepper. If you want to marinate the squabs, puree 1 pint fresh raspberries or one thawed 10-ounce package unsweetened frozen raspberries in a food processor. Holding a strainer over a medium bowl, strain the puree. (Alternatively, if you have a strainer with fairly large holes, rather than pureeing them, just use a rubber spatula to press the whole raspberries through the strainer.) Add the squabs and 2 thyme sprigs and coat completely. Marinate at least 2 hours, or overnight, in the refrigerator.

Rinse the marinade off the birds and pat dry with paper towels. Rub the birds with olive oil. Panfry the bird(s) under a 2 to 3-pound weight over medium high to high heat, about 5 minutes on each side, starting skin side up; the skin should be crisp and the flesh red-pink.

## Herb-Rubbed Brick-Fried Quail    Serves 2

*Quail are delectable little birds with dark, mild-flavored flesh. They are often available in packages of 4 or 8 in supermarkets. (Bone-in or semiboneless quail will work equally well for this recipe.) Since they defrost and cook so quickly, I like to keep some in my freezer to make quick elegant little meals. For 4 quail, you'll need one 12-inch nonstick or well-seasoned cast-iron skillet or two 10-inch skillets. If you don't have two skillets, cook the quail in two batches.*

In a small bowl or mortar, combine ½ teaspoon dried sage, a scant ½ teaspoon dried rosemary, ¼ teaspoon dried thyme, and a scant ½ teaspoon dried savory. Crush the herbs with the back of a spoon or a pestle and stir until they are the texture of coarse sand. Butterfly 4 medium quail, about 4 ounces each. Rub the quail on both sides with the cut side of a halved garlic clove. Season on both sides with the herb mixture, salt, and pepper, and let sit at least an hour, or up to 24 hours in the refrigerator. Blot dry before cooking.

Heat the skillet(s) over medium-high heat until very hot; add 2 teaspoons olive or grapeseed oil and swirl to coat. Add the quail skin side up. Place a flat heavy lid (slightly smaller than the skillet) and, if necessary, a weight on top of the quail to keep them flat. Cook for 1 minute, and remove the lid. Cook 1 minute longer for medium rare (add 30 seconds more if you like them more well done) and turn the quail over. Weight them again and cook for another minute, or until the skin is crisp and brown (add 30 seconds more if you like them more well done).

# Chicken with Root Vegetables in Fragrant Lemongrass Broth

- Rabbit Rillettes
- Chicken with Red Wine, Bacon, and Mushrooms
- Guinea Hen with Bacon and Madeira

On my first trip to France many years ago, the unassuming poulet au pot, a whole chicken poached in a barely simmering stock with carrots, leeks, and turnips, made a profound impression. The sliced chicken and vegetables were served in a large bowl, with broth poured around to moisten them; a small dish of sea salt was placed alongside to lift the flavors. The flavor of each element was distinct and clear, and contributed to an extraordinary sense of comfort, well-being, and connection that is the enduring appeal of such dishes. The problem is, it requires a lot of excellent *real* chicken broth to make it, something I don't always have on hand. So I improvised a radically different way to have poulet au pot–style dishes, including the delicious broth, with little effort or forethought.

I cook an organic bird in a tightly sealed Dutch oven in the oven with white wine and aromatics; garlic, lemongrass, and ginger are my current favorites. To ensure flavorful, perfectly cooked vegetables, I add them during the last half hour of cooking. When I open the pot I find, through this method's mysterious alchemy, a succulent bird surrounded by tender root vegetables and a limpid, flavorful broth, redolent with lemongrass and ginger. This modern poulet au pot is the perfect family or Sunday night supper, along with a salad. It is also an ideal restorative for anyone under the weather.

This recipe builds on a simple cooking technique I use often: roasting birds in a snug, tightly sealed vessel or foil package with just a few tablespoons of wine or broth, some fat, and some aromatics: a braise with very little liquid. The bird essentially cooks in its own juices, yielding extraordinarily succulent, flavorful flesh and a delectable brothy sauce with a very pure flavor. I've used this method with various combinations of wines, fats, and flavorings to make fuss-free versions of classic dishes. White wine, a good dose of olive oil, and lots of unpeeled whole garlic cloves becomes Chicken with 40 Cloves of Garlic. A chicken larded under the skin with thin slices of black truffle and drizzled with Madeira becomes Poulet Demi-Deuil (Chicken in Half-Mourning). To make a classic poulet au pot, use thyme and bay leaf with white wine and butter and add carrots, leeks, and turnips during the last half hour.

The main variables for improvising are the cooking liquid and flavorings. The liquid adds flavor and becomes the base for a sauce; white wine, Madeira, sherry, sake, hard cider, reductions of red or fortified wines, even cream all work well. Just a tablespoon or two is all that is necessary, particularly with more strongly flavored liquids. Dry white wine is so neutral, though, you can add up to a cup of it to accentuate the brothiness of the dish. The flavorings can vary wildly: from the subtleties of aromatic vegetables such as leeks, or herbs—tarragon leaves slipped under the chicken's skin, for example—to robust spice mixtures such as curry powder or Thai green curry, to other flavorful combinations such as saffron, coriander, cumin, fennel seed, ginger, lemongrass, even Mexican mole paste. Some fat is essential to give body to the resulting broth and keep it from tasting hollow: olive oil, butter, sesame oil . . . bacon and pancetta being the ultimate.

Any vegetables that you add at the beginning will, in the course of cooking, give up much of their flavor to the broth and become very soft, the way they do in a stock. This works fine for whole cloves of garlic, which need radical mellowing; for vegetables, from carrots to potatoes, to keep their texture and flavor intact, add them during the last half hour. I generally figure about 1 cup vegetables per person and use a greater proportion of mild sweet ones, such as carrots, parsnips, and parsley root, and fewer "strong" ones like turnips or whole uncut members of the onion family, such as spring onions, pearl onions, or shallots or largish sections of leek (cut-up onions become too assertive). Cutting the vegetables into a uniform thickness will ensure they are done at the same time. Add separately cooked embellishments, such as wilted spinach or chard as well. The chicken and vegetables would also be lovely spooned over mashed potatoes or buttered egg noodles.

Although a whole chicken makes the most dramatic presentation, you can use chicken parts or other white-fleshed birds: 4 small poussins or game hens, for example. This is an excellent way to cook a whole turkey breast to have on hand for sandwiches and salads during the week, with a dividend of rich broth to use for soups or to freeze.

Take this method a step further to make poultry in a rich red wine sauce similar to a coq au vin but with much less fuss. Instead of white wine, use a highly reduced concentrate of red wine, fortified wine, and caramelized shallots. See Chicken with Red Wine, Bacon, and Mushrooms (page 222).

. . . . . .

# Chicken with Root Vegetables in Fragrant Lemongrass Broth    Serves 4

One 3-pound chicken, preferably free-range and organic,
   rinsed and patted dry
2 teaspoons kosher salt
2 fresh lemongrass stalks
6 thin fresh ginger coins, bruised
About 8 or 9 unpeeled large garlic cloves
¾ cup dry white wine
1 tablespoon unsalted butter or extra virgin olive oil
Freshly ground black pepper
5 to 6 cups sliced root vegetables, such as carrots, parsnips,
   parsley root, or new potatoes, in any combination, peeled
   and sliced ½ inch thick
Pinch of sugar if necessary
About ½ cup coarsely chopped cilantro

**Season the bird.** If possible, salt the chicken at least 2 hours and up to 24 hours in advance. Rub the bird inside and out with salt; place on a platter and cover. Refrigerate if salting more than 1 hour before cooking the bird.

**Assemble the bird, wine, and flavorings in a pot.** Pat the chicken dry with paper towels and place in a snug-fitting casserole with a lid. Trim the woody ends off the lemongrass and pull off the tough loose outer leaves. Slice the stalks in half lengthwise, and pound with a pestle or other heavy object to crush them lightly. Cut the pieces in half crosswise. Place a few pieces each of lemongrass, ginger, and garlic in the chicken's cavity and nestle the remainder around the bird; drizzle over the wine and dot with the butter. Pepper generously. Place a large sheet of aluminum foil over the pot and press down until it just touches the bird; the object is to remove the airspace around the bird to prevent it from steaming. Press down the lid. The oven-ready bird can sit up to 1 hour at room temperature.

**Roast, adding the vegetables during the last half hour.** Preheat the oven to 350°F. Put the pot in the oven and bake 30 minutes. Remove the lid and foil and nestle the vegetables around the chicken. Replace the foil and lid and continue baking 30 minutes longer.

To test the chicken for doneness, insert an instant-read thermometer between the thigh and body; it should read 170°F. Or prick the thickest part of the thigh deeply with a kitchen fork to see if the juices run clear. Remove the chicken from the oven and let rest 5 minutes.

**Defat the broth, if desired, and serve.** Defatting the sauce is not essential, but if you wish to, transfer the chicken and vegetables to a platter and cover with the foil. Pour the juices into a small deep bowl or sauceboat; discard the lemongrass and ginger. Let sit while you carve the chicken (discarding the skin). Skim the fat off the juices. Pepper generously and stir in the sugar if necessary to round the flavors. Serve the chicken and vegetables in large soup bowls; spoon the broth over the top. Sprinkle liberally with cilantro.

**Note:** If you want to cook a larger bird, add 10 minutes per ½ pound to the cooking time. To figure when to add the vegetables, calculate the total cooking time and subtract 30 minutes. For example, a 4-pound chicken will take 1 hour 20 minutes; add the vegetables after 50 minutes. Figure ½ to scant ¾ teaspoon salt per pound of chicken.

## Improvisations

### Rabbit Rillettes    Makes about 4 cups

*Rillettes are like a free form pâté, a rich shredded paste of meats—commonly pork and rabbit—that have been cooked slowly in fat until spoon-tender. Taking a cue from the chicken-in-a-sealed-casserole method (above) and the similar Close-Roasted Pork with Ancho, Cinnamon, and Cocoa (page 235), which produce exceedingly tender flesh, this is an easier way to make rabbit rillettes using less fat. I sealed peppery seasoned rabbit in aluminum foil with olive oil and a little Madeira, garlic, and lemon zest and roasted it slowly. Then I shredded the meat and beat in the gelatinous broth and olive oil as the binder, which became creamy as the mixture chilled. The results were truly delicious rillettes with a clear flavor of rabbit. Although you can do this with a whole rabbit, it is best made with the "dark meat" legs and bony parts of a rabbit. So I divide my rabbit into parts, using the loin for special dishes and stockpiling the rest in the freezer until I have enough for rillettes. Serve with crusty bread and Caramelized Onions (page 143), Pickled Cherries (page 316), or Sweet-and-Sour Spiced Prunes (page 75). You can halve the recipe if you wish.*

Prepare Duck, Rabbit, Game, and Charcuterie Seasoning (page 48). Rub 2½ to 2¾ pounds rabbit pieces (either a whole cut-up rabbit or the bony parts and legs) with the seasoning, arrange on a platter, and let sit at least 2 hours, or overnight, refrigerated.

Preheat the oven to 275°F. Pat the rabbit dry. Lay an 18 × 26-inch rectangle of heavy-duty aluminum foil shiny side up on the counter. Arrange the rabbit pieces on one half of the foil. Nestle in 2 lightly bruised unpeeled garlic cloves and a 2-inch strip of lemon zest. Drizzle over 3 tablespoons extra virgin olive oil and 1 tablespoon Rainwater or Sercial Madeira. Fold the empty half of the foil over the rabbit. Beginning at one creased corner, fold the edges over in neat pleats, being sure to fold each successive pleat so it overlaps the previous one to make a tight seal, until you get to the opposite creased corner, to make a neat, tightly sealed package. Then crimp around the edges again with your finger.

Place on a baking sheet and bake for 2 hours. Let cool slightly, then open the package. Transfer the rabbit to a bowl; pour the juices into a measuring cup. When cool enough to handle but still warm, pull the meat off the bones (freeze the bones for broth or discard), shredding it as you go. With a pestle, or the back of a kitchen spoon, pound and mash the meat to a coarse paste, gradually drizzling in ¼ cup or more of the juices, until it is moist but not wet. Adjust the seasoning, peppering the rillettes generously. Pack into clean jars, cover, and refrigerate until firm.

Bring to room temperature and stir vigorously before serving.

## Chicken with Red Wine, Bacon, and Mushrooms   Serves 4

*When he was a new, and newly divorced, cook, a friend decided to try my recipe for coq au vin. I arrived at his apartment to find him wild-eyed and stressed out, and his small kitchen a disarray of dirty pots, utensils, and platters. He had never browned chicken parts before, much less peeled pearl onions or rendered lardons; he was in over his head.*

*Still, the dish, which had taken him hours to make, was delicious. And it made me realize that I'd avoided making the dish I love more often because it was time-consuming, and browning the chicken left my apartment in a cloud of fat that lingered for days. I wondered if there was another way to have coq au vin without quite the drama. So, I improvised a hybrid: coq au vin flavors applied to a simple technique of cooking a bird in a tightly sealed vessel. To achieve the rich "brown" flavors of browned chicken, I used lots of sliced shallots caramelized in bacon fat and simmered them in reducing red wine, Madeira, and port. Sealed in a pot with this rich red wine essence and some mushrooms, the chicken adds its juices to the wine to make a rich sauce, very much in the spirit of a coq au vin. Serve over buttered egg noodles. This stripped-down classic also freezes beautifully. A mandoline or Benriner makes short work of slicing the shallots.*

You'll need a 3- to 3½-pound chicken, cut into 8 pieces; rinse and pat dry. Rub with 2 teaspoons kosher salt and some freshly ground black pepper at least 2 hours before cooking. Refrigerate.

Toss ½ cup diced bacon, preferably applewood-smoked (about 2 ounces), into a flameproof casserole just large enough to hold the chicken snugly in one layer; cover and cook, stirring occasionally, about 7 minutes, until the bacon is brown and crisp and most of the fat has rendered out. With a slotted spoon, transfer the crisp bacon to a bowl; reserve. Although it's not essential, for slightly richer flavor you can brown the chicken pieces (patted dry first) skin side down in the pot until golden brown, about 5 minutes on each side; transfer to a platter.

Preheat the oven to 350°F. Add 8 medium shallots, thinly sliced (about 1 cup), to the pot, cover, and sauté, stirring frequently, until the shallots are softened and golden, about 6 minutes. Add 1½ cups dry full-bodied red wine, ½ cup ruby port, and ¼ cup Rainwater or Sercial Madeira and bring to a boil over high heat; boil until the wine has almost completely evaporated and the shallots are a dark burgundy color, about 15 minutes. Meanwhile, trim the stems from 8 ounces cremini mushrooms and rub with a damp cloth to remove the dirt. Nestle the chicken pieces and mushrooms in the pot; add the reserved bacon. Cover with a large sheet of aluminum foil pressed down so it just touches the bird; then press down the lid to make a tight seal.

Bake the chicken for 1 hour. Remove from the oven and let rest 10 minutes. Transfer the chicken to a platter and keep warm. Tilt the pot to pool the juice in one end; skim the fat and discard. Return the chicken to the pot and serve.

## Guinea Hen with Bacon and Madeira     Serves 3

*The inspiration for this delectable guinea hen in its own smoky juices is an extravagant dish I used to make when a fresh black truffle would come my way: I slid thin slices of truffle under the bird's skin and left it to infuse overnight, then sealed it in a foil package with a drizzle of Madeira and roasted it. The result was a moist bird in a heady truffled broth. But it was the method, rather than the truffles, that brought out the best in the bird. Substituting bacon as the aromatic flavoring element, I added just enough Madeira, and some lemon zest to enhance the natural flavors of the bird, to make an elemental dish that is marvelous served with Root Vegetable Puree with Vanilla (page 101) or a gratin such as Lemon-Infused Potatoes with Thyme (page 150)—an example of economic constraints yielding a satisfying improvisation.*

Rub a 3-pound guinea hen inside and out with 2 teaspoons kosher salt and some freshly ground black pepper at least 2 hours before cooking. Meanwhile, cut 2 thick bacon slices, preferably applewood-smoked, into ½-inch-thick pieces and cook, covered, over moderate heat in a small heavy skillet until crisp. Set aside.

Preheat the oven to 325°F. Lay an 18 × 26-inch rectangle of heavy-duty aluminum foil shiny side up on the counter; smear or brush about a tablespoon of the bacon fat on the foil, then rub with a cut clove of garlic. Pat the guinea hen dry and arrange on one half of the foil. Coarsely chop the garlic and sliver a 2-inch piece of lemon zest. Stuff half the garlic, zest, and bacon, drained, plus 2 fresh thyme sprigs into the cavity. Scatter the remaining garlic, zest, and bacon around the bird and drizzle over 3 tablespoons Rainwater or Sercial Madeira. Fold the empty half of the foil over the hen. Beginning at one creased corner, fold the edges over in neat pleats, being sure to fold each successive pleat so it overlaps the previous one to make a tight seal, until you get to the opposite creased corner, to make a neat, tightly sealed package. Then crimp around the edges again with your finger.

Bake about 1 hour on a baking sheet, 10 minutes more for a larger hen. Place the package on a deep serving platter and let rest 10 minutes. Open it and transfer the bird onto the platter. Pour the juices into a small deep bowl or sauceboat; degrease, if desired. Carve the chicken and spoon some of the juices over each serving.

# Panfried Duck Steaks with Caramelized Shallots

- Panfried Duck Steaks without the Skin
- Duck Breasts with Confited Dried Cherries
- Duck Breasts with Confited Kumquats
- Warm Salad of Duck Breasts, Walnuts, Figs, and Caramelized Shallots
- "Steak Frites"
- Panfried Duck Breasts with Cauliflower-Apple Puree and Caramelized Shallots

A duck breast makes an ideal steak, boneless, easy to cook, and with the satisfactions of red meat. I briefly marinate duck breasts in a mixture of salt, sugar, and pepper, which tenderizes the meat and accentuates their natural flavor. Then I cook them with the skin on by a method that renders out most of the fat and leaves it crackling, like crisp-skin roast duck. Duck steaks are so versatile I keep them on hand in the freezer (they defrost in a few hours) for quick, elegant, satisfying meals.

Duck steaks can easily stand on their own, like a beef steak without a sauce, paired simply with separately made side dishes. Wild rice, risottos, mashed potatoes, Hazelnut-Scented Sweet Potato Puree (page 157), and polenta all work well. Any of the braised root vegetable dishes on pages 149 to 152, such as Root Vegetables with White Wine and Rosemary, are perfect. Caramelized shallots—fried at the last minute in the hot duck fat—add a unifying element that make these simple combinations seem somehow luxurious.

One caveat: Duck breasts are best cooked medium rare like a steak; cook them longer, and they begin to taste livery and lose much of their savor. If you are a well-done steak person, this recipe is not for you.

Like boneless chicken breasts, duck breasts are easy to cook and versatile but with a lot more dazzle; they are, in essence, a game bird, whose rich, winey flavor goes especially well with sweet, spicy elements: root vegetables such as turnips and parsnips; fruits, fresh and dried, such as figs, peaches, mango, cherries, and oranges; sweet, aromatic spices such as coriander, allspice, or ancho chile powder; and woody herbs such as rosemary, thyme, and savory.

Since the great virtue of duck breasts is that they yield a sophisticated dish for little work, I like to keep improvisations simple. Add flavorings to the salt-sugar rub to flavor the meat itself, such as ¼ to ½ teaspoon coarsely cracked coriander, grated orange zest, or minced rosemary or thyme. Or use Duck, Rabbit, Game, and Charcuterie Seasoning, page 48. An abundance of duck fat will render out of the skin as it cooks; you can add all sorts of garnishes to the fat to fry along with the breasts, such as sliced shallots or leeks, whole garlic cloves, or fat black olives, to name a few.

Because the duck meat is so rich, it needs robust, slightly sweet sauces or accompaniments to stand up to it: Salsas work well, as do fruit-based sauces in tandem with fortified wines such as Madeira (Sercial or Rainwater), dry Marsala, or tawny port. Traditional pan sauces made by sautéing shallots in a little of the fat (once the cooked breasts have been left to rest on a cutting board) and deglazing with fortified wine will have a hollow flavor unless enriched by chicken broth or demi-glace, something often lacking in home kitchens. As an alternative, I came up with some interesting solutions, such as cooking fruits like dried cherries and thinly sliced kumquats in Marsala or Madeira until they resembled confits.

Duck breasts are available at many supermarkets and specialty stores. Muscovy duck breasts and magrets, the large breasts from the Moulard duck, weigh from 12 to 16 ounces and have a full flavor and dense texture. The breasts from Pekin (Long Island) duckling average about 6 ounces each and are more delicately flavored. When calculating quantities, figure 6 to 8 ounces duck (uncooked) per person.

• • • • • •

## Panfried Duck Steaks with Caramelized Shallots     Serves 4

2 Muscovy or Moulard duck breast halves (12 to 16 ounces each)
   or 4 boneless Pekin (Long Island) duck breast halves
   (about 6 ounces each)
1¼ teaspoons kosher salt
¼ teaspoon freshly ground black pepper
¼ teaspoon sugar
4 shallots, thinly sliced crosswise (optional)

**Remove the tenderloins and score the skin.** Place the duck steaks skin side down on the work surface. With a thin sharp knife, remove the tenderloin (if any), the thin strip of meat that runs lengthwise down the underside of each breast; reserve. Turn the breasts over. Make a series of shallow parallel cuts across the fatty skin, spaced about ¼ inch apart, without cutting into the meat. Turn the breasts 90 degrees and make a second series of cuts at right angles to the first, to make a crosshatch pattern of shallow cuts. This will allow the fat to melt out of the skin as the breast cooks, rendering it both leaner and crisper.

**Season the breasts.** In a small bowl, combine the salt, pepper, and sugar. Sprinkle evenly over both sides of the breasts; rub a pinch of the mixture into the tenderloins. Cover with plastic wrap. If possible, let marinate for at least an hour (unrefrigerated) or up to 4 hours in the refrigerator. If they've been refrigerated, bring the breasts to room temperature about 30 minutes before cooking. Pat dry with paper towels.

**Panfry the breasts.** Arrange the breasts skin side down in a heavy 10-inch skillet set over moderately low heat. After a few minutes, the fat under the skin will begin to melt and run into the pan. Cook until the skin is crisp and brown, a great deal of fat has rendered out, and a few droplets of blood are visible on top, 9 to 10 minutes for Muscovy or Moulard breasts, 5 to 6 minutes for Pekin breasts. Turn the breasts over, increase the heat slightly, and cook until the bottom is brown and the breasts feel springy when poked, 4 to 5 minutes longer for Muscovy or Moulard breasts, 2 minutes for Pekin breasts. About a minute before they are done, add the tenderloins; cook 1 minute on each side. Transfer the breasts (and tenderloins) skin side up to a cutting board and let rest for 5 to 10 minutes.

**Fry the shallots (optional).** Add the shallot slices to the hot duck fat. Fry, rearranging occasionally, until tender and caramelized, about 4 minutes. Remove with a slotted spoon and drain on paper towels.

**Slice and serve the steaks.** Using a thin sharp knife, slice each breast on a diagonal ⅛ inch thick. Fan the duck slices onto each plate and spoon the sauce over. Serve at once.

## Improvisations

### Panfried Duck Steaks without the Skin

*If you don't wish to eat duck skin, you can make any of the following improvisations with skinned meat using oil instead of duck fat. Once the skin is removed, duck flesh is among the leaner, and most delicious, of red meats.*

Rather than scoring the skin, remove it by prying an edge of it away from the flesh with your fingers. Then use a thin sharp knife to release the membrane that attaches it to the flesh and peel the skin off in one sheet. Discard.

Season the breasts as directed with salt, pepper, and sugar.

To cook the breasts, heat 2 teaspoons peanut, grapeseed, or olive oil in the pan and add the duck breasts; cook until browned on both sides but still springy to the touch, 3 to 4 minutes on each side for Muscovy or Moulard breasts, or 2 to 4 minutes on each side for Pekin duck breasts. Transfer the breasts to a cutting board and fry the shallots in additional oil, if desired, while they rest. Slice and serve the duck.

### Duck Breasts with Confited Dried Cherries    Serves 4

*Dried cherries are a wonderful pantry staple; they keep indefinitely and reconstitute quickly, providing inspiration for improvised dishes at a moment's notice, like this play on the classic duck with cherries. Rather than making the usual involved sauce, I tried cooking them like Confited Kumquats. The result were confited cherries, plumped and preserved in Marsala, that taste as if they were cooked in a rich wine-laced stock.*

Season 2 Muscovy or Moulard duck breast halves (12 to 16 ounces each) or 4 boneless Pekin duck breast halves (about 6 ounces each) as above. Panfry the breasts. While the duck is cooking, start the **Confited Dried Cherries**: combine 8 ounces dried cherries and 2 cups dry Marsala or Madeira (Sercial or Rainwater) in a small saucepan; bring to a simmer over moderate heat. Mince 1 shallot.

Transfer the duck skin side up to a cutting board and cover loosely to keep warm. Discard all but 1 teaspoon of the fat; return the pan to moderate heat. Add the minced shallot and cook, stirring, until it is translucent and golden, about 2 minutes. Add the dried cherries and Marsala and bring to a boil. Cook at a low boil until the cherries are soft and glazed and the liquid is almost completely evaporated, 15 to 20 minutes. Stir in $\frac{1}{4}$ teaspoon fresh thyme leaves and freshly ground black pepper to taste. Remove from the heat and add a pinch of salt and a squeeze of lemon juice to pick up the flavors.

Slice and serve the duck, arranging some of the cherries on top or alongside.

### Duck Breasts with Confited Kumquats    Serves 4

*Kumquats look like tiny blimp-shaped oranges and have a unique sweet-sour citrusy taste reminiscent of the pleasantly bitter Seville oranges usually used in the French classic canard à l'orange. Because they last for weeks in the fridge, they are great to keep on hand to use, thinly sliced, in fruit or lettuce salads, in cooked fruit desserts, and in sauces, as in this delicious savory confit. Chasing after the rich flavors of the classic duck à l'orange, I discovered that thinly sliced kumquats, cooked slowly in a fortified wine like dry Marsala or Madeira, gain that classic, sophisticated bitter-orange-peel-in-stock-and-wine flavor. You can make the Confited Kumquats separately to serve as an accompaniment to classic roast duck.*

Season 2 Muscovy or Moulard duck breast halves (12 to 16 ounces each) or 4 boneless Pekin duck breast halves (about 6 ounces each) as above. Pan-fry the breasts. Transfer the breasts skin side up to a cutting board and cover to keep warm.

To make the **Confited Kumquats**: Discard all but 1 teaspoon of the duck fat and return the pan to moderate heat. Add 2 tablespoons minced shallot (1 medium shallot) and cook, stirring, until translucent and golden, about 2 minutes. Add 8 kumquats, sliced crosswise as thin as possible, and stir to coat with fat, about 30 seconds. Pour in $1\frac{1}{2}$ cups dry Marsala or Madeira (Rainwater or Sercial) and bring to a boil. Cook at a low boil until the kumquats are soft and glazed and the liquid is almost completely evaporated, 15 to 20 minutes. Remove from the heat and add a pinch of salt and a squeeze of lemon juice to pick up the flavors.

Slice and serve the duck steaks. Arrange the Confited Kumquats alongside.

### Warm Salad of Duck Breasts, Walnuts, Figs, and Caramelized Shallots   **Serves 4**

*This elegant warm salad sounds elaborate but is really very easy to put together; it is more an assemblage of simple elements. A salad and main course all rolled into one, it makes a lovely lunch or supper dish. The warm duck wilts the greens slightly, and its juices become part of the dressing. Use this basic model for making warm salads with other seared meats and poultry. If figs aren't available, use other sliceable fruits, or leave out altogether.*

Prepare Pan-Fried Duck Steaks with Caramelized Shallots.

While the duck breasts are cooking, in a small bowl, combine 2 teaspoons each balsamic and sherry vinegars and a pinch of salt. Stir in 2 tablespoons roasted walnut oil or extra virgin olive oil and 1 teaspoon water. Place 8 cups washed frisée or mesclun salad and ¼ cup coarsely chopped walnuts or pecans in a large bowl. If desired, add 4 ripe figs, quartered.

Drizzle the dressing over the salad, toss to coat, and divide among 4 dinner plates. Slice the duck breasts into thin slices and arrange on top of the salad. Scatter the caramelized shallots over the salad and serve.

### "Steak Frites"   **Serves 4**

*My version of steak frites, the wonderfully satisfying bistro classic, is a duck steak served with either Parsnip Fries (page 129) or Post-Modern Fries (page 128), both of which are fried in the oven. The scenario is simple: Salt the duck steaks and marinate, then pat dry. Prepare the fries and start roasting them. To figure out when to start the duck steaks so they are ready at the same time as the fries, subtract the 20 minutes or so you need to cook the duck steaks from the fry cooking time.*

### Panfried Duck Breasts with Cauliflower-Apple Puree and Caramelized Shallots   **Serves 4**

*Duck with turnips is a classic of French cooking. Thinking about that flavor affinity, I realized cauliflower has a similar flavor to turnips, but is more ethereal when pureed. I serve the Panfried Duck Steaks with Caramelized Shallots, thinly sliced, fanned out on a pool of velvety Cauliflower and Apple Puree (page 161) that acts as sauce and vegetable; the shallots add a crispy oniony note that completes the dish. It is a great example of combining two or three separately made recipes to improvise a dish.*

Start preparing the Cauliflower and Apple Puree at least ½ hour before cooking the duck. Keep the puree warm in a double boiler while you panfry the breasts and shallots. Slice each cooked breast on a diagonal ⅛ inch thick. Pool some of the puree onto each of 4 dinner plates; fan the duck slices over the puree and sprinkle with the Caramelized Shallots. Serve at once.

# Close-Roasted Pork with Ancho, Cinnamon, and Cocoa

Over the years, I've made mental notes of interesting recipes I've read for pork shoulder rubbed with various combinations of garlic and chiles and slowly roasted in a covered casserole until the meat was falling off the bone. The spoon-soft meat was then rolled in tortillas, Mexican style, with cilantro and avocado. An organic pork shoulder at my local market inspired me to finally experiment with the idea. I rubbed the pork in an improvised seasoning mix with the flavors of mole sauce—ancho chile, cinnamon, and clove—and roasted it slowly in a sealed pot. In a kind of Mexican/Southern fusion, I served it with a pan of Crackling Corn Bread (page 261) and Creamy Cilantro Slaw (page 122) to a gathering of hungry friends and their kids. The pork was delectable: succulent, tender, utterly satisfying, a practically effortless way to serve a crowd. It affirmed my love of slow roasting as a great technique for cooking meat.

This recipe is perfect for a casual dinner party or gathering because it's hardly any work, you can make it ahead, and you can't overcook it. To feed more, just cook another pork shoulder or two.

Slowly cooking meats, covered, for a long time in a very low oven–what I call "close roasting"–is the modern version of hearth cooking, both in approach and effect. The low oven heat acts like the penetrating heat of coals; the tightly sealed, lidded casserole or foil package is akin to an earthenware vessel. When large or tough cuts of meat are cooked this way, an extraordinary process occurs that renders the meat spoon-tender, juicy, and deeply flavored. Heat builds up within the meat, creating steam and causing its collagen to break down; the pressure of the steam opens up the meat fibers, causing the fat in the meat to melt and the juices to move from the center to the outside. The food essentially cooks in its own juices.

Apply the basic method to many cuts of meat: from large ones such as leg of lamb to tougher cuts such as pork shoulder or beef rump roast to smaller cuts such as shanks–lamb or veal, oxtails, or short ribs. It is far and away the best way to cook cheap, tough cuts.

Flavorings for the meat can be dry or wet. Dry ones take the form of rubs made from various combinations of spices and/or herbs mixed with kosher salt. (See Fragrant Herb Salt and the other seasonings on pages 46 to 48, for examples.) Figure about ¾ teaspoon of salt per pound and, as always, salt the meat well ahead to give it time to penetrate and season deeply. Mix the spices and herbs right into the salt; as the salt penetrates, it will carry the flavors into the flesh. Flavorings can run the gamut from Moroccan-Style Seasoning with Cinnamon, Coriander, and Cumin (page 46) to various mixes of herbs, such as the classic Italian rosemary, garlic, and fennel seed seasoning often used on pork. Pork in particular goes well with spices, especially chiles, that offset the richness of the meat and enhance its porky flavors. Generally, allow about 1 teaspoon per pound of a hot chili powder such as chipotle and up to a tablespoon per pound of milder chile or spice rubs.

As with the pork, any meat sealed in a vessel or foil will cook just fine in its own juices–there's no need to add any. If you do add liquid, it should be a small amount and calculated to build in more flavor, such as red, white, or sweet wines; fortified wines such as Madeira, port, and Marsala; broths and aromatics, such as garlic, shallot, leek, bay leaf, fruit zest, and so on, can work in tandem.

The beauty of this method is that you don't have to do a lot to the meat to make it delicious, as the pork and the seven-hour leg of lamb illustrate. But add further flavors as you're inspired to, browning shallots or onions, for example, and reducing red and fortified wines to a rich concentrate, as in Short Ribs Bourguignon. Browning the meat itself adds richness and savor, especially when you want the juices to act as a sauce.

The other area of improvisation with slow-roasted meats is what to do with them after they are cooked. They offer so many possibilities, I've created a separate section (see Days-After Improvisations for Close-Roasted Meats, page 239).

•    •    •    •    •    •

# Close-Roasted Pork with Ancho, Cinnamon, and Cocoa   Serves 8

> 2½ tablespoons Mole-Inspired Seasoning with Ancho, Cinnamon, and Cocoa
>   (page 47)
> 1 tablespoon plus ½ teaspoon kosher salt
> 1 teaspoon sugar
> About 3½ pounds pork shoulder, trimmed of excess fat, tied to make a
>   compact roast (bone-in is preferable, though boned is fine)
> 1 head of garlic, broken into cloves but not peeled

**Season the meat.** In a small bowl, combine the mole seasoning, salt, and sugar. Rub all over the pork shoulder and place on a plate. Marinate for 1 hour unrefrigerated, or 2 to 24 hours refrigerated.

**Prepare the meat for roasting.** Preheat the oven to 275°F. Place the pork in a Dutch oven or deep-lidded roaster just big enough to hold the roast snugly. Scatter the garlic cloves around the roast. Place a large piece of aluminum foil over the pot, then press the lid down securely. Alternatively, wrap the meat in a tightly sealed foil package (make sure the seam is at the top so the juices don't leak out) and place the package in an ovenproof skillet or casserole.

**Roast the meat.** Roast the pork until very tender and practically falling apart, 3¾ to 4 hours. Transfer the roast to a platter and cover with foil.

**Defat the roasting juices.** Pour the juices into a sauceboat and place in the freezer for 10 minutes. Spoon off the fat that has risen to the top.

**Serve the meat.** Pull the meat apart or slice it across the grain and arrange on a platter. Pour some of the juices over and pass the rest. Save any remaining juices for heating up leftovers.

## Improvisations

### Spoon Lamb with Masses of Garlic, after Paula Wolfert   Serves 6 to 8

*Among the decades of wonderful recipes that Paula Wolfert has written, perhaps the most famous is her seven-hour leg of lamb, roasted slowly until the meat is tender enough to eat with a spoon. In the original, the lamb is first boiled for 15 minutes, then browned, then cooked with dessert wine and lots of peeled garlic cloves. My version is an example of taking improvisational liberties with an actual recipe, viewing it as a guide rather than a topographical map. I skipped the boiling because I was too lazy, couldn't figure out why it was necessary, and figured the long roasting would yield tender results without it; lacking a dessert wine, I devised a reasonable facsimile with white wine, honey, and a strip of orange zest. I also skipped the time-consuming job of peeling 60 garlic cloves and threw them in unpeeled, figuring I could: (a) pass the soft cooked cloves through a food mill into the sauce or (b) my guests would happily squeeze the softened flesh out of the husks right into their mouth. I'd make that decision at the last minute.*

*This is a spectacular dinner party dish that will drive your guests wild. It takes ½ hour max to put together, then cooks unattended. Serve with buttered egg pasta or Celery Root and Pear Puree (page 162).*

*This dish yields more than 3 cups of rich juices, a kind of concentrated lamb consommé that is a treasure; heat some in a small saucepan and float ravioli or tortellini in it for a divine supper.*

A 5-pound leg of lamb works best for this dish because it is small enough to fit in a casserole. Larger legs should be semiboneless and tied into a compact shape. (Have the butcher trim off the shank bone.) A few hours before cooking the lamb, rub it with 1 tablespoon kosher salt. Place on a platter in the fridge to marinate. Meanwhile, break apart 5 heads of garlic and separate the cloves, pulling off any papery skin; don't peel unless you want to.

Preheat the oven to 200°F. Heat about 1 tablespoon olive oil in a large flameproof casserole (enamel on cast iron is perfect) over moderate heat. Pat the lamb dry and brown to golden, about 5 minutes per side, 20 minutes total. Pour off the fat and add a scant ¼ cup Cognac or Armagnac. Tilt the pan to ignite, taking care to stand back. When the flames have died out, add 1⅓ cups dry white wine, 2 tablespoons wildflower honey, 1 strip orange zest, 2 to 3 fresh thyme sprigs, and the garlic cloves. Cover with a sheet of aluminum foil and press the lid down to seal.

Roast until the lamb is fork-tender, about 7 hours, turning the lamb over once halfway through.

Transfer the lamb to a platter and cover with the foil. Pour the juices into a cup and degrease. If desired, boil the juices to concentrate their flavor.

Pull the meat apart or slice it across the grain and arrange on a platter. Pour some of the juices over, and pass the rest.

### Veal Shanks with Melting Onions and Lemon Gremolata   Serves 4

*I was given a windfall of organic veal shanks, but I was tired of the usual tomato-based braises for shanks. Inspiration came from what was in the fridge. An open bottle of white wine, lemons, parsley, and lots of onions became the braising liquid in which I close-roasted the shanks. The onions melted into a rough puree, giving mellow flavor and body to the sauce. The flavor of the shanks, accentuated by the gremolata's last-minute hit of flavor, shone through.*

Preheat the oven to 300°F. Sprinkle 4 veal shanks (about 12 ounces each) with 2 teaspoons kosher salt. Heat 1 tablespoon vegetable oil in a flame-proof casserole large enough to hold the shanks in a single layer. Pat the shanks dry and add to the pot. Brown well, 4 to 5 minutes on each side; transfer to a platter.

Add a little more oil, if necessary, 2 pounds onions, thinly sliced, and ½ teaspoon kosher salt; stir, turn the heat to moderately low, and cover the pot. Sweat the onions 10 minutes. Uncover, increase the heat slightly, and sauté, stirring frequently, until golden, about 7 minutes.

Stir in 4 anchovy fillets packed in oil, rinsed and chopped, and 1 cup dry white wine. Boil until the wine is almost completely evaporated. Stir in 1 teaspoon slivered lemon zest and 1 teaspoon fresh thyme leaves. Nestle the shanks in the onions. Cover the pot with aluminum foil and press the lid down to make a tight seal.

Bake, turning the shanks halfway through, until the meat is fork-tender, about 2 hours.

Transfer the meat to a serving dish. Strain the juices into a tall measuring cup; spoon the onions over the shanks and cover to keep warm. While you're waiting for the fat to rise, quickly make the **Lemon Gremolata:** Mince 1 teaspoon coarsely chopped garlic with ¼ teaspoon kosher salt. Add ¼ cup flat-leaf parsley leaves and 1½ teaspoons grated lemon zest; chop fine.

Skim the fat off the juices and pour over the meat. Scatter the gremolata on top and serve at once.

## Short Ribs Bourguignon    Serves 4

*Boeuf Bourguignon is a classic French concoction: beef cooked in red wine with mushrooms, pearl onions, and little lardons (bits of fried fatback or bacon)—beef stew elevated to celestial heights.*

*Chasing after those flavors one day, I decided to fashion something bourguignonish with some organically raised beef short ribs I found at my local market. I browned the ribs and braised them in a concoction I use with great success for coq au vin–style dishes: red wine, port, and Madeira in league with lots of sautéed sliced shallots. Instead of canned beef or chicken broth, I used a quickly made porcini mushroom broth to augment the braising liquid. The result was tender short ribs with the onion-and-mushroom flavors of bourguignon garnishes built right into the rich sauce. (If you wish, add the traditional peeled pearl onions, sautéed button mushrooms, and diced bacon or pancetta garnishes to the defatted dish: Get them ready while the beef is cooking.)*

At least 2 hours before cooking, rub 2 teaspoons kosher salt into 3 pounds beef short ribs. Just before cooking, pat dry and dust evenly with 1 tablespoon flour. Place ⅓ cup dried porcini mushrooms in a small bowl and cover with 1 cup boiling water.

Preheat the oven to 275°F. Heat 1 tablespoon vegetable oil in a large shallow flameproof casserole over moderate heat. Add the ribs and brown on all sides, 12 to 15 minutes total. Transfer to a platter.

Add 7 or 8 shallots, thinly sliced (about 1 cup), to the pot, stir to coat with the oil, reduce the heat, and cover. Cook, stirring frequently, until the shallots are soft and golden, about 5 minutes. Add 1½ cups dry red wine, ½ cup ruby port, and ¼ cup Rainwater or Sercial Madeira. Turn the heat to high and boil the wine until reduced by half. With a slotted spoon, scoop the dried mushrooms out of the liquid and add to the pot. Then slowly pour in the soaking liquid, leaving any sediment behind. Nestle the ribs in the pot, cover with aluminum foil, and press the lid down to seal.

Bake, turning the ribs once, until they are very tender, about 2½ hours.

Transfer the ribs to a platter and cover with the foil. Pour the juices into a cup and put in the freezer for 10 minutes to allow the fat to rise to the surface; skim. Pour the juices over the ribs and serve. Alternatively, pull the meat off the bones and add to the sauce to serve like a stew.

# Days-After Improvisations for Close-Roasted Meats

- Shredded Close-Roasted Meat Soft Tacos
- Crackling Cornmeal Cakes with Sour Cream and
  Shredded Close-Roasted Meat
- Close-Roasted Pork, Lamb, or Beef and Bean Stew or Cassoulet
- Close-Roasted Lamb or Beef "Ragù" with Pasta and Parmigiano
- Impromptu Rillettes

For years, I've been looking for another word for leftovers, the surplus of a delicious dish stored in the fridge for the days that follow. The word "leftovers" is dreary, evoking reheated dishes that are a pale shadow of their former selves, rather than the gold out of which I can make something delicious: raw materials that come from finished dishes. They are an essential part of my gastronomic survival, one of the strategies I employ for eating well with almost no time spent on preparation when I'm working hard and my life gets wild. Anne Disrude, one of the best improvisational cooks I know, calls leftovers "money in the bank."

Slow-cooked, close-roasted, falling-off-the-bone meats such as the ones on pages 235 to 238 make great leftovers because they get better with age and build in rich, deep flavors to any dish. They keep 5 days in the refrigerator in a plastic container with the juices poured over and freeze fine up to 2 months (I freeze them in 1-cup portions), so it's worth making big batches. Close-Roasted Pork with Ancho, Cinnamon, and Cocoa (page 235) in particular is so easy to cook and so good that I often make it just to keep it in the fridge for such a purpose. The following are some spur-of-the-moment improvisations for these slow-cooked treasures.

Close-roasted meats are very much like stews; during the slow, moist-heat cooking, the meat becomes fork-tender and contributes its juices to a concentrated "sauce." Their flavor gets better in the days to follow, so they are ideal for improvisations. Simply warm the meat slowly in its rich juices, covered, over low heat. Once warm, it will separate easily into melting shreds and chunks. Use as a filling–for ravioli, empanada-style turnovers, hot sandwiches, and soft tacos–or as a rich, ragùlike sauce for pasta, polenta, or risotto, or to embellish cooked dried beans and hashes of potatoes or root vegetables.

### Shredded Close-Roasted Meat Soft Tacos

*Shredded slow-roasted meats warmed in their juices make perfect fillings for soft tacos (plain corn tortillas keep for weeks in the fridge). I usually eat these at the stove, one by one as they come out of the pan. If I have a guest, I'll fire up two skillets so that two tacos will be ready at the same time.*

Heat a cast-iron skillet over moderate heat. Throw in a corn tortilla, flip it when it begins to get spotty, then put it on a plate, and roll it with warmed Close-Roasted Pork with Ancho, Cinnamon, and Cocoa (page 235) or another shredded slow-cooked meat and sour cream, cilantro, avocado, sweet onion, a squeeze of lime, depending on what you have on hand.

### Crackling Cornmeal Cakes with Sour Cream and Shredded Close-Roasted Meat

*The simultaneous occurrence of great leftovers is often the source of my improvisations. The best ones, like this one, are so good that they are worth making from scratch.*

*I had some batter left over from a breakfast of Crackling Cornmeal Cakes (page 264) and about a cup of Short Ribs Bourguignon (page 238) that I'd pulled off the bone. So I heated the meat in a saucepan, fired up a skillet, and cooked up a few pancakes. The only assembly required was to put the corn cakes on a dinner plate, top each one with a small dollop of sour cream as a creamy liaison between the two parts, and then a spoonful of the warm meat. Perfect.*

*I've since made these with Spoon Lamb with Masses of Garlic, after Paula Wolfert (page 235) and Close-Roasted Pork with Ancho, Cinnamon, and Cocoa (page 235), sprinkled with chopped cilantro.*

*If I have no cornmeal, I pile some of the warm shredded meats onto a Shallot (or Garlic) Toast (page 274) or crushed boiled new potatoes, with a little dab of sour cream to smooth the way.*

### Close-Roasted Pork, Lamb, or Beef and Bean Stew or Cassoulet

*Sometimes I pile shredded pork, lamb, or beef right onto a plate of beans. Just about any kind of bean will do: cannellini, borlotti, black-eyed peas, or an exotic pinto, cooked simply (see page 167), and dressed with some of the meat juices and fresh herbs, a gremolata made of parsley or basil (see page 237) for lamb or short ribs, or cilantro for pork. Or, veering toward cassoulet, pile a mix of slow-roasted meat, cooked beans, and meat juices into a small casserole rubbed with garlic, then sprinkle over fresh bread crumbs, dot with butter, and bake until golden.*

## Close-Roasted Lamb or Beef "Ragù" with Pasta and Parmigiano   Serves 2

*Close-roasted meats are meant to fall apart; they naturally separate into tender shreds and chunks that, when combined with their rich juices, make an instant pasta sauce, a ragù.*

*Rather than mixing the ragù right into the pasta, I like to toss the cooked pasta with grated aged cheese, such as Parmigiano, pecorino Romano, Fiore Sardo, Grana Padano, Roncal, or Pepato, and a little pasta cooking water to form a creamy coating; then I spoon the slow-cooked meat "ragù" on top. The sharp cheese acts as a catalyst between the rich sauce and the pasta, heightening and balancing all the flavors. Figure about ¾ to 1 cup shredded slow-cooked meats and 3 or 4 ounces of dried pasta per serving.*

Shred about 2 cups leftover slow-roasted meat, discarding any bone, fat, and gristle; add any cooking liquid. Place in a saucepan over moderately low heat and add a couple of tablespoons of water. Cover and bring to a simmer, stirring occasionally. Reduce the heat to very low to keep the meat warm; add another tablespoon of water if it begins to dry out.

Cook 6 to 8 ounces dried pasta in plenty of boiling salted water until tender but still slightly firm to the bite (al dente). Drain the pasta in a large strainer or colander held over a measuring cup in the sink, reserving about ½ cup of the cooking water. Return the pasta to the pot and set over high heat. Pour ¼ cup of the reserved cooking water over the pasta. Sprinkle with 2 or 3 tablespoons grated hard cheese. Toss until the cheese has melted into a creamy sauce and the pasta is thoroughly coated. Add salt and pepper to taste. Divide the pasta between heated shallow bowls and spoon the ragù on top. Pass more cheese separately.

### Impromptu Rillettes

*One day, I'd invited a friend over for a glass of wine and was trying to figure out a snack to serve with it. I had about ½ cup of close-roasted veal shanks (page 237) I'd pulled off the bone and some of the gelatinous cooking liquid. So I heated them in a covered saucepan until they were warm but still cool enough to handle. I shredded the meat, put it in a mortar, and, with a pestle (you can also use a bowl and the back of a spoon), pounded and mashed it as I gradually drizzled in some of the juices until I had a coarse paste. I peppered it liberally and packed it into a bowl. Served at room temperature with warm Shallot (or Garlic) Toasts (page 274), it was like a rough, delicious pâté. You can do this with all kinds of slow-cooked meats and poultry, as long as they are very soft and shreddy when warmed. If you don't have any cooking liquids or if the pounded meats aren't mellow enough, beat in some softened unsalted butter.*

# An Ever-Improvisational Meat Loaf

- Spicy Smoky Pork Meat Loaf with Cumin and Chipotles
- Lamb Meat Loaf with Cumin, Coriander, and Fennel
- Faux Pâté Campagne with Pistachios

My meat loaf has evolved over the years as I've given rein to my personal idiosyncrasies—preferring other meats to the usual beef, for example and guided by what I had in my pantry. Recently, I incorporated ricotta cheese, an idea from a meatball recipe I'd heard about; ricotta lightens and moistens the meat loaf, giving it a fluffier texture and ensuring against its being dry. It's become part of my basic meat loaf formula, a forgiving essential mix that seems to accommodate endless variations.

Served warm, it makes for a simple, satisfying supper. Served cold, thinly sliced and sandwiched between slices of toasted country bread, it gains in sophistication, an American-style terrine.

Meat loaves all tend to follow a basic formula: ground meats mixed with eggs and bread crumbs and flavored with onions, herbs, and other seasonings, formed into a loaf, and baked. The basic meat loaf notion has a kitchen sink quality—whatever is around finds its way in—so it lends itself to improvisation.

Meat loaves can be made from just about any ground meat and/or poultry, singly or in combination, including beef, pork, lamb, veal, turkey, duck, rabbit, uncooked bulk sausage meat, bacon, and pancetta. If you make a meat loaf with "white meats" such as pork, veal, turkey, rabbit, you get something closer to a pâté. Using 50 percent or so ground beef steers it back toward traditional meat loaf. Because the fat in the meat helps keep the loaf moist, the leaner the meats are, the more you'll need to compensate by adding flavorful, moistening ingredients: sautéed vegetables, such as onions, mushrooms, or sweet bell peppers; ricotta cheese, yogurt, milk, or cream; ketchup, chili sauce, or mustard. Thin slices of bacon or pancetta help ensure that a meat loaf will be moist by basting it with fat as it cooks. Eggs and bread crumbs bind the ground meats together into a loaf and give them an airier, moister texture. Because turkey is so lean, turkey meat loaves tend to be a bit dry and thinly flavored; the good ones have a lot of moistening ingredients to pull them through.

Meat loaves accommodate many flavorings and additions, including fresh or dried herbs, such as rosemary, thyme, savory, sage (used sparingly), or flat-leaf parsley; ground or cracked spices such as chili powders, cumin, coriander, fennel seed; lemon zest; condiments from ketchup, mustard, and Worcestershire sauce to hot sauce, chipotle adobo sauce, and ancho chile puree. A few teaspoons of lemon juice or balsamic vinegar can brighten flavors, as can freshly ground pepper. Chopped onions or shallots are essential; cooking them beforehand will give the loaf a sweeter flavor. Grated Parmigiano magically improves almost any meat loaf. To get a sense of how the cooked loaf will taste, fry up a small patty of the meat mixture and taste it.

Finally, many recipes for meatballs share the same basic formula as meat loaves, adding further possibilities for improvisation. The uncooked Lamb Meat Loaf with Cumin, Coriander, and Fennel would do well rolled into small balls and browned in a skillet for an improvisation on Middle Eastern *kofta*.

. . . . . .

# An Ever-Improvisational Meat Loaf    Serves 6 to 8

2 teaspoons vegetable oil

1 medium onion, chopped

2 garlic cloves, minced

½ cup dry white wine

1¼ pounds lean ground pork

12 ounces ground turkey

1½ cups fresh bread crumbs (see page 247)

¾ cup grated Parmigiano

½ cup chopped flat-leaf parsley

1 cup ricotta

½ cup milk

2 large eggs

1 tablespoon fresh rosemary leaves, minced, or 1 teaspoon
  crumbled dried rosemary

1 tablespoon fresh thyme leaves, minced, or 1 teaspoon
  dried thyme

1¼ teaspoons coarsely ground black pepper

1 teaspoon kosher salt

4 ounces thinly sliced bacon

**Sauté the onion and other aromatics or vegetables.** Preheat the oven to 325°F. In a small skillet, combine the oil and onion; cover and cook over low heat until the onion is translucent, about 3 minutes. Uncover, increase the heat to moderate, and sauté, stirring frequently, until browned, 3 to 4 minutes. Add the garlic and cook, stirring, 1 minute longer. Then add the wine and simmer until the liquid has evaporated, 3 minutes. Remove from the heat.

**Combine the meats with the bread crumbs and flavorings.** In a large bowl, combine the pork, turkey, the onion mixture, bread crumbs, Parmigiano, parsley, ricotta, milk, eggs, rosemary, thyme, pepper, and salt. Mix by hand until well blended.

**Form the loaf.** Scoop the mixture into the center of a large heavy baking pan. Shape into a loaf about 10 × 5 inches. Lay the strips of bacon over the loaf.

**Bake.** Bake the meat loaf for 1 hour 15 minutes to 1 hour 30 minutes, until an instant-read thermometer inserted in the center reads 160°F. Let cool slightly and remove the bacon, if desired. Blot up the fat in the pan with paper towels before slicing.

## To make fresh bread crumbs

Trim the crusts off white bread and tear the bread into pieces. Pulse them in a food processor until they are reduced to crumbs. Six ounces of bread, crusts trimmed, will yield about 1½ cups crumbs (3 ounces).

• • • • • •

## Improvisations

### Spicy Smoky Pork Meat Loaf with Cumin and Chipotles    Serves 8

*I used only pork in my basic formula and flavored it with rendered bacon bits and cumin for a robustly flavored meat loaf. For an additional spicy kick, add 3 tablespoons adobo sauce from a can of chipotles in adobo.*

Preheat the oven to 350°F. In a medium heavy skillet over moderately low heat, cook 8 ounces bacon, preferably applewood-smoked, cut into ½-inch-wide pieces, until crisp and browned, 8 to 10 minutes. Drain the bacon on paper towels and pour off all but 1 tablespoon of the fat. Add 2 medium onions, chopped; cook until soft and browned. Add 2 garlic cloves, minced, and a jalapeño pepper, chopped, and cook 1 minute longer. Add ½ cup dry white wine and simmer until evaporated. Remove from the heat.

In a large bowl, combine 2 pounds lean ground pork, the onion mixture, 1¼ cups fresh bread crumbs, ⅓ cup milk, 2 large eggs, ½ cup grated Parmigiano, ¼ cup chopped flat-leaf parsley, 1 tablespoon fresh thyme leaves, minced, 2 teaspoons ground cumin, 1½ teaspoons coarsely ground black pepper, 1¼ teaspoons kosher salt, 1 tablespoon Dijon mustard, and 1 tablespoon fresh lemon juice. Mix by hand until well blended.

Scoop the mixture into the center of a large heavy baking pan. Shape into a loaf about 10 × 5 inches. Lay 4 or 5 additional strips of smoked bacon over the loaf, cutting them to fit.

Bake until an instant-read thermometer inserted in the center reads 160°F, about 55 minutes. Let cool slightly and remove the bacon, if desired. Transfer to a platter and serve.

## Lamb Meat Loaf with Cumin, Coriander, and Fennel    Serves 8

*This unusual lamb meat loaf, seasoned with cumin, coriander, fennel, and cinnamon was inspired by the flavors of a Moroccan lamb tagine. The thin core of pitted prunes baked into the center gives a hint of sweetness that balances the spices, an interesting, though not essential, embellishment.*

In a small skillet, cook 1 medium onion, chopped (scant 1¼ cups), in 1 tablespoon extra virgin olive oil, covered, over low heat until translucent, about 3 minutes. Uncover, increase the heat slightly, and sauté, stirring frequently, until browned, 3 to 4 minutes. Add 2 garlic cloves, minced (1 tablespoon), and cook, stirring, 1 minute longer. Then add ½ cup dry white wine and simmer until the liquid has evaporated, 3 minutes. Remove from the heat.

Preheat the oven to 350°F. In a large bowl, combine 1½ pounds lean ground lamb, ½ pound lean ground veal, the onion mixture, 1½ cups fresh bread crumbs, ¼ cup yogurt, 2 large eggs, ½ cup grated Parmigiano, ¼ cup chopped flat-leaf parsley, 1¼ teaspoons coarsely ground black pepper, 1¼ teaspoons kosher salt, 1 teaspoon chopped fresh thyme leaves, 1¼ teaspoons ground cumin, 1¼ teaspoons ground coriander, ½ teaspoon fennel seed, ¼ teaspoon cayenne pepper, ⅛ teaspoon ground cinnamon, 3 tablespoons tahini or 2 tablespoons Dijon mustard, and 2½ to 3 teaspoons grated lemon zest. Mix by hand until well blended.

Scoop half the mixture into the center of a large heavy baking pan and smooth into a squat loaf about 10 × 5 inches. Arrange 8 to 10 pitted prunes end to end in a line down the center of the loaf. Pile the remaining meat mixture on top and smooth into a neat loaf.

Bake until an instant-read thermometer inserted in the center reads 150°F, about 55 minutes. Let cool 10 minutes before transferring to a platter.

## Faux Pâté Campagne with Pistachios    Serves about 8

*This meat loaf is modeled after a classic country pâté: ground pork and veal seasoned with Cognac, herbs, spices, and pistachios, but without the usual dose of pork fat. Placing a weight on the cooked terrine for a few hours gives it a denser, more sliceable texture. Serve it chilled or at room temperature with crusty bread, grainy mustard, and cornichons or Pickled Cherries (see page 316).*

Preheat the oven to 350°F. In a small skillet, cook ½ cup finely chopped shallots in 1 tablespoon extra virgin olive oil, covered, over low heat until the shallots are translucent, about 3 minutes. Uncover, increase the heat slightly, and sauté, stirring frequently, until browned, 3 to 4 minutes. Add 2 garlic cloves, finely chopped, and cook, stirring, 1 minute longer. Add 2 tablespoons Cognac or Armagnac and cook until evaporated. Add ½ cup dry white wine and simmer until the liquid has evaporated, 3 minutes. Remove from the heat.

In a large bowl, combine 1 pound each ground pork and veal, the shallot mixture, 1½ cups fresh bread crumbs, ½ cup milk or yogurt, 2 large eggs, 3 tablespoons chopped flat-leaf parsley, 2 teaspoons kosher salt, and ⅛ teaspoon cayenne. Add 2 teaspoons All-Purpose Aromatic Pepper (page 48) or the following spice mix: Using a pepper mill, a spice grinder, or a mortar and pestle, coarsely grind 1 tablespoon each white and black peppercorns and ¾ teaspoon each allspice berries and coriander seed. Use the remainder as you would the Aromatic Pepper. Mix the meat mixture by hand until well blended. Quickly work in ½ cup shelled pistachios.

Arrange 3 small imported bay leaves in the bottom of a 9 × 5 × 2 ¾-inch (8-cup) terrine or loaf pan. Press the meat mixture into the loaf pan and smooth the top. Rap the terrine gently on a folded kitchen towel on the counter several times to eliminate any air pockets. Cover with 5 or 6 thin pancetta slices.

Bake until an instant-read thermometer inserted into the center of the terrine reads 150°F, 1 hour. Let cool for ¼ hour.

Press a piece of aluminum foil directly onto the top of the terrine and place another loaf pan on top of the meat; place a 2-pound weight such as a can or a rock inside the empty pan. Let sit at room temperature until completely cool, about 3 hours. Remove the weight and refrigerate for at least 6 hours before slicing.

To serve, pry the loaf out of the pan and wipe off the jellied juices and fat; discard the bay leaves. Slice into ¾-inch slices.

# Herb-Scented Roast Leg of Lamb, Venison Style

- Rolled, Boneless Leg of Lamb for Improvising
- Lamb Chops or Steaks with Olive Paste
- Double Pork Tenderloin Roast with Rosemary-Sage Salt
- Roast Leg of Wild Venison

One fall day in hunting season, a man showed up at my New York apartment with a leg of young venison about the size of a leg of lamb, a gift from a friend in West Virginia. It was a treasure, to be sure, as all wild foods are to my mind, though being a city kid, I didn't have much experience cooking real—as opposed to farm-raised—venison. I winged it, applying a leisurely two-day salting and gentle roasting that resulted in a perfectly seasoned, truly tender, uniformly rosy roast. This approach proved an excellent way to roast legs of lamb, bone in or out, without the usual extremes of well done outside and raw at the bone. It has become an essential recipe—technique, I should say—in my repertoire.

Although I've cooked lamb with any number of flavorings, from Moroccan-style mixes of cumin, coriander, and cinnamon to anchovies and garlic, my favorite remains a mix of Provençal herbs—rosemary, thyme, and a breath of lavender—with garlic. I mince them with salt to make a fragrant instant seasoning that tenderizes the lamb and carries mellow herb-and-garlic flavors into the flesh, to give it a subtle herbal perfume. It's a fine example of the adage: "Foods that grow together, go together."

Leg of lamb is an ideal dinner party dish, accompanied by Lemon-Infused Potatoes with Thyme (page 150) or Celery Root and Pear Puree (page 162).

This recipe illustrates some essential principles for roasting different kinds and cuts of meats that will guarantee tender, succulent results with just about any roast; it is especially useful for ones thicker than about 3 inches or over about 5 pounds, which can be tough and unevenly cooked.

Seasoning, that is, salting the meat well in advance of cooking, gives the salt time to penetrate to the center, to bring out the meat's own flavors. It also tenderizes the flesh by slightly curing it. (Figure about ¾ teaspoon kosher salt per pound of meat or poultry.) Seasoning salts like the Rosemary, Thyme, and Lavender Salt are endlessly variable; blend in just about any combination of herbs or spices, in league with garlic or shallot, if you like, chopping them right into the salt. Vary the herbs in this essential mix, blending in savory, basil, chile peppers, lemon zest, and so on. (Read more about making Fragrant Herb Salt on page 46.) Because salt mellows the flavors of whatever it is blended with, there is no danger of garlic or shallot flavors becoming harsh within a roast, as is often the case when raw slivers are inserted into the flesh.

Or, in place of salt, use salty condiments that act in the same way: Anchovy with meat might seem like a dissonant pairing, but it brings out the flavor of the meat without seeming fishy. It has an affinity for Provençal herbs and garlic, as do Dijon mustard and olive paste, made from naturally salty olives; pungent Asian fish sauce also offers possibilities, in tandem with ginger, garlic, or lemongrass, as does miso tempered with rice wine, sake, and sesame oil.

The smaller the cut, the more quickly the salty seasoning will penetrate to the center—4 hours to overnight for a rack of lamb. Larger cuts need more time; 2 to 3 days is ideal for a leg of lamb or fresh ham. That being said, if you don't have much time, seasoning salts are the quickest, most powerful way to imbue meats with flavor. Even salting within an hour of cooking will add a good dose of flavor. A caveat, though: Do not wrap seasoned meat in plastic wrap, which locks in moisture. Rather, leave it unwrapped or wrapped in freezer or butcher's paper, which allows the meat to age a bit and its surface to dry out and brown well in the oven.

For extremely lean roasts, such as pork tenderloin or a leg of venison, cover the roasts with thin slices of pancetta, which will baste the meat with fat as it cooks and add another level of flavoring, slightly porky and peppery. Bacon will add a smoky flavor.

Let the roast come to room temperature well in advance of roasting so the center won't be cold when roasted; this ensures even roasting, avoiding rare-at-the-bone meat with a well-done exterior.

Generally speaking, the larger the cut, the more gently it should be cooked, that is, the lower the temperature to prevent the outside from becoming over-cooked and tough. A temperature of 325°F is perfect for leg of lamb and fresh ham. Use a higher temperature, about 450°F, for thinner cuts such as rack of lamb; to sear the outside, heat the roasting pan for 10 minutes before adding the rack.

. . . . . .

# Herb-Scented Roast Leg of Lamb, Venison Style   Serves 8 to 10

Rosemary, Thyme, and Lavender Salt
> 1 medium garlic clove
> 1 tablespoon plus 1 teaspoon kosher salt
> 2/3 cup loosely packed fresh rosemary and thyme leaves,
>    in any combination
> 1/4 teaspoon unsprayed dried lavender flowers or minced fresh lavender
>    leaves (optional)
> 3/4 teaspoon freshly ground black pepper

> One 6-pound bone-in leg of lamb, trimmed of excess fat
> 2 teaspoons extra virgin olive oil
> Fresh rosemary, thyme, and/or lavender sprigs for garnishing

**Make the flavored salt or salt-based seasoning.** On a cutting board, mince the garlic with the salt. Place the rosemary, thyme, and lavender in a mound and coarsely chop them. Add the garlic salt and the pepper, and chop them together to make a coarse rub.

**Season the meat.** Rub the lamb with the herb salt to coat completely. Wrap in freezer or butcher's paper or simply set the roast on a platter. Refrigerate, preferably for 48 hours, although even a few hours will do. Before roasting, bring the leg to room temperature; allow 4 hours for a bone-in leg of lamb, and proportionally less time for smaller cuts.

**Preheat the oven.** Position an oven rack in the center of the oven. Preheat the oven to 325°F about 20 minutes before roasting.

**Massage the roast with oil.** Blot the lamb dry with paper towels. Massage the whole leg with the olive oil (this will help it to brown as it roasts).

**Roast the meat.** Roast about 1 hour and 25 minutes until an instant-read thermometer inserted into the thickest part reads 125°F to 130°F for medium rare (the temperature will rise about 10 degrees once out of the oven).

**Allow the meat to rest.** Remove the roast from the oven, cover loosely with aluminum foil, and let rest in a warm place for 20 minutes before carving. This will allow the juices in the roast to redistribute, making for a much more tender roast.

**Slice the meat.** Slice across the grain at right angles to the direction of the faint striations or muscle fibers. Because there are several different muscles in a bone-in leg of lamb, the grain will shift. Hold the shank end with a towel, with the meaty part of the leg facing up. Using a thin sharp knife, beginning at the shank end, make thin vertical slices down to the bone. Then cut the slices free from the bone by cutting parallel to and against the bone. Continue from end to end, rotating the leg to carve the meat from all sides. If you can, keep an eye on the changes in the grain, changing the angle of your knife accordingly to keep cutting at right angles to it. Arrange the slices on a platter and garnish with herb sprigs. Serve.

## Improvisations

### Rolled, Boneless Leg of Lamb for Improvising   Serves 8 to 10

*Boneless legs of lamb take seasoning more quickly than bone-in ones and are easier to slice, though they don't have quite the richness of flavor. They are usually rolled into a slightly bulbous shape, with one thicker end, which makes it difficult to cook. I devised this simple method to roll boneless legs into a uniform log, which ensures even cooking and easy slicing.*

Open out the lamb skin side down on a work surface, with the grain of the meat running from right to left (or parallel to the edge of the counter). Season the lamb with a salt-based seasoning as desired. Working on a slight diagonal, roll the lamb lengthwise into a uniform sausage shape about 5 inches in diameter. Cut off the small sinewy flap of skin left at the end that you have no way of tucking in. (Sauté it up as a snack or light meal.) Tie the rolled lamb with cotton string at 1-inch intervals.

Marinate and proceed as directed in Herb-Scented Roast Leg of Lamb, Venison Style.

### Lamb Chops or Steaks with Olive Paste

*Improvisations on a theme can be like a ball being tossed back and forth. I once wrote a recipe for a boneless leg of lamb that I smeared with black olive paste, rolled, tied, and roasted. A friend told me he took the idea and just rubbed a whole bone-in leg with olive paste and roasted it, with great success. In a hurry to make dinner one night, I took his idea and smeared lamb chops with olive paste, sprinkled them with savory, and seared them in a grill pan for a delicious quick dinner. The olive paste acts like salt to season the meat.*

Pat 1-inch-thick lamb chops or leg of lamb steaks, trimmed of fat, dry with paper towels. Massage prepared black olive paste or tapenade onto them, leaving a thin coating on each side. Sprinkle a little chopped fresh savory, thyme, or rosemary on each side. Heat a grill pan or a broiler to very hot. Cook the chops several minutes on each side until seared and caramelized on the outside and pink inside, or until an instant-read thermometer inserted near the bone reads 125°F.

## Double Pork Tenderloin Roast with Rosemary-Sage Salt    Serves 4 to 6

*Pork tenderloin—the thin, tapered strip of meat that runs along the loin—is a lean, flavorful cut that can be tricky to roast because it is so thin—under 2 inches at the thickest part. As a solution, I lashed two tenderloins together to make a roast of uniform thickness. First, though, I rubbed each one with a Tuscan-style rosemary-sage salt—the same idea as in the Herb-Scented Roast Leg of Lamb, Venison Style, with a different combination of herbs. The sides that are bound together create a flavorful seam through the center of the roast. Wrapping the roast in thin sheets of pancetta keeps it moist and adds back some porky savor. It is delicious hot or cold.*

Preheat the oven to 450°F. Rinse 2 pork tenderloins, 1 pound each, and pat dry with paper toweling. Set aside.

To make **Rosemary-Sage Salt:** Mound 1¼ teaspoons kosher salt and a small peeled garlic clove on a cutting board. Use a chef's knife to mince the garlic, blending it with the salt as you work. Place 2 tablespoons fresh rosemary leaves and about 15 fresh sage leaves in a mound and coarsely chop them. Add the herbs to the garlic salt and chop them together to the texture of fine sand.

Rub the salt into the tenderloins. Place one loin on the work surface. Arrange the second loin on top with the thin end parallel to the thick end of the other. Press the tenderloins together to form a log of uniform thickness. If desired, sprinkle lightly with fennel seeds. Arrange 4 or 5 thin pancetta slices, slightly overlapping each other, down the length of the roast. Tie the roast at 1-inch intervals with cotton string to give it a neat shape. Place, pancetta side up, on a rack in a shallow roasting pan.

Roast the pork for 10 minutes. Reduce the temperature to 350°F and roast 20 to 25 minutes longer, until an instant-read thermometer inserted into the center reads 145°F. Let rest for 10 minutes before slicing.

## Roast Leg of Wild Venison

*If by some good fortune you happen to find yourself with a leg of wild venison, follow the recipe for Herb-Scented Leg of Lamb with these changes: Omit the herbs (to allow the taste of the venison itself to shine through) and simply salt and pepper the leg 2 to 3 days ahead. Before roasting, cover the leg with thin slices of pancetta, securing them with cotton string. Roast about 12 minutes per pound, until an instant-read thermometer inserted in the thickest part reads 120°F. Allow to rest for 20 minutes before slicing across the grain.*

➤ BREADS, GRAINS, AND PASTA

# Crackling Corn Bread

I serve corn bread often as an accompaniment to foods that are not at all Southern—fish stews; all manner of pork, crab, or lobster salads; Sunday roast chicken scented with herbs—as the starch of the meal, instead of potatoes, rice, or pasta. I see it as a fusion of two cultures I love—the American South and Italy—that know cornmeal to be savory, mutable, and compatible with so many foods: polenta by way of quick bread.

There is corn bread and there is corn bread. I learned to make real, truly crackling corn bread from Mary Hicks in Helvetia, West Virginia, who taught me that a well-greased and very hot cast-iron skillet is the secret to crisping the outside, to making it crackle. That is the key to having something that seems so ordinary be both surprising and delightful. Guests at my table are always charmed by it, and amazed that they never think to make it themselves, because it adds so much to a simple meal.

Here is my corn bread recipe, honed over years of making and eating other cooks' corn bread in the South; it is fine as is, and a great starting point for improvisation.

Great cornmeal is essential to great corn bread, for both texture and flavor. It's worth searching out a source for it, whether local or mail-order. I love the white cornmeal favored in parts of the South, such as Martha White or White Lily, for its subtly steely, earthy flavor. Yellow polenta meal or stone-ground cornmeal, ground medium-coarse, is also excellent.

You can vary the proportion of cornmeal to flour to change the texture of the corn bread, as long as it totals 2 cups dry ingredients. More cornmeal will make a grittier, cornier, denser corn bread; more flour will make it lighter, milder, and more cakelike. All cornmeal and no flour will result in a dense, corny, crackly bread that needs to be eaten while hot; it dries out as it cools. Sugar should only, if ever, be used like salt, in fractional amounts, to enhance flavor.

The fat you use will also alter the flavor. Smoky bacon fat provides a fabulous background flavor that seems to sweeten and enhance that of the corn, with a Southern flair. Pancetta lends an earthy, complex hint of pig, but no smoke. Butter is fine, sweeter and more delicate. For the health-conscious, olive oil works too, especially when you are adding somewhat Italianate flavors to the corn bread.

Buttermilk ensures a more tender crumb, and its slight acidity brings out that of the corn. In a pinch, use whole milk mixed with yogurt in equal proportions.

You can incorporate all manner of flavorings into corn bread batter. I find the classic American additions such as Jack cheese, fried onions, scallions, and chile peppers problematic; corn bread gets too heavy and slightly stodgy from these moist additions. Viewing corn bread in an Italian light, I prefer to apply polenta's affinities, using herbs such as rosemary and sage; aged fairly dry and piquant cheese such as Parmigiano-Reggiano, Manchego, or long-aged Gouda; and bits of cooked pancetta.

The basic formula—cornmeal and flour in varying proportions, leavening, eggs, buttermilk, some fat—can be adjusted not only to make corn breads of different textures, but also cornmeal griddle cakes, corn muffins, and so on. Since corn bread is really like a batter cake—quickly made and leavened with baking powder—it is an easy leap into imagining cornmeal or polenta dessert cakes with the addition of another egg, a cup or so of sugar—brown, white, or maple—and up to ½ cup butter.

Once made, corn bread is so friendly to many foods that it lends itself to interesting marriages: with Close-Roasted Pork with Ancho, Cinnamon, and Cocoa (page 235), baked hams, and long-cooked ragoutlike dishes, such as Spoon Lamb with Masses of Garlic, after Paula Wolfert (page 235). It is also marvelous with lobster or shrimp salads and crab Louis, and as an accompaniment to fish or shellfish stews. Use toasted leftover corn bread as a bread base for quick hors d'oeuvres, again thinking of polenta, pairing it with olive paste, mozzarella, or goat cheese, and for satisfying open-faced sandwiches.

# Crackling Corn Bread    Serves 6 to 8

1 1/2 cups medium-coarse white or yellow cornmeal, preferably stone-ground

1/2 cup all-purpose flour

2 teaspoons baking powder

1/4 teaspoon baking soda

1 teaspoon kosher salt

1 3/4 to 2 cups buttermilk or plain yogurt mixed with milk in equal
   proportions

1 large egg, beaten

2 to 4 tablespoons rendered bacon fat or unsalted butter

**Heat a cast-iron skillet.** Preheat the oven to 400°F. Place a 9- or 10-inch well-seasoned cast-iron skillet in the oven for 5 minutes while you mix up the batter.

**Mix the batter.** In a medium bowl, combine the cornmeal, flour, baking powder, soda, and salt. Stir in 1 3/4 cups of the buttermilk and egg. Add more buttermilk if necessary to make a thick, just-pourable batter—a wet sand consistency is too thick.

**Coat the skillet with the fat and add the remainder to the batter.** Remove the skillet from the oven and add the fat; swirl it around to melt it and coat the inside completely. Then pour the remainder of the fat into the batter. Stir until just combined. Pour the batter into the skillet.

**Bake.** Bake until the top is golden and a knife inserted in the center comes out clean, about 30 minutes.

**Note:** To render bacon fat, cook several slices of bacon in a covered skillet over moderate heat until crisp. Strain the fat into a bowl for easy measuring. Refrigerate unused fat. (Eat the crisp bacon.)

# Improvisations

### Rosemary- or Sage-Scented Corn Bread    Serves 6 to 8

*Playing on cornmeal's affinity for herbs, I often arrange sage or rosemary leaves in the bottom of an oiled skillet before spooning the corn bread batter on top. When the corn bread is inverted onto a platter, it displays a charming pattern of leaves, which also flavor the bread.*

Preheat the oven to 400°F. Heat the skillet and mix up the batter for Crackling Corn Bread. Instead of bacon or butter, swirl 2 or 3 tablespoons extra virgin olive oil or pancetta fat in the hot skillet and stir the remainder into the batter. Arrange 16 fresh sage leaves or sprinkle 2 tablespoons fresh rosemary leaves evenly over the bottom of the pan. Carefully spoon the batter over the herbs without disturbing them, to "set" the pattern of leaves in the bottom of the corn bread.

Bake until the top is golden and a knife inserted in the center comes out clean, about 30 minutes. Cool on a rack for 5 minutes, then loosen the edges of the corn bread with a knife. Place a round platter on top of the skillet; using pot holders to hold the platter and skillet together, invert the two so the corn bread falls onto the platter, revealing the herbs. Serve at once.

### Parmigiano Corn Bread, after Polenta    Serves 6 to 8

*My free associations with cornmeal jump back and forth between polenta and corn bread. Parmigiano almost always flavors polenta, so why not bake it into a corn bread? It makes an intriguing savory bread that is the perfect accompaniment to rich French- or Italian-style stews and slow roasts, such as Spoon Lamb with Masses of Garlic, after Paula Wolfert (page 235) or Short Ribs Bourguignon (page 238). I often whip up a batch for a simple supper and eat it with a couple of fried eggs and a plate of garlicky greens: my Italian-Southern fusion comfort food.*

Make Crackling Corn Bread, adding 1 cup grated Parmigiano (or other grated long-aged cheese like Manchego or aged Gouda) and a few grinds of pepper to the cornmeal-flour mixture. Butter works fine as the fat, though substituting rendered pancetta fat adds another layer of unexpected flavor.

### Corn Bread Crostini

*Although day-old corn bread is usually too dry and pebbly to eat as is, I consider it a great resource. It makes a fine, quick play on crostini, brushed with garlicky olive oil, dusted with grated Parmigiano, and toasted under a hot broiler until golden and glazed. Serve these little toasts as an hors d'oeuvre or accompaniment to a rustic soup or stew. You can also use them as a base for Slow-Roasted Tomatoes (page 95), olive paste, roasted peppers, or goat cheese.*

Pour a few tablespoons extra virgin olive oil into a small bowl and add a peeled, lightly smashed garlic clove. Slice leftover corn bread ½ inch thick. Brush with the garlic oil and sprinkle with grated Parmigiano and some freshly ground black pepper. Toast under a preheated broiler as close to the heat source as possible until the cheese is golden and tinged with brown. Serve at once.

### Maple Sugar Pecan Cornmeal Cake    Serves 8

*This cake rolls the Crackling Corn Bread recipe and the basic Lightning Cake formula on page 321 into one. Whipped cream, served alongside, is an essential part of this dessert. Maple sugar—dehydrated maple syrup—yields a true maple flavor and tender crumb. You can find it in gourmet and natural food stores.*

Preheat the oven to 350°F. Butter and flour a 9-inch springform pan or a deep fluted tart pan with a removable bottom. In a small bowl, combine ½ cup coarsely chopped pecans and 1 tablespoon maple sugar; reserve. Sift together 1 cup all-purpose flour, 2 teaspoons baking powder, and ¼ teaspoon salt; stir in ½ cup yellow cornmeal, and set aside. In a medium bowl, beat 2 large eggs with 1 cup less 1 tablespoon maple sugar until light and frothy; stir in 2 teaspoons vanilla extract. Whisk in the flour mixture until almost incorporated, then whisk in ½ cup buttermilk and ½ cup (1 stick) unsalted butter, melted. Pour the batter into the prepared pan and sprinkle the pecan mixture evenly over the top.

Bake until a skewer inserted in the center comes out clean, about 30 minutes. Cool the cake on a rack. Transfer to a platter and sift confectioners' sugar over the top. Serve with whipped cream.

### Sweet or Savory Crackling Cornmeal Cakes  Makes 24 to 30 griddle cakes

*Occasionally I retreat to a friend's cabin in the West Virginia Appalachians to rest and cook with what is there: a rudimentary kitchen and whatever the local store offers me. Hankering for pancakes one morning, I decided to wing it and see if I could make them out of my basic corn bread formula, which I keep in my head. I mixed up the recipe with a slightly greater proportion of cornmeal, an additional egg, and enough milk mixed with plain yogurt to simulate buttermilk to make a batter. I fried bacon in the one skillet, both for crisp strips to accompany the cakes and for the fat to flavor them.*

*Homemade raspberry jam dressed the barely sweet, corny cakes: perfect, along with the lesson that it's easy to slide from Crackling Corn Bread to Crackling Cornmeal Cakes. These would also be great topped with sour cream and smoked salmon or caviar for an elegant hors d'oeuvre or New Year's Eve supper. Or with goat cheese that's been warmed in the oven for a few minutes. Or with a small dollop of sour cream and a shredded close-roasted meat (see pages 235–238).*

In a medium bowl, combine 1⅔ cups cornmeal, ⅓ cup all-purpose flour, 2 teaspoons baking powder, ¼ teaspoon baking soda, and ¾ teaspoon plus a pinch of salt. Stir in 1½ to 2 cups buttermilk (less will make a puffy ¼-inch-thick cake; more, a thinner, crisper one), 2 eggs, beaten, and 2 tablespoons melted rendered bacon fat or unsalted butter.

Heat a large heavy griddle or skillet over medium heat until a drop of water bounces across the surface. Brush the surface lightly with melted butter or bacon fat. Drop the batter 2 tablespoons at a time onto the surface, leaving enough room for the pancakes to spread (the corn cakes will be about 3 inches in diameter). Adjust the heat if necessary to keep the butter from burning. Cook the cakes until the surface is bubbled and set and the edges on the underside are brown. Flip the cakes and cook until the second side is brown. Repeat until all the batter is used, brushing the pan with butter before each batch.

Serve the cakes as they come off the griddle or keep them warm, layered in (and covered with) clean tea towels in a 200°F oven.

## Crab, Shrimp, or Lobster and Corn Bread Sandwich

*Corn bread is fabulous paired with lobster, shrimp, or crab salads; so in summer, or when I am yearning for summer, I whip up a sandwich with the two. The individual components of the sandwich are simple to prepare and may be done in advance, to assemble at the last minute. Because corn bread is crumbly and thick, I split the slices and pile fresh seafood on top, to serve the sandwich open face. The corn bread is best served still warm from the oven. If made the day before, it can be split and toasted before making the sandwich, or use Corn Bread Crostini (page 263). Garlic Mayonnaise (page 67) provides the perfect bridge between the two, and lettuces—watercress, arugula, field greens, plus a few basil leaves—provide a fresh green foil. If there's a good tomato around, slice it and pile it on, or a few strips of roasted peppers. The availability of cooked and shelled lobster, crab, or shrimp from local fish markets makes life even easier. Figure 5 to 6 ounces cooked crab or sliced lobster or shrimp for each sandwich.*

Make a pan of Crackling Corn Bread and cut into wedges; split each wedge into two horizontally. Place the bottom and top half of each wedge cut side up on a dinner plate and spread with Garlic Mayonnaise (page 67). Arrange a few lettuce leaves over the corn bread halves and a slice of tomato or roasted pepper, if you have it. Pile cooked crabmeat, lobster, or shrimp on top. Place some basil leaves in a neat stack and slice into a fine julienne, or chiffonade. Sprinkle over each sandwich. Serve at once.

# French-Fried Cheese Toast

A few years ago, I tried making French toast savory instead of sweet. I left out the traditional sugar and sweet flavorings and added grated Parmigiano to the egg-and-milk batter to make a crisp, chewy toast with a custardy inside that tasted something like a cheese soufflé. It was a revelation of the possibilities for savory French toast.

Serve the cheese toast with a frisée-and-walnut salad (dressed with a fine roasted-walnut oil) and a glass of dry white wine. Cut into squares, the cheese toasts make a satisfying hors d'oeuvre.

I recommend a mildly flavored, holey peasant-style bread, such as a ciabatta, or one with a light mix of unbleached and whole-grain flours, or a rustic rosemary-scented bread. If the bread is baguette-shaped, slice it on an extreme angle to get a bigger slice. Use prosciutto bread for an Italianate croque monsieur.

The constants in French toast are the bread and the custard mixture: egg, salt, and milk, half-and-half, or cream. Adding flavorings to the basic custard is the key to quick improvisations.

If you add savory flavorings to the custard, as in the French-Fried Cheese Toast, it transmutes into a quick lunch, brunch, or supper. These include pungent, not-too-sharp grating cheeses such as Parmigiano, Coach Farm's grating stick, or aged Gouda and herbs such as minced chives, basil, or rosemary, or a fines herbes mixture of parsley, chives, and tarragon.

To make French toast sweet, for breakfast or dessert, add a sweetener such as sugar, maple sugar, or interesting honey and fruity/floral flavorings, such as spices, citrus zests, vanilla, almond extract, orange flower or rose water, brandy, or even pear or cherry eau-de-vie. Chocolate and cocoa offer interesting possibilities. Or the sweetener can be left out of the batter and served on the side, for an interesting play of flavors, as in some of the improvisations.

Next to varying the flavorings, the other big option is the bread you use. Brioche will be buttery and yeasty; raisin bread fruity and cinnamony; fennel or rosemary bread will add herbal flavors that complement savory French toasts. The bread's texture will greatly affect the outcome: Coarse peasant bread needs time to soak up the custard and will produce a toast that is appealingly chewy and robust. The best all-purpose bread is an unsliced white sandwich or Pullman loaf, a blank palette for endless flavor improvisations. A softer bread will soak up the custard quickly and make a more traditional French toast with a creamy center. The thicker the slice of bread, the longer it will take to absorb the custard.

Slices ¾ inch and thicker can be covered during cooking to help the custard cook through.

. . . . . .

## French-Fried Cheese Toast  Serves 4

2 large eggs, preferably organic

⅔ cup milk, whole or low fat (2%), or half-and-half, depending upon how rich
  you want the custard to be

¼ teaspoon kosher salt

Pinch of cayenne pepper

Freshly ground black pepper

¾ cup plus 1½ tablespoons grated Parmigiano

Four ½-inch slices white sandwich bread

About 2 tablespoons unsalted butter

**Make the custard.** In a shallow pan large enough to hold the bread slices side by side, whisk together the eggs, milk, and salt.

**Add the flavorings and/or any sweetener.** Stir in the cayenne, pepper, and Parmigiano. Whisk to combine.

**Soak the bread in the custard.** Arrange the bread in the custard and poke holes in it with a fork to help it absorb the liquid. Let sit several minutes, until the bottom side is soft, then carefully flip the slices to coat the other side. Soak until the bread has absorbed most of the liquid, turning once or twice, at least 10 minutes.

**Fry the toast.** Heat two heavy 10- or 12-inch nonstick skillets over medium-high heat. Add 2 teaspoons of the butter to each pan and swirl to coat. When the butter stops sizzling and is fragrant, carefully place 2 soaked bread slices in each pan. (Once you place the slices, do not move them, or you will disturb the coating.) Lower the heat to medium and cook until the bottom is golden, about 3 minutes. Flip the slices, adding additional butter if necessary; cook 2 to 3 minutes longer, or until the custard is set and the second side is golden.

# Improvisations

### Chive French Toast    Serves 4

*In another foray into making a savory rather than a sweet French toast, I added minced chives to the unsweetened custard for a chewy, holey peasant bread. It was like a warm onion bread, chewy-crisp on the outside, eggy and delicious inside. Serve it cut into squares as an hors d'oeuvre with drinks or with sour cream and smoked salmon for an unexpected brunch.*

In a shallow pan large enough to hold the bread slices side by side, whisk together 2 large eggs, ⅔ cup milk, and ¼ plus ⅛ teaspoon salt. Stir in 2 tablespoons minced fresh chives.

Arrange four ½-inch slices peasant or white sandwich bread in the custard and poke holes in it with a fork to help it absorb the liquid. Let sit several minutes, until the bottom side is soft, then carefully flip the slices to coat the other side. Soak until the toast has absorbed most of the liquid, turning once or twice, at least 15 minutes.

Heat two heavy 10- or 12-inch nonstick skillets over moderately high heat. Add 2 teaspoons butter to each pan and swirl to coat. When the butter stops sizzling and is fragrant, carefully place 2 soaked bread slices in each one. (Once you place the slices, do not move them, or you will disturb the coating.) Lower the heat slightly. When the underside is deep brown and releases easily from the pan, after about 3 minutes, turn the slices over with a spatula, adding more butter to the pans as you lift each one to flip it. Cook until the underside is deep brown, 2 or 3 minutes longer.

### Bittersweet Chocolate French Toast    Serves 4

*"What would happen if," I asked myself, "I melted really great chocolate into a French toast custard?" I panfried thick slices of bread soaked in a barely sweet chocolate custard-soaked bread and served them with little mounds of granulated sugar on the side. You dip each bite in the sugar; bitter and sweet hit the tongue all at once, making a surprising, complex, and satisfying dessert, a cross between warm beignets and chocolate soufflé.*

Cut four ¾-inch slices from a white sandwich or Pullman loaf and trim off the crusts. Place in a shallow pan large enough to hold the bread slices side by side.

Combine 1⅓ cups whole or low-fat (2%) milk, 4 ounces bittersweet (at least 70% cocoa solids) chocolate, coarsely chopped, and 2 teaspoons sugar in a small saucepan; heat over very low heat, whisking frequently, until the chocolate is melted. Set aside to cool 15 minutes.

In a medium bowl, beat 4 large eggs with ½ teaspoon salt; slowly whisk in the chocolate mixture and 2 teaspoons vanilla extract.

Pour the chocolate custard over the bread; with a spatula, lift up each bread slice to allow the custard to flow under it. Refrigerate, turning once or twice, until the bread has absorbed the custard, at least 4 hours, or overnight.

Heat two heavy 10- to 12-inch nonstick skillets over medium-high heat. Add 2 teaspoons unsalted butter to each and swirl to coat the pans. When the butter stops sizzling and is fragrant, carefully place 2 soaked bread slices in each one. (Once you place the slices, do not move them, or you will disturb the coating.) Lower the heat to low and cook, covered, until just golden on the bottom and the custard has begun to firm up. Flip the bread, adding more butter to the pans if necessary; cover and cook until the toasts are firm, 5 minutes longer. Uncover and cook until brown and crusty, taking care that the toasts don't burn, 2 minutes longer on each side. To serve, place one toast on each of 4 dinner plates and mound a small pile of granulated sugar—about 1 tablespoon each—alongside for dipping.

### Jill's Sea-Salted French Toast   Serves 4

*My assistant, Jill Anton, figured out a perfect solution for people who don't like the blast of sweet in classic breakfast French toast. She leaves the custard unsweetened and serves the toast lightly sprinkled with sea salt. Maple syrup is served in little bowls on the side, for dipping or pouring over the toast. It works in the same way a pinch of sea salt illuminates the flavors of a caramel.*

In a shallow pan large enough to hold the bread slices side by side, whisk together 4 large eggs, 1⅓ cups milk, and ⅓ teaspoon kosher salt. Arrange four ¾-inch slices white sandwich bread in the custard and poke holes in it with a fork to help it absorb the liquid. Let sit several minutes, until the bottom side is soft, then carefully flip the slices to coat the other side. Soak until the toast has absorbed most of the liquid, turning once or twice, at least 2 hours, or overnight.

Heat two heavy 10- or 12-inch nonstick skillets over medium-high heat. Add 2 or 3 teaspoons unsalted butter to each pan and swirl to coat the pans. When the butter stops sizzling and is fragrant, carefully place 2 soaked bread slices in each pan. (Once you place the slices, do not move them, or you will disturb the coating.) Lower the heat to medium, cover, and cook until the bottom is golden, 6 minutes. Flip the slices, adding additional butter if necessary; cover and cook until the custard is set and the toast is golden, 10 minutes longer. Sprinkle each serving with flaky sea salt, such as Maldon, or kosher salt, and serve maple syrup on the side.

### French Toast Gratin    Serves 8

*French toast baked in a casserole becomes a charming, rustic-looking dessert or brunch dish, with overtones of a bread pudding. Turbinado sugar sprinkled over the top before baking makes a crackly crust with a subtle caramel flavor. Assemble the casserole, without the pecans and final sprinkling of sugar, up to a day ahead and bake 45 minutes before serving.*

Butter a 13 × 9 × 2-inch baking dish and sprinkle the sides and bottom with ½ cup turbinado sugar. Cut six 1¼-inch slices from a white Pullman or sandwich loaf in half; then cut each half slice in half again to make squares. Arrange the squares in one layer in the dish so that the crust edges are placed randomly throughout, abutting crustless edges.

In a medium bowl, whisk together 7 large eggs, 3 cups milk, 1 cup heavy cream, 2 teaspoons vanilla extract, 1 teaspoon bourbon, and ½ teaspoon salt. Pour over the bread. Cover and chill until the bread has absorbed all the custard, at least 4 hours, or overnight.

Bring the bread to room temperature. Preheat the oven to 425°F. Push 2 cups toasted pecans down into the seams between the slices and along the edges, so that they are level with the top of the bread. Sprinkle the top evenly with an additional ½ cup turbinado sugar. Bake until puffed and golden, about 35 minutes. Serve warm.

# Shallot (or Garlic) Toasts

For years, my favorite way of making more of a simple soup, stew, or salad was to serve it with rustic toasts brushed with olive oil and rubbed with a cut clove of garlic to gently perfume them. Then I thought, Why not rub the toasts with a cut shallot instead of garlic? The result was shalloty toasts, a superquick version of onion bread. It's a good example of the way a simple shift in thinking on the obvious can yield something really useful. Both Shallot and Garlic Toasts have endless uses.

When the cut side of a garlic clove or a shallot is rubbed across rough toast, its juices are released, permeating the toast with flavor. Theoretically, you could do this with other members of the onion family, from scallions to the pungent ramps that grow wild in the spring.

Shallot (or Garlic) Toasts are not only fine accompaniments to dishes such as fish soups or stews such as Tuscan Island–Style Shellfish Stew (page 174), or an Herb Salad (page 112), they also make great bases on which to improvise. To make bruschetta and crostini for hors d'oeuvres, top them as they come out of the oven with savory mixtures from thinly sliced prosciutto or smoked salmon to ripe summer tomatoes, chopped and seasoned with salt, olive oil, and herbs.

The toasts can be embellished before baking with shredded cheeses to make crisp-chewy cheese toasts, or with cured fatty meats such as pancetta, bacon, or guanciale for the ultimate ham sandwich.

There is an ever-expanding selection of artisanal breads to choose from—sour dough to whole grain to herb or seed-laced breads. My favorite all-purpose breads for rustic toasts are chewy, crusty, holey, white flour–based peasant breads or baguettes, for their satisfying texture and the way they take to flavors without losing their own character.

How you slice the bread offers lots of possibilities. Baguettes can be sliced on an extreme diagonal to make dramatic long, narrow slices. Slicing loaves lengthwise, with the knife running parallel to the work surface, will yield large slabs of bread that can be toasted as is or cut into smaller pieces. For a more tender toast, trim off the crusts.

. . . . . .

## Shallot (or Garlic) Toasts    Serves 4

> Four ½-inch slices crusty peasant bread or baguette
> 1 tablespoon extra virgin olive oil or unsalted butter, melted
> 1 shallot or 2 garlic cloves, halved
> About ½ teaspoon kosher or coarse sea salt

**Brush the bread slices with the olive oil.** Preheat the oven to 425°F. Arrange the bread slices on a baking sheet and brush both sides with the olive oil or melted butter.

**Toast the bread** until golden, 2 to 3 minutes.

**Rub each slice lightly with a cut shallot or garlic clove;** sprinkle with salt.

**Note:** If you are in a hurry, toast the bread slices, without oil, in a toaster or toaster oven. When golden, brush each slice with extra virgin olive oil and rub lightly with a halved shallot or garlic clove; sprinkle with salt. (These are a little less chewy.)

## Improvisations

### Simple Bruschetta and Crostini Improvisations

*Shallot (and Garlic) Toasts make great bases for bruschetta or crostini, topped with savory leftovers such as:*

Slow-Roasted Tomatoes (page 95). Coarsely chop, pile on, drizzle with extra virgin olive oil, and sprinkle with fresh herbs.

Ramp, Garlic, and Other Oniony Confits (page 53). Drain the garlic or ramps and mash onto the toasts. Sprinkle with a few grains of sea salt.

Ragout of Green Soybeans (page 140). Drain some of the beans and mash onto the toasts. Garnish with a few slivers of lemon zest and Parmigiano.

Caramelized Onions (page 143). Spoon some onions onto each toast. Top each with a thin shaving of ricotta salata or aged goat cheese and a few grindings of fresh black pepper.

White Beans with Fried Sage Leaves (page 167). Spoon some white beans onto each toast. Garnish with the crispy sage leaves.

Impromptu Rillettes (page 243). Spread each toast with some rillettes. Sprinkle a few grains of coarse salt and some freshly ground black pepper over the top.

Ricotta cheese. Gently warm the cheese and spread on the toasts; sprinkle with a few chopped oregano leaves.

## Pancetta Tartines

*Inspired by the Onion Tartines on page 144, I roasted slabs of peasant bread with thin slices of pancetta on top; as the fat renders out of the pancetta, it bastes the bread, leaving the bottom and the pancetta top crisp, the center tender. It is at once indulgent, elemental, and somehow slightly taboo, a perfect hors d'oeuvre or snack.*

Preheat the oven to 375°F. Cut ½-inch slices from a loaf of rustic peasant or sourdough bread and trim the crusts. Brush the slices on one side with extra virgin olive oil. Rub both sides with a cut clove of garlic. Arrange the slices oiled side down on a baking sheet. Cover each slice completely with a thin slice of pancetta or guanciale (cured pork cheeks); they should overhang the edges a little. Grind over some pepper. Bake until the bottoms are golden and crisp, 25 minutes. Serve at once.

## Smoke-Grilled Bread

*This is my makeshift way of smoking bread on the stovetop so that it tastes as if it has been grilled over a wood fire. Use it as you would Shallot (or Garlic) Toasts.*

Heat a large cast-iron skillet over moderate heat until very hot, about 5 minutes. Pile a scant tablespoon smoking chips, such as mesquite, hickory, or alderwood, or a 1-inch piece of grapevine in the bottom of the pan. Place a round footed rack in the skillet. Brush ½-inch slices of peasant bread with extra virgin olive oil. When the chips begin to smoke, arrange the slices on the rack. Cover and toast 3 to 4 minutes on each side, until golden. Rub each slice with a halved garlic clove or shallot and sprinkle lightly with kosher salt or coarse sea salt. Serve at once.

## Manchego Toasts    Serves 4

*If you slice a holey bread thin and bake it with shredded aged cheese, some of the cheese will melt through the holes and caramelize on the pan, to make delight-fully chewy, caramelized cheese toasts. When cool, they become more cracker-like. Serve them alongside soups or rustic bean dishes, or as an hors d'oeuvre.*

Preheat the oven to 375°F. Coarsely shred 4 ounces or more of Manchego, aged Gouda, or Gruyère and toss with a pinch or two of pimentón de la Vera or another sweet, smoky paprika or some fresh thyme leaves. Slice a peas-ant loaf or baguette (preferably somewhat holey) lengthwise, with the knife running parallel, to the work surface, into two or three ¼-inch slices and trim off the crusts; or, alternatively, slice a baguette on an extreme di-agonal into eight ¼-inch slices. Brush one side of each slice with extra vir-gin olive oil and arrange oiled side down on a baking sheet. Rub each side lightly with a cut clove of garlic and top with a thin, even layer of shredded cheese. Bake 7 to 8 minutes, until the cheese is bubbling and the toasts are golden with crisp edges.

# Risotto with Dry Sherry and Lemon

I devised this recipe as a way of making a worthy risotto with canned chicken broth and little else in the larder. Dry sherry and lemon—which I always have on hand—provide a rich, nuanced flavor that more than makes up for lackluster broth and allows the flavor of the rice—another pantry staple—to shine through. I use Carnaroli rice because of its lovely balance of tenderness and firmness, with its truly luxurious creaminess. This risotto can be served as a main course or as a side dish to accompany roasted or braised chicken, rabbit, game birds, or shellfish preparations. It makes a fine base on which to spoon shredded left-over meats or poultry, braised wild mushrooms, or roasted onions or root vegetables.

Replace the fino sherry in this recipe with dry white wine, and use saffron instead of lemon zest, and you have a classic risotto Milanese, THE most basic formula for any kind of risotto you make. Using this model, there are literally hundreds of possibilities for manipulating the broth, wine, cheese, and embellishments to improvise interesting risottos.

Risotto recipes generally call for real chicken broth—something busy cooks don't always have on hand—because of its purity of flavor. If you wish to use canned chicken broth, plan to add flavorings to either the broth or the risotto and use very low-sodium brands of broth, which generally have a truer flavor than high-sodium ones. Or simmer the broth with chicken, duck, or rabbit trimmings and trimmings from any vegetable you might wish to add to the risotto, as well as wild mushrooms, saffron, spices, or herbs. Vegetable, beef, and seafood broths can be used as well. (The lobster broth on page 193 is spectacular.) To make dessert risottos (in essence, rice puddings), use milk instead of broth, in tandem with a sweetener such as sugar or honey.

The wine is another opportunity for flavoring a risotto, as in this one; red wine, sherry or Madeira, or an herbal white wine can make interestingly flavored risottos for little work. Vegetables stirred into the cooking rice will give their flavors to the broth and provide texture and distinct character. Add longer-cooking vegetables such as winter squash early in the process; add quicker-cooking vegetables such as leafy greens later.

Last-minute flavorings for risotto include herbs, particularly soft-leaf ones such as basil, chives, chervil, and flat-leaf parsley; spices—ground pepper, saffron, coriander; citrus zest; and white truffles. Parmigiano, traditionally added at the end, acts like a great salt to enrich and complete the risotto; use other hard-grating cheeses for their unique flavors. A Spanish Manchego, for example, would complement this sherry-based risotto, an example of "foods that grow together, go together."

For rustic, chewy-creamy "risottos," replace the rice with whole grains, such as farro, barley, and brown rice; use additional broth and cook the grains longer. You can even plug pasta into the basic approach, as in the Lobster Noodles on page 195.

. . . . . .

# Risotto with Dry Sherry and Lemon    Serves 4 as a main course, 6 as an appetizer

5 to 6 cups homemade or canned low-sodium chicken broth

2 tablespoons unsalted butter or olive oil

1/4 to 1/3 cup finely chopped shallots or onions

1 1/2 cups (10 ounces) Italian rice for risotto, such as Carnaroli, Vialone Nano, or Arborio

1/2 cup dry sherry, such as Tío Pepe or La Ina

1 teaspoon grated lemon zest

One 1-inch strip lemon zest, slivered

3/4 cup grated Parmigiano

Kosher salt and freshly ground black pepper

1 to 2 tablespoons heavy cream, crème fraîche, or sour cream (optional)

**Heat the broth with flavorings, if desired.** In a medium saucepan, bring the chicken broth to a boil over high heat, lower the heat to maintain a simmer until ready to use.

**Sauté the shallots and rice.** In a large heavy saucepan over medium-low heat, combine the butter and shallots, cover, and cook, stirring occasionally, until the shallots are translucent, about 4 minutes. Uncover, increase the heat to moderate, and cook, stirring, until the shallots are golden, about 1 1/2 minutes longer. Add the rice and cook, stirring constantly, until the grains look chalky with a white dot in the center of each, 4 to 5 minutes. Do not allow the rice to brown.

**Add the wine, flavorings, and broth in increments.** Add about 1/3 cup of the sherry and cook, stirring, until it has been absorbed by the rice. Stir in 1/2 cup of the broth. Cook at a very low boil, stirring frequently, until the liquid is almost absorbed, 3 to 5 minutes. Continue adding the broth in this fashion, 1/2 cup at a time, until the rice is tender yet still firm in the center and the risotto is creamy but not soupy. This will take about 25 minutes. Stir in the remaining sherry and the grated and slivered zest.

**Enrich the risotto and adjust the seasoning.** Stir in 1/4 cup of the cheese and salt to taste. Pepper generously and add the cream, if desired. Serve at once, passing the remaining cheese on the side.

### Warm Dessert Risotto with Bay Leaf and Vanilla    Makes about 6 cups, 6 to 8 servings

*Arborio, one of the more tender-cooking risotto rices, is perfect for dessert risottos and rice puddings. Its abundant starches bind with milk to make a rich, custardy sauce without eggs or cream; bay leaf and vanilla give it a haunting flavor.*

In a large heavy saucepan, bring 6 cups whole milk to a simmer over moderate heat; add ¾ cup sugar and ½ teaspoon salt and stir to dissolve. With a thin sharp knife, slice 1 vanilla bean in half lengthwise and scrape out the seeds; add the seeds and pod to the milk. Stir in 1½ cups arborio rice and 1 medium imported bay leaf (California bay leaves are too strong) and cook over medium-low heat, stirring frequently, until the rice is very tender and suspended in a thick custardlike sauce, 35 to 40 minutes. If the risotto is getting too thick and the rice still needs cooking, stir in additional milk, ¼ cup at a time. Allow the risotto to cool to warm or room temperature before serving. Discard the vanilla bean.

To rewarm, place the pan over a medium-low flame and stir, adding milk a tablespoon at a time, until creamy and warm. Alternatively, keep the risotto warm in a double boiler.

### Crispy Panfried Risotto Cakes

*The best way to use up leftover risotto is to form it into cakes and panfry them until the outside is crisp and the interior creamy. Serve them hot out of the pan as an hors d'oeuvre or snack, or with a salad for a simple meal. To get a really crisp crust, I dust the cakes with Wondra flour or white rice flour (see page 203), although all-purpose flour will do. Use a simple risotto—that is, without vegetables, meats, or seafood, which can make the cakes fall apart.*

Shape leftover risotto into 2½-inch patties about ½ inch thick (about ¼ cup risotto each). Sprinkle a layer of Wondra flour, rice flour, or all-purpose flour in a shallow dish and nestle the formed cakes into it. Sift more flour over the top to coat lightly. In a nonstick or well-seasoned cast-iron skillet, heat a thin film of extra virgin olive oil over moderate heat. When hot but not smoking, use a metal spatula to transfer the cakes—be sure to knock off excess flour—into the pan. Cook until golden, 3 to 4 minutes on each side, taking care not to break the cakes when you flip them. Repeat with as much risotto as you have.

Another approach is to spread leftover risotto 1 inch thick on a buttered jelly-roll pan or in an ovenproof skillet. Sprinkle the top liberally with grated Parmigiano and bake in a preheated 475°F oven until the top is golden and crisp, about 20 minutes. Cut into squares or wedges.

## Farro Risotto with Red Wine and Rosemary    Serves 4

*One evening I used farro, an Italian grain with a sweet, subtle barley-hazelnut flavor, instead of rice in a red wine risotto I learned to make from my friend Alan Tardi. This earthy risotto is lovely on its own as well as for a side dish for roasted game meats and poultry, and can serve as a model for other whole-grain risottos, such as barley or brown rice.*

In a medium saucepan, bring 6 cups homemade or canned low-sodium chicken broth to a boil over high heat; lower the heat to maintain a simmer until ready to use.

In a large heavy saucepan, melt 2 teaspoons each butter and extra virgin olive oil over low heat. Add ¼ cup finely chopped shallots or onions and a 2-inch fresh rosemary sprig; cover and cook, stirring occasionally, until the shallots are translucent, about 4 minutes. Uncover, increase the heat to moderate, and cook, stirring, until they are golden. Add 1½ cups farro and cook, stirring constantly, 2 minutes. Do not allow the farro to brown.

Add 1½ cups dry red wine and cook, stirring, until the wine has been absorbed by the farro. Stir in ½ cup of the chicken broth. Simmer, stirring frequently, until the liquid is almost absorbed, 3 to 5 minutes. Continue adding the broth in this fashion, ½ cup at a time, until the farro is tender and the mixture is fairly creamy but not soupy, 55 to 60 minutes. If you need more liquid, add boiling water ¼ cup at a time. Discard the rosemary and stir in about ¼ cup grated Parmigiano and pepper to taste; adjust the seasoning. Pass additional grated cheese on the side.

## Lobster Paella    Serves 6

*Paella is risotto's Spanish cousin; it shares the same type of medium-grain rice and general approach, to a different end. Because paellas are not stirred, rather than being creamy, the grains are firm and separate, dry on top and moist and melded together in the center, with a crunchy crust on the bottom.*

*This paella made with Lobster Essence (page 193) has such a rich lobster flavor a friend proclaimed it "better than eating a lobster." Although it is completely satisfying as is, you can gild the lily by adding slices of chorizo, peeled raw shrimp or strips of chicken, and/or roasted red peppers during the last few minutes of cooking.*

In a medium saucepan, heat 6 cups Lobster Essence (page 193); crumble in a large pinch of saffron and bring to a simmer over moderate heat.

Heat 2 tablespoons extra virgin olive oil in a very large (14-inch) nonstick or seasoned cast-iron skillet. Sauté ¼ cup finely chopped shallots until golden, about 3 minutes. Add 1 pound short-grain rice, such as Italian Arborio or Spanish granza, and sauté until barely golden, about 4 minutes. Pour in the warm broth and stir to combine. Cook at a gentle boil, without stirring, 35 to 40 minutes, until all of the liquid has been absorbed and the rice is tender. During the last 15 minutes, periodically stir the top of the rice into the center, without disturbing the brown crust on the bottom. If the rice needs more liquid, add boiling water in ¼-cup increments. Five or 10 minutes before the paella is done, nestle thin slices of chorizo or any other embellishments, if desired, into the rice.

Cover the paella with a tea towel and let rest 5 to 10 minutes before serving. Serve the paella directly from the pan, making sure to scrape up some of the crispy layer that has formed on the bottom.

# Sage-and-Garlic Popcorn

- Brown Butter Popcorn
- Caramelized Shallot Popcorn
- Rosemary Popcorn
- Smoky Bacon Popcorn
- White Truffle Popcorn

My improvisations with popcorn arose out of an attempt to panfry white beans in sage-and-garlic-flavored oil. The beans came out crispy with a flavor that reminded me of popcorn. I considered calling them "popcorn beans," then I thought: Why not actually try the oil on popcorn, instead of the usual melted butter? So I made a quick garlic-and-sage-flavored olive oil to drizzle over hot popcorn and used the crispy sage as a garnish.

It proved to be an addictive, grown-up popcorn to serve with cocktails or wine, while watching TV, or anytime you want a crunchy snack. I've been known to take it to the movies. It was just the beginning of a continuing exploration into popcorn possibilities.

I use an inexpensive hot-air popper that pops corn kernels in minutes without oil. If you pop your corn in a microwave, use plain kernels; steer clear of those with "butter flavor" or other additives. If you don't want to pop your own, use unflavored store-bought popcorn.

The classic flavoring for popcorn is melted butter, a liquid fat. Using other flavorful fats is an unlimited strategy for improvising. Simmering garlic and sage in olive oil is just one example of the different kinds of flavored oils that could be made to dress popcorn, using thinly sliced shallots, leeks, or ramps (wild leeks); herbs, such as rosemary, thyme, savory, or sage, singly or in combination; spices, such as ground or cracked coriander, fennel seed, curry powder, or ground chili powders. (Read the "Understanding" section on page 50 for in-depth thinking on making flavored oils.) The by-products of many of these flavored fats are delicious crispy bits, such as shallots, sage leaves, or garlic chips, which make a nice counterpoint to the popcorn. For a buttery-flavored oil, mix extra virgin olive oil with unsalted butter; butter alone would burn from the prolonged heat. Rendering bacon yields a smoky fat and crisp pieces of bacon. Here's the basic formula for dressing popcorn: ½ cup kernels yields about 12 cups popcorn, which needs about ¼ cup fat to flavor it.

Grated sharp cheeses make a satisfying, deeply flavored, and additive-free cheese popcorn. Toss hot buttered or olive oil–dressed popcorn liberally with grated Parmigiano, pecorino Romano, or aged Gouda.

If you don't want to pour fat on your popcorn, use a seasoned salt (not commercial garlic or onion salt, which has an acrid flavor). Consider Real Garlic Salt (page 46), fragrant Moroccan-Style Seasoning (page 46), or the Japanese seasoning called gomasio, a toasted sesame-flavored salt; or improvise salts with crushed cumin, fennel or coriander seeds, pink or Szechuan peppercorns, . . . and so on, using the method outlined on page 45.

Exotically flavored popcorns make terrific gifts. Bear in mind, though, if you want to make popcorn well in advance of eating it, that butter-dressed popcorn doesn't stay as crisp as popcorn dressed with oil.

. . . . . .

# Sage-and-Garlic Popcorn    Makes 12 cups, 4 to 6 servings

½ cup white or yellow popping corn kernels
2 tablespoons unsalted peanut or canola oil (if necessary)

### Sage-and-Garlic Butter
3 tablespoons unsalted butter
2 tablespoons extra virgin olive oil
8 to 10 medium garlic cloves, thinly sliced (about ¼ cup)
½ cup loosely packed fresh sage leaves (about 40)
Fine sea salt or kosher salt

**Pop the popcorn.** Pop the kernels in a hot-air popper or a microwave according to the manufacturer's instructions. Or, to pop on the stovetop, pour the peanut oil into a large saucepan (at least 4 quarts). Heat over medium heat until hot but not smoking. Add a few kernels and cover. When they pop, the oil is hot enough. Add the popping corn kernels and cover. Shake the pan back and forth on the burner, holding down the lid if necessary. Cook, shaking, until the popping stops, 3 to 4 minutes. Pour the popcorn into a large bowl.

**Make a flavorful fat.** In a large nonstick skillet, combine the butter, olive oil, and garlic. Cover and cook over low heat, stirring frequently, until the garlic is barely golden, about 5 minutes. Uncover and cook until the garlic is crisp and golden, about 1 minute; do not allow it to brown. With a slotted spoon, transfer the garlic to a plate lined with paper toweling. Add the sage leaves to the skillet and cook, turning once, until the leaves are darkened, fragrant, and crisp, 2 to 3 minutes. Drain the leaves on paper towels. Remove the oil from the heat.

**Toss the popcorn with the fat.** Drizzle the sage oil over the popcorn, tossing it with tongs to distribute it evenly. Then sprinkle the popcorn liberally with salt and toss again. Scatter the crispy sage leaves and garlic over the popcorn and serve at once.

### Brown Butter Popcorn   Makes 12 cups, 4 to 6 servings

*Brown butter is butter toasted in a pan until it smells like roasting nuts. It takes classic buttered popcorn a big step further with no extra effort, deepening the flavor with roasty caramel overtones.*

For **brown butter,** melt ⅓ cup unsalted butter in a small saucepan over moderately low heat until the clear fat is amber colored and smells like roasted nuts.

Place 12 cups popcorn (from ½ cup kernels) in a large bowl. Drizzle the brown butter over, tossing it to distribute it evenly. Then sprinkle the popcorn liberally with salt and toss again.

### Caramelized Shallot Popcorn   Makes 12 cups, 4 to 6 servings

*If you thinly slice shallots crosswise and fry them in peanut oil, you get something like tiny onion rings, along with a shallot-flavored oil. They are a perfect match for popcorn.*

For **Caramelized Shallots** and **shallot oil,** in a medium (10-inch) heavy skillet over medium-high heat, combine ¼ cup peanut oil and 5 to 6 medium shallots, thinly sliced crosswise (¾ cup). Simmer until the shallots are golden and crispy, 8 to 10 minutes. Scoop the shallots out of the oil with a slotted spoon, drain, and transfer to a plate; sprinkle with sea salt.

Place 12 cups popcorn (from ½ cup kernels) in a large bowl. Drizzle the shallot oil over, tossing it to distribute it evenly. Then sprinkle the popcorn liberally with salt and toss again. Scatter the crispy shallots over the top.

### Rosemary Popcorn   Makes 12 cups, 4 to 6 servings

*Rosemary makes an appealingly fragrant popcorn.*

For **garlic and rosemary oil,** in a large nonstick skillet, combine ¼ cup extra virgin olive oil, 2 medium garlic cloves, thinly sliced, and 2 tablespoons minced fresh rosemary. Cover and cook over low heat, stirring frequently, until the garlic is barely golden, about 5 minutes. Uncover and cook until the garlic is crisp and golden, about 1 minute.

Place 12 cups popcorn (from ½ cup kernels) in a large bowl. Drizzle the rosemary oil over, tossing it to distribute it evenly. Then sprinkle the popcorn liberally with salt and toss again.

### Smoky Bacon Popcorn     Makes 12 cups, 4 to 6 servings

*This is a completely over-the-top popcorn that makes perfect sense when you think of the affinity of bacon and corn. Since bacons vary wildly, it's difficult to calculate exactly how much fat it will yield when cooked. If you have more fat than you need, store it in a little jar in the fridge to use in the future.*

Slice about 6 ounces bacon, preferably applewood-smoked, crosswise ¼ inch thick, and place in a medium heavy skillet. Cook, covered, over medium-low heat until the bacon is crisp, about 7 minutes. Use a slotted spoon to transfer the bacon to a plate; measure ¼ cup liquid bacon fat.

Place 12 cups popcorn in a large bowl. Drizzle the bacon fat over the popcorn, tossing it to distribute it evenly. Then sprinkle the popcorn liberally with sea salt and toss again. Scatter the crisp bacon over the popcorn.

### White Truffle Popcorn     Makes 12 cups, 4 to 6 servings

*It's worth investing in a small bottle of white truffle oil just to make this popcorn. Two or three teaspoons will flavor 12 cups of popcorn, so it's an inexpensive way to get a heady dose of truffle.*

Combine 4 tablespoons (½ stick) unsalted butter, melted, or extra virgin olive oil with 2½ to 3 teaspoons white truffle oil, or to taste. Place 12 cups popcorn in a large bowl. Drizzle the truffle butter over the popcorn, tossing well to coat. Season liberally with salt.

# Macaroni and Cheese with Extra Top

- Saffron Pasta Gratin
- Fried Mac-and-Cheese
- Unbelievably Rich Manchego Gratin
- Frittata di Pasta

I once won an informal, but heated, macaroni-and-cheese cook-off with a leaner version that was so good no one ever guessed it was missing quantities of fat. Over the years I've continued to improvise on the basic approach, and I use an easy-to-make pasta cream–pasta boiled in milk and pureed–for an exceptionally creamy base while eliminating a few hundred calories. (see Pasta Cream, page 290). Because there is never enough crusty top, half the macaroni and cheese is baked in a casserole and half is baked in a flat sheet pan, to make an extra pan of crust.

Macaroni and cheese is basically an American version of a classic French noodle gratin: shredded cheeses melted into a creamy liquid, then mixed with cooked pasta and baked in a casserole until the top is crisp and golden, the center molten. Each element—cheese, creamy base, and pasta—offers possibilities for improvising. The permutations on this basic formula are endless.

The real lesson in my leaner version is the power of great cheeses to provide complex flavor and satisfying richness. Choose pungent aged cheeses, such as Manchego, Asiago, Raclette, or Boucheron. For an American-style mac-and-cheese, use sharp Vermont Cheddar and a hard aged Gouda or Monterey Jack to take it from the ordinary to the memorable. For a classic French-style gratin, use Gruyère and/or Parmigiano. Figure about ½ to 1 pound cheese per pound of pasta; the harder and more pungent the cheese, the less you'll need (this translates to about 2½ cups grated Parmigiano, about 4 cups Cheddar, and so on). Or blend cheeses, say, Italian Fontina, Gruyère, Bel Paese, and Parmigiano to make a "maccheroni quatro formaggi." Melting the cheeses into the base allows you to taste for cheesiness, adding more until you get the level you like.

To create a creamy base, I use a faux cream I devised by cooking pasta in milk and pureeing it; it has a silky texture and tastes as if it's made with butter. It simmers while I prep the other parts of the dish. There are several other possible creamy bases you can use instead to save time or achieve different textures. The more fat your base has, the richer the gratin will be, and the less you'll need to use. For an exceptionally rich casserole, for 1 pound of pasta, figure 2½ cups or more heavy cream, crème fraîche, or evaporated milk; or 3 cups milk whisked with 4 or 5 beaten egg yolks over low heat until thick but not boiling; or 3½ to 4 cups of a starch- or flour-thickened milk or classic cream sauce per pound of pasta.

And then, there are embellishments. Layer in sautéed greens such as chard or spinach; caramelized onions, leeks, or shallots (ramps would be great); sautéed wild mushrooms; roasted peppers; oven-roasted tomatoes; slivered prosciutto; crisp bacon. Flavor with minced fresh herbs, saffron, ancho chile powder, cracked coriander, pepper mixes, or a few scrapings of grated nutmeg.

. . . . . .

# Macaroni and Cheese with Extra Top   Serves 6

Pasta Cream

   1 quart whole or 2% fat milk

   ½ cup water

   1 small shallot, peeled, halved, and stuck with a clove

   1 small imported bay leaf

   ¼ teaspoon kosher salt

   2 ounces dried eggless pasta, such as elbow macaroni (⅓ cup) or thin
      spaghetti, broken into 2-inch pieces

   8 ounces sharp Vermont Cheddar, shredded (2½ to 3 cups)

   8 ounces aged Monterey Jack or aged Gouda, grated (2 to 2½ cups)

   ¼ to ½ teaspoon sweet Hungarian paprika, ancho chile powder,
      or sweet smoky pimentón de la Vera

   Kosher salt and freshly ground black pepper

   1 pound elbow macaroni

   ½ teaspoon softened butter or vegetable oil

**Prepare the creamy base.** Rinse a medium saucepan with cold water and add the milk, water, shallot, bay leaf, and salt. Bring to a gentle boil and stir in the pasta; cook, stirring occasionally, until the pasta is very soft, 10 or 15 minutes longer than the package directions. Discard the shallot and bay leaf and ladle about ¼ cup of the pasta mixture into a blender container; cover, leaving the center steam cap open (to prevent the hot liquid from spurting). Blend the mixture on low. With the motor running, gradually ladle in more liquid; blend on high for 1 to 2 minutes, until the mixture is perfectly smooth. You should have 3½ to 4 cups. Return it to the saucepan.

**Add the cheese and flavorings.** Set aside ½ cup each Cheddar and aged Jack. Stir the remaining cheeses and the paprika into the Pasta Cream. Cook, stirring, over low heat until the cheese is barely melted. Remove from the heat and add salt and pepper to taste.

**Cook the pasta and prepare the pans.** Preheat the oven to 425°F. Bring a large pot of water to a boil; salt liberally. Add the macaroni and cook until it is almost tender but still quite firm to the bite. Meanwhile, lightly butter the inside of a 2-quart ovenproof casserole (13 × 9 inches or an 11 × 8-inch oval) and a 13 to 14 × 9-inch baking sheet; set aside.

**Combine the pasta and cheese mixture.** Drain the pasta well and return to the pot. Stir in the cheese mixture and adjust the seasoning. Pour half the macaroni into the casserole and half onto the baking sheet, smoothing it into an even layer. Sprinkle the tops of both with the remaining cheeses.

**Bake.** Bake until the top is golden brown, about 30 minutes. Serve at once.

**Note:** You can assemble the casserole up to 2 hours ahead. Cover and leave at room temperature until ready to bake.

## Improvisations

### Saffron Pasta Gratin    Serves 6

*This elegant play on mac-and-cheese is like saffron-infused fettuccine Alfredo.*

Prepare the Pasta Cream. (Alternatively, you can make this dish with 2½ cups heavy cream.) Bring to a simmer over medium heat and stir in a large pinch of saffron, crumbled. Remove from the heat and stir in 2 cups grated Parmigiano; set aside.

Preheat the oven to 450°F. Boil 12 ounces egg fettuccine or 1 pound ziti in a large pot of salted water until it is barely tender but still quite firm to the bite. Drain well, return to the pot, and toss with the reserved cheese sauce. Season with salt and plenty of freshly ground black pepper. If the sauce is too thick, stir in a few tablespoons of half-and-half or heavy cream.

Pour into a 2-quart ovenproof casserole, such as a 13 to 14 × 9-inch oval. Sprinkle the top evenly with ¼ to ½ cup additional grated Parmigiano. Bake until the top is tinged with brown, 25 to 30 minutes. Serve at once.

### Fried Mac-and-Cheese

*On a dare I tried a recipe that involved boiling spaghetti for half an hour, mixing it with ketchup and Velveeta, molding it into a loaf, and, the next day, slicing and frying it in a skillet. Flying as it did against everything I believed in—such as not using processed foods and never overcooking pasta—I imagined it would be awful. In fact, it was delicious. I served it as an hors d'oeuvre with cocktails.*

*The lesson I learned from it was to panfry slices of a cold leftover cheese-and-pasta loaf—whether macaroni and cheese or a sophisticated saffron pasta gratin—until the outside is crisp, the interior molten. The elegance of presentation will depend on the thickness and neatness of your mac-and-cheese—and, hence, the slices. But it will all be delicious, and perfect for a homely supper or private snack.*

Slice chilled leftover macaroni and cheese into ⅓- to ½-inch slices. Sprinkle Wondra flour, rice flour, or grated Parmigiano into a pie plate and dredge the slices to coat each side. Heat some extra virgin olive oil or butter in a nonstick skillet until hot but not smoking. Lift the slices out of the flour, knock off the excess, and transfer them in one layer to the pan. Fry about 3 minutes on each side, until golden and crisp. Serve at once.

### Unbelievably Rich Manchego Gratin    Serves 6

*This is an over-the-top version of a classic French gratin, made with Spanish Manchego instead of Gruyère. It has a luxuriousness and purity of flavor that can only be achieved with cream.*

Preheat the oven to 450°F. Boil 1 pound ziti or penne in a large pot of salted water until it is almost tender but still quite firm to the bite. Drain the pasta and return to the pot. Add 2⅔ cups heavy cream and bring to a simmer over medium heat. Stir in 2 to 2½ cups shredded Manchego (8 ounces) and about ½ cup grated Parmigiano until barely melted; season with salt and plenty of freshly ground black pepper. Pour into a 2-quart ovenproof casserole, such as a 13 to 14 × 9-inch oval. Spoon ⅓ cup crème fraîche over the top. Bake until the top is tinged with brown, about 30 minutes. Serve at once.

### Frittata di Pasta    Serves 4 to 6

*I devised this frittata one night when I had a lot of unsauced pasta left over from a dinner party; it is a satisfying, stripped-down macaroni and cheese, perfect for an informal supper or lunch with a salad.*

Preheat the oven to 400°F. In a bowl, whisk together 6 eggs, ¼ cup milk, 1 cup grated Parmigiano, ¼ cup minced fresh chives, about 1 teaspoon salt, and freshly ground black pepper to taste. Stir in 4 cups cooked, drained egg fettuccine or any other pasta you like.

Heat 1 tablespoon extra virgin olive oil in a 10-inch nonstick skillet over medium heat until hot but not smoking. Pour the pasta mixture into the pan and smooth with a spatula. Sprinkle the top with an additional ¼ cup grated Parmigiano. Place in the oven and bake until set, about 20 minutes. Invert onto a plate, if desired, or serve right from the pan.

# Pasta with Pancetta or Guanciale and Sherry Vinegar

I constantly cannibalize my own recipes, taking a piece of one to plug into another, building and improvising endlessly on what I know. I especially like to improvise pasta dishes this way; the blank-canvas nature of pasta lends itself to many embellishments. So, one evening I lifted a section of the Squid Pasta recipe (page 201)—pancetta, garlic, and sherry vinegar, in league with some Parmigiano and black pepper, all long-keeping staples—to make a pasta sauce that is simple, rustic, and utterly satisfying, a great deal more than the sum of its parts. It is spectacular made with guanciale, cured pork cheeks, which are increasingly available in fine stores; they have a rich, luxurious texture and porky savor. Like pancetta, guanciale makes just about everything delicious. Because it is freezable, it is easy to keep on hand.

As a further elaboration, after you've rendered the pancetta, add a few cups of thinly sliced vegetables (about 1½ pounds), such as leeks, radicchio, greens, or wild mushrooms, to the fat with several tablespoons of water; cover and cook until tender. Then toss with the pasta as directed.

This recipe is an example of a simple, versatile formula for improvising pasta dishes: just-cooked pasta, plus a cooked, flavorful, slightly saucy embellishment, plus a few tablespoons of the hot pasta cooking water and some cheese. Pasta cooking water has the viscosity and some of the flavor of mild chicken broth; a few tablespoons emulsify the fat in the saucy embellishment, to gloss the pasta and spread its flavors. This technique can even transform simple grated cheese, butter, and black pepper, elements of a bare-bones larder, into a rustic, creamy sauce.

"Cooked, flavorful, and slightly saucy" can mean a great many things, as long as it has some fat in it for the cooking water to bind with. In fact, just a flavorful fat will do, from butter, pancetta, guanciale, or bacon fat (with the chewy rendered bits) to a flavored oil, such as Sage and Garlic Oil with Fried Sage Leaves (page 52). Or think olive paste or a pesto made with basil or sun-dried tomatoes; or cooked vegetables and beans, from simple sautés in garlic and olive oil to braises, stews, and roasted vegetables, as in Jumbo Shells with Peppers, Pine Nuts, and Molten Mozzarella (page 90). Leftovers will find new purpose in this pasta formula: bits of shredded long-cooked meat or poultry with some of the cooking juices; roasted vegetables; sautéed greens; beans; any from the long list in the following Simple Pasta Improvisations. The range of pastas to choose from is vast, from classic spaghetti to wild-shaped dried pastas to filled pastas such as ravioli and pansotti.

A hard grating or shaving cheese is an essential component, as it works like salt to bring out flavors and melts slightly to add creaminess and substance. This could be goes-with-everything Parmigiano, a hard aged goat cheese, pecorino Romano (used sparingly), or shards of ricotta salata. In addition, little cubes of smoked or fresh mozzarella can be a nice touch, thrown into the hot mix just before serving so the cheese is melted and stringy by the time it hits the plate.

Finishing touches can add instant personality. They include black or green olives; capers; toasted nuts, particularly pine nuts or walnuts; chopped fresh soft herbs, such as flat-leaf parsley or basil; lemon zest; and, finally, freshly ground black pepper.

## Pasta with Pancetta or Guanciale and Sherry Vinegar   Serves 4

> 4 ounces pancetta or guanciale, sliced into thin strips or pieces
> 1 tablespoon plus 1 teaspoon finely chopped garlic
> 1/4 teaspoon hot red pepper flakes
> Kosher salt
> 12 ounces narrow, tubular pasta, such as catanisella lunga, casarecci,
>    ziti or penne, or linguine or spaghetti
> 1/4 cup grated Parmigiano
> 2 teaspoons sherry or Banyuls vinegar
> Freshly ground black pepper or All-Purpose Aromatic Pepper (page 48)
> 1/3 cup chopped flat-leaf parsley (optional)

**Prepare or warm the sauce.** Place the pancetta in a large heavy skillet and cook, covered, over moderately low heat until golden brown and chewy (on the verge of crisp), about 6 minutes. Turn off the heat, let the pan cool for 30 seconds, and stir in the garlic and pepper flakes; continue stirring until the garlic is soft and golden. Set aside.

**Cook the pasta.** Bring a large pot of water to a boil; salt liberally and add the pasta. Cook until tender but still slightly firm to the bite. Drain, reserving 1/2 cup of the pasta water.

**Combine the pasta and sauce with some cooking water.** Heat the skillet of pancetta fat over moderately low heat for about 1 minute. Reduce the heat to low. Add the pasta and 1/4 cup of the pasta water; toss well. Add the Parmigiano and toss until the cheese is melted and creamy. If necessary, stir in a few more tablespoons of the pasta water so that the pasta is lightly glossed with the sauce. Stir in the vinegar and adjust the seasoning; pepper generously. Sprinkle with the parsley, if desired. Serve at once.

## Improvisations

### Simple Pasta Improvisations

*Use Pasta with Pancetta or Guanciale and Sherry Vinegar as a model for many improvisations, substituting the pancetta-garlic-hot pepper sauce with any recipes you can imagine doubling as a pasta sauce, like the ones listed below.*

Warm Vegetables with Anchovies, Currants, and Pine Nuts (page 58)

Sage and Garlic Oil with Fried Sage Leaves (page 52)

Basil, Lemon, and Tomato Oil (page 51)

Magic Peppers (page 89), chopped with additional oil

Slow-Roasted Tomato Sauce (page 96) or chopped Slow-Roasted
   Tomatoes (page 95)

Ragout of Green Soybeans with Rosemary and Thyme (page 140)

Caramelized Onions (page 143)

White Beans with Rosemary, Thyme, and Lavender (page 168)

White Beans with Fried Sage Leaves (page 167)

Tuscan Island–Style Shellfish Stew (page 174)

Essential Caesar Sauce (page 57)

Veal Shanks with Melting Onions and Lemon Gremolata (page 237),
   pulled off the bone and shredded

Warm the sauce, and cook the pasta in salted water; drain, reserving some of the pasta water. Add the sauce to the pasta pot and stir in a few tablespoons of the pasta water to loosen it slightly. Stir in the pasta, bring to a simmer, and add a little additional pasta water to moisten and slick the pasta with the sauce. Adjust the seasoning, pepper, and garnish, if desired, with chopped flat-leaf parsley. Serve, passing grated Parmigiano separately (except with seafood-based sauces).

### Ravioli with a Handful of Herbs     Serves 4

*Here I made a quick flavored oil with herbs I had in the fridge, then emulsified it with pasta cooking water. It makes a limpid, fragrant sauce for ravioli. Even in the dead of winter, this combination has a bright, summery flavor.*

*Vary the combination according to what herbs you have on hand. The rule of thumb when blending herbs is to use more of the milder herbs, such as parsley and basil, and small amounts of the powerful herbs, such as thyme and rose-*

*mary. Chives, tarragon, and sage fall somewhere in the middle. You can pretty much tell the balance of your herb mixture by smelling it or by tasting it once the herbs have been steeped in the oil. You can always add more of one herb or another to balance out the mixture. A few slivers of lemon zest do wonders to lift and balance the flavors. Sometimes I add shavings of ricotta salata at the last minute.*

In a small saucepan, combine ½ cup extra virgin olive oil, ¼ cup chopped flat-leaf parsley, ¼ cup fresh basil leaves, 2 tablespoons chopped fresh chives, 2 tablespoons chopped fresh sage, 2 teaspoons finely chopped fresh rosemary, 2 teaspoons finely chopped fresh thyme, 1 teaspoon finely chopped garlic, and ¼ teaspoon hot red pepper flakes. Set aside.

Bring a large pot of water to a boil; salt well. Add 4 servings of cheese ravioli and cook until al dente. A few minutes before the pasta is done, heat the herb mixture over low heat until it is fragrant and bright green, about 3 minutes; turn off the heat.

Drain the pasta, reserving about ½ cup of the cooking water. Return the pasta to the pot and pour the herb mixture over it, along with about ¼ cup of the cooking water. Turn the heat to medium and toss until the pasta is coated with herbs. Adjust the seasoning, peppering liberally. Serve at once, with grated Parmigiano on the side.

## Panfried Ravioli

*Ravioli are so dumplinglike—dough wrapped around a filling—that one day it occurred to me to panfry them, rather than boiling and saucing them. They are a cross between a blintz and a fried wonton, with a caramelized exterior and soft filling. Serve them with a sprinkling of sea salt or a pungent dipping sauce, such as Balsamic Caramel (page 64), Essential Caesar Sauce (page 57), without the lemon juice, or Roasted Romesco (page 91). My favorite ravioli for this is cheese, wild mushroom, or pumpkin. I always keep a good supply in the freezer.*

Boil some ravioli in salted water until al dente. Drain well, then blot dry with paper toweling. Over moderate heat, cook 2 or 3 teaspoons unsalted butter in a heavy skillet large enough to hold the ravioli in one layer. When the butter has just turned golden and smells like roasting nuts, add an equal amount of olive oil. Add the ravioli and cook until the bottom sides are golden, about 3 minutes; flip and continue cooking until the other sides are golden, 2 to 3 minutes. Serve at once.

## Pasta with Baby Artichokes   Serves 4

*The olive oil-stewed artichokes in Shrimp with Confited Baby Artichokes (page 199) were the inspiration for this simple pasta. The thinly sliced artichokes and garlic are cooked until they melt into a sauce, then tossed with a bite-sized dry pasta like strozzapreti. Baby artichokes have no chokes and are much easier to prepare than the large ones, so I use them when they're in season.*

You'll need 2 pounds baby artichokes. Squeeze a lemon into a medium bowl and fill it with cold water. Working with 1 artichoke at a time, pull off 4 or 5 layers of the tough green outer leaves from the base to reveal the pale yellow ones; they will resemble closed rosebuds. Cut off the top third of each artichoke and trim all but ¼ inch off the stem. Using a mandoline, a Benriner, or a thin sharp knife, slice each artichoke lengthwise through the stem into ⅛-inch slices. Or cut the artichokes lengthwise into wedges. Place the slices in the lemon water as you work. (You may prepare the artichokes up to 1 hour ahead.)

In a heavy medium skillet, combine ⅓ cup extra virgin olive oil, 4 or 5 garlic cloves, thinly sliced, and ¼ teaspoon hot red pepper flakes. Cook over moderate heat until the garlic is tender and golden, about 5 minutes. Use a slotted spoon to remove the garlic to a plate. Drain the artichokes and add them to the skillet, along with ¼ cup water, ¼ teaspoon salt, and 2 fresh thyme, rosemary, or sage sprigs. Cover and cook over medium-low heat, stirring occasionally, until the artichokes are tender, 12 to 15 minutes. Uncover and continue cooking, if necessary, until the water has evaporated. Stir in the reserved garlic.

Cook 12 ounces of a fun bite-sized pasta shape, such as strozzapreti, campanelle, or creste di galli, in boiling salted water until tender but still slightly firm to the bite. Drain, reserving about ½ cup of the cooking liquid. Add the artichokes to the pasta pot with about ¼ cup of the reserved pasta water. Bring to a boil and boil for 30 seconds. Add the drained pasta and toss to coat, seasoning with salt, plenty of pepper, and a sprinkling of sherry vinegar or Banyuls vinegar. Toss with ¼ cup each coarsely chopped flat-leaf parsley and toasted pine nuts. Serve at once, with grated Parmigiano on the side.

➤ DESSERTS

# Ethereal Brown Sugar Butter Cookies

When I am asked to bring a dessert to a dinner party, I invariably turn to this recipe for delectable, melt-in-your-mouth cookies fragrant with butter and the caramel flavors of light brown sugar. When I want to whip up something dazzling for my own impromptu dinners, it can double as a pastry dough for tarts. A few drops of orange flower water subtly intensifies the flavor of the butter, a trick I learned from my Greek grandmother.

For a memorable dessert for a dinner party, bake the cookies at the last minute and place the cookie sheet hot out of the oven in the center of the table (on trivets, of course), along with a metal spatula for the guests to serve themselves.

Best of all, the cookies will last several weeks when stored in an airtight container. They make much-appreciated gifts.

The beauty of this dough is that it is extraordinarily mutable. Its essential structure—butter, sugar, flour, cornstarch—yields a tender cookie into which you can plug all kinds of interesting flavorings.

The sugar itself even poses interesting possibilities: Replace some of the light brown sugar with varying proportions of granulated sugar to mute the caramel-toffee effect, depending on flavorings. Use exotic sugars such as turbinado, muscovado, or maple sugar, each with its own distinctive flavor.

Possible flavorings for this dough are so vast that I have only scratched the surface with the improvisations suggested here. They include fruit zests, such as lemon, orange, or lime, and ground sweet spices, such as cloves, cinnamon, nutmeg, coriander, and white pepper—singly or in combination. Replace the vanilla extract with a flavorful alcohol such as brandy, bourbon, Kahlúa, or rum. Rose water, instead of orange flower water, and grated nutmeg would make Shaker-inspired cookies. About 2 tablespoons minced fresh herbs, such as rosemary, thyme, lemon thyme, or lemon verbena, or about 1 tablespoon flowers, such as lavender or rose geranium, finely minced, alone, in combination, or in tandem with grated lemon or orange zest, make lovely surprising tea cookies and pastry for free-form fruit tarts. The seeds scraped out of a split vanilla bean and mixed with the sugar up the ante in any improvisation with its haunting flavor. Add the flavorings to the butter-sugar mixture to blend them thoroughly.

Incorporate interesting elements into the dough: crushed toffee; ground roasted pecans, almonds, or hazelnuts; shredded coconut; fine bits of crystallized ginger; grated chocolate; and so on. Replace a tablespoon or two of the butter with a fragrant roasted hazelnut or walnut oil for a nuttier cookie.

Ground tea—Earl Grey to be exact, with its citrus-floral scent of bergamot—yields an astonishing cookie and makes me wonder which other teas would work.

This versatile dough can be formed in a variety of shapes, for a variety of purposes: Wedges, squares, or rounds can serve as cookies, or as "top crusts" for free-form tarts (page 311). Pressed into a tart tin, the dough makes a great tart base.

. . . . . .

# Ethereal Brown Sugar Butter Cookies

Makes about thirty 1½-inch round cookies or 12 to 16 wedges or squares

½ cup (1 stick) cold unsalted butter, cut into pieces

⅓ cup packed light brown sugar

A scant ¼ teaspoon kosher salt

1 teaspoon pure vanilla extract or ½ vanilla bean, split lengthwise in half, seeds scraped out, and stirred into the sugar

¼ teaspoon orange flower water (optional)

¾ cup plus 2 tablespoons all-purpose flour

3 tablespoons cornstarch

**Prepare the dough.** In a food processor, combine the butter, sugar, salt, vanilla, and orange flower water, if desired, and process to a light, fluffy paste, 20 to 30 seconds. Remove the lid and add the flour and cornstarch. Pulse until the dough begins to clump together and the mixture is fairly uniform, 8 to 10 times. Gather the dough together into a rough ball, kneading a few times if necessary. (You can also mix the dough by hand or with an electric mixer.)

**Alternative 1: Form the dough into a freezable log, chill, slice into rounds, and bake.** Form the soft dough into a log about 1½ inches in diameter. Gently roll up the log in plastic wrap and refrigerate to firm up, at least 1 hour, or until ready to use.

To bake, preheat the oven to 325°F. Arrange the oven rack in the lower half of the oven.

Using a thin knife, slice the chilled log into ⅛-inch slices and arrange them 1½ inches apart on a cookie sheet. (If the dough is very soft, place the cookie sheet in the freezer for 10 minutes to firm up.) Bake until the tops are firm and the edges are barely colored, about 20 minutes. With a thin metal spatula, transfer the cookies to a cooling rack. Cool completely before packing into a tin.

**Alternative 2 (quicker method): Press the dough into a pan, bake, and slice into shortbread-style wedges or squares.** Press the dough into a 9- or 10-inch tart pan, preferably with a removable bottom, or an 8- or 9-inch square pan. Prick the dough at 2-inch intervals with the tines of a fork. Place the pan on a baking sheet and freeze for 10 to 15 minutes.

To bake, preheat the oven to 325°F. Arrange an oven rack in the lower half of the oven. Bake until the edges are barely colored and the center is no longer puffy, 30 to 35 minutes for a 9-inch round or an 8-inch square, 25 to 30 minutes for a 10-inch round or a 9-inch square.

Transfer the pan to a cooling rack and cool for 5 minutes. With a thin sharp knife or a serrated knife, carefully cut the shortbread rounds into wedges or cut squares into squares, rectangles, or strips.

**Note:** You can refrigerate the dough up to 2 weeks or freeze up to 2 months; thaw in the refrigerator for 8 hours before using.

## Improvisations

### Earl Grey Tea Cookies    Makes about thirty 1½-inch-round cookies or 12 to 16 wedges or squares

*Earl Grey tea is flavored with bergamot, a fragrant essential oil from the peel of a small acidic orange. The tea itself makes a spectacular, very surprising, and very adult flavoring for butter cookies.*

In a food processor, combine ½ cup (1 stick) cold unsalted butter, cut into pieces, 3 tablespoons light brown sugar, 2 tablespoons granulated sugar, a scant ¼ teaspoon kosher salt, 1 teaspoon vanilla, and 4 teaspoons finely ground Earl Grey tea (cut open 4 tea bags and extract the tea; or use loose tea; grind it to a powder in a blender or clean coffee grinder). Process to a light, fluffy paste, 20 to 30 seconds. Remove the lid and add ¾ cup plus 2 tablespoons flour and 3 tablespoons cornstarch. Pulse until the dough begins to clump together and the mixture is fairly uniform, 8 to 10 times. Gather the dough together into a rough ball, kneading a few times if necessary.

Shape the dough as desired into rounds (sliced from a chilled log) or press into a pan; chill. Bake in a preheated 325°F oven until the edges are barely colored.

### Fleur de Sel Cookies    Makes about thirty 1½-inch-round cookies or 12 to 16 wedges or squares

*This fabulous cookie is a perfect example of the kind of free association that can spur a cook's mind. The caramel flavors of the butter and brown sugar shortbread reminded me of a caramel I once tasted that had been sprinkled with a few grains of fleur de sel—the famous French sea salt that is said to have the faintest perfume of violets. Inspired, I took some of the salt out of the Ethereal Brown Sugar Butter Cookie dough and sprinkled some fine sea salt on the surface just before baking: Its taste was delightful, a gentle surprise on the tongue. Use the best sea salt you can find with fine or flaky, not coarse, crystals. Maldon sea salt is a particularly nice one.*

Prepare the Ethereal Brown Sugar Butter Cookie dough, using only a pinch of salt in place of the scant ¼ teaspoon. Shape the dough as desired into rounds (sliced from a chilled log) or press into a pan; chill. Just before baking, sprinkle the cookies evenly with a scant ¼ teaspoon sea salt. Press lightly into the dough. Bake in a preheated 325°F oven until the edges are barely colored.

## Holton's Coffee Vanilla Bean Cookies

**Makes about thirty 1½-inch-round cookies or 12 to 16 wedges or squares**

*I created this recipe for my friend Holton, to re-create the flavors of a delectable cookie we had tasted years before, a gift from an acquaintance who never told us where she got the cookies. I worked my way through version after version—fine-tuning the balance of flavors—until I had the subtle blend of coffee, caramel, and vanilla. For more-overtly coffee cookies, increase the instant coffee to 2 or 3 teaspoons; omit the vanilla bean and just use vanilla extract.*

Pour 2 teaspoons Kahlúa into a small bowl and stir in 1 teaspoon instant espresso powder; set aside. In a food processor, combine ½ cup (1 stick) cold unsalted butter, cut into pieces, ¼ cup granulated sugar, 1 tablespoon light brown sugar, and a scant ¼ teaspoon kosher salt. With a thin sharp knife, slice half a vanilla bean in half lengthwise; scrape out the seeds and add to the sugar mixture. Process to a light, fluffy paste, 20 to 30 seconds. Add the Kahlúa mixture and process until combined. Remove the lid and add ¾ cup plus 2 tablespoons flour and 3 tablespoons cornstarch. Pulse until the dough begins to clump together and the mixture is fairly uniform, 8 to 10 times. Gather the dough together into a rough ball, kneading a few times if necessary.

Shape the dough as desired into rounds (sliced from a chilled log) or press into a pan; chill. Bake in a preheated 325°F oven until the edges are barely colored.

## Brown Sugar Butter Pastry Shells and Lids for Tarts

**Makes one 10-inch tart shell, six 4-inch tart shells, or 6 pastry lids**

*Unbaked Ethereal Brown Sugar Butter Cookie dough makes an easy-to-work pastry dough for dessert tarts. To give it a more neutral, less caramel flavor, use half granulated sugar and half light brown sugar in the dough.*

Make 1 recipe Ethereal Brown Sugar Butter Cookie dough; do not chill. To make a tart shell, press the dough into a 10-inch tart tin with a removable bottom, building up the edge slightly to make a ¼-inch-high rim. To make 6 individual tartlet shells, press the dough into 4-inch tart tins, building up the edges in the same way. Chill ½ hour before filling and/or baking. To bake without a filling, bake in a preheated 325°F oven until the edges are barely colored, 30 to 35 minutes; cool before filling.

To make individual pastry lids for free-form tarts, don't build up the edge when you press the dough into tartlet tins; just bake them as flat disks you can pop out of the tins. Use to top individual portions of cooked fruit, such as Boozy Prunes (page 315) or Warm "Wild" Blackberries or blueberries (page 310), along with some whipped cream.

## Brown Sugar Lime Curd Tart     Serves 6 to 8

*The Caribbean origins of brown sugar and lime inspired me to pair the Ethereal Brown Sugar Butter Cookie dough baked in a tart tin with an unusually light tangy lime curd to make this charming tart. Make the Lime Curd up to 5 days ahead. (You can also use the basic method to make lemon curd or Meyer lemon curd; just adjust the sugar accordingly.) In a pinch, use good-quality store-bought lemon curd, stirring in a few teaspoons fresh lemon juice to make it sufficiently tart.*

Prepare the Lime Curd (page 306) and chill. Follow the directions for forming and baking a 10-inch tart shell in Brown Sugar Butter Pastry Shells and Lids for Tarts, above.

Within 1 hour of serving, gently fold ¼ to ½ cup whipped cream, whipped crème fraîche, or sour cream into the Lime Curd. Spread evenly into the tart shell. Serve with whipped cream or crème fraîche on the side.

**Lime Curd.** For 1 cup Lime Curd, you'll need ½ cup fresh lime juice (Key limes are particularly good). In a small bowl, sprinkle ½ teaspoon unflavored gelatin over 2 tablespoons of the lime juice. Set aside to soften. In a medium stainless steel bowl or the top of a double boiler, combine the remaining (6 tablespoons) lime juice, 7 tablespoons sugar, 1 large egg, 1 egg white, and one 3 × 1-inch strip lime zest. Set the bowl over, but not in, simmering water. Whisk constantly until the curd is thick and coats the back of a spoon, about 5 minutes. Stir in the gelatin mixture and cook 1 minute longer. Strain into a medium bowl and allow to cool to room temperature, whisking occasionally. Discard the zest, cover, and refrigerate until ready to use.

# Warm Fresh Cherries with Vanilla Ice Cream and Balsamic Caramel (Warm Pie Fruit)

- Warm "Wild" Blackberries with Ice Cream and Balsamic Caramel
- Warm Raspberry Plums with Lavender and Crème Fraîche
- Impromptu Jam
- Free-Form Fruit Tart in a Bowl

If good cherries were available all year round, I would dish up this dessert at every dinner party: pitted cherries cooked with vanilla bean and sugar until they just release their juices, served warm in a shallow bowl with fine vanilla ice cream and a drizzle of Balsamic Caramel. It is like eating the inside of a just-baked cherry pie so I've nicknamed them Warm Pie Fruit. Pitting cherries takes no more effort than peeling apples for pie.

The Balsamic Caramel gives a surprisingly sophisticated edge to the dessert. It is a poor man's version of the extraordinarily expensive artisan-made balsamics from Modena, whose deeply complex, resonant, sweet-tart flavor transform anything they come in contact with. They are famously served over vanilla ice cream, a startling combination that inspired the Balsamic Caramel.

In this recipe, ripe fresh cherries are gently cooked with sugar and a table-spoon or two of water in a covered pan until their juices begins to run. A split vanilla bean amplifies their natural sweetness and perfume while adding a sub-tle, haunting quality. A teaspoon or two of fresh lemon juice also punches up the flavor. This is the easiest way to bring out the best in all kinds of fresh fruit and transform them into something memorable. You can use raspberries, blackberries, or blueberries; sliced peeled peaches, nectarines, mangos, pears, or apples; sliced or halved apricots, figs, or plums. Sweet or Savory Quinces in White Wine and Honey (page 72) is a variation on this theme. (When no fresh fruit looks appealing, use this method with frozen unsweetened berries.)

Fruits cooked this way go well with all kinds of creamy accompaniments and sauces: whipped cream or crème fraîche, custard sauces, thick full-fat yogurt, fresh ricotta cheese, zabaglione (sweet wine, yolks, and sugar beaten to a warm froth), and, of course, premium vanilla ice cream, with or without the Balsamic Caramel. Match ice creams to the fruit: pistachio with warm raspber-ries or cherries; buttercrunch or pecan with apples; coconut with mango; strawberry with peach; and so on. I spill the warm fruits into shallow soup bowls and pool or plunk the creamy embellishment right in the center.

Since the warm fruits are like the inside of a pie, I use them to make free-form tarts and pastries. Ladle some into a shallow bowl and top with prebaked pastry lids, such as Brown Sugar Butter Pastry Shells and Lids for Tarts (page 305), free-form pastry lids made from your favorite pie dough or Easy Butter Dough for Tarts, Pies, and Free-Form Pastries (page 355). For shortcake, split buttermilk bis-cuits and sandwich the warm fruit in between, with fresh whipped cream.

You can also add other flavors besides vanilla to the basic mix. Lavender is delightful with plums, berries, and figs; fresh thyme or a single juniper berry will bring out a wild berry flavor in purple fruit such as blueberries and blackberries. You can combine fruits: raspberries and peaches or figs, mangoes, and black-berries, for example. The less sweet combinations can be used as sweet-savory accompaniments to roasted meats and poultry. Splash the fruit with red or white wine instead of water and cut back on the sugar: plums with red wine and a pinch of thyme, for example, or mango with lime juice, chile pepper, scallion, and cilantro—no vanilla bean—makes a great warm salsa for duck or pork.

. . . . . .

## Warm Fresh Cherries with Vanilla Ice Cream and Balsamic Caramel (Warm Pie Fruit) Serves 4

3 cups fresh sweet cherries, pitted

About 3 tablespoons sugar or honey

2 tablespoons water

1 vanilla bean

A teaspoon or two of fresh lemon juice (optional)

1 pint premium vanilla ice cream

Balsamic Caramel (page 64) or fine long-aged artisanal balsamic vinegar (optional)

**Combine the fruit with the sugar and cook, covered, to release the juices.** In a medium saucepan, combine the cherries, sugar to taste, and water. With a sharp paring knife, split the vanilla bean lengthwise and scrape out the seeds. Add the seeds and bean to the pan. Cook over moderate heat until the cherries release their juices, about 2 minutes.

**Cook uncovered to concentrate the juices.** Uncover and cook over high heat until the cherries are tender, about 2 minutes longer. Taste and add lemon juice if necessary to clarify the flavor. Discard the vanilla bean. Let the cherries cool a few minutes.

**Serve.** Spoon the cherries into 4 shallow soup bowls. Spoon a scoop of ice cream on top of each. Drizzle with Balsamic Caramel, if desired.

**Note:** There are several well-designed cherry pitters available that can pit a pound of cherries in just a few minutes, from simple hand-held pitters to more elaborate plunger-and-chute models. Or use the makeshift technique on page 354.

### Warm "Wild" Blackberries with Ice Cream and Balsamic Caramel    Serves 4

*The blackberries available in supermarkets are often a pale version of wild ones. Cooking them with some sugar, vanilla bean, and thyme brings out their flavors. Then they are marvelous with vanilla ice cream and Balsamic Caramel, or with peach ice cream or crème fraîche.*

*Substitute blueberries, alone or in combination with the blackberries. Another trick to bring the most out of cultivated or frozen berries is to cook half the berries until they become jammy and their flavors are quite concentrated. Add the remaining berries and cook until their juices run but they are not falling apart. A handful of fresh raspberries added at the end and just warmed through adds a blast of concentrated berry flavor.*

In a medium saucepan, combine 3 cups blackberries and/or blueberries, about 3 tablespoons sugar (to taste), 2 tablespoons water, and 2 fresh thyme sprigs. Scrape the seeds from a split vanilla bean into the pan and add the bean. Cook over moderate heat until the berries release their juices, about 2 minutes. Uncover and cook over high heat until the berries are tender, about 1 minute longer. Taste and add lemon juice if necessary to clarify the flavor. Discard the vanilla bean and thyme sprigs. Let the berries cool for a few minutes before serving.

### Warm Raspberry Plums with Lavender and Crème Fraîche    Serves 4

*This improvisation is an example of the way simple elements can converge to produce unexpectedly delicious results. I put them together on a hunch one evening and discovered that plums and raspberries make a hauntingly flavored compote with a luxurious texture. A touch of lavender boosts the fruits' perfume without being obtrusive. Lavender is often available with other fresh herbs in the produce section of supermarkets, or at farmers' markets, and dried at spice and flower stores. (Be sure to use only unsprayed lavender.)*

In a medium saucepan, combine 1¾ pounds medium plums, halved, pitted, and sliced into ½-inch wedges; ¼ cup wildflower or lavender honey; 2 teaspoons water; 1½ teaspoons fresh lemon juice; and a scant ¼ teaspoon lavender flowers, if desired. Cover and cook over moderate heat until the plums release their juices, 3 to 4 minutes. Uncover and stir in 2 cups raspberries; continue cooking until the plums are very tender and the mixture is a thick stew, 2 to 3 minutes longer. Adjust the sweetness if necessary. Let the fruit cool a few minutes before serving. Serve warm with crème fraîche.

### Impromptu Jam

*When you have a surplus of berries or soft fruits, turn them into a small-batch jam that will keep several weeks in the refrigerator by simply cooking Warm Pie Fruit for a longer amount of time. These easy-to-make jams have a vivid flavor that is great on breakfast breads or French toast, or for the ultimate peanut-butter-and-jelly sandwiches. Warm Raspberry Plums make a particularly lovely and unusual jam.*

Follow the preceding method to cook any of the fruit-sweetener-vanilla combinations you like over low heat, stirring frequently, until the fruits have all but fallen apart and become jammy, about 20 minutes. (For firmer fruits that take longer to cook, such as Sweet or Savory Quinces in White Wine and Honey on page 72, add a little water to keep them from sticking to the pan.) Allow to cool before adjusting the flavoring with lemon juice and additional sweetener. Pack into clean, dry jars and refrigerate.

### Free-Form Fruit Tart in a Bowl

*This is my all-time favorite dessert: an upside-down free-form tart in a bowl that is more an approach than a recipe. I make Warm Pie Fruit with seasonal fruit, such as cherries, blueberries, raspberries, peaches, or figs; spill them into shallow soup bowls, and top them with a prebaked pastry lid and a dollop of whipped cream or crème fraîche on the side. (Crème fraîche is the lazy man's whipped cream; spooned right out of the container, it gives a luxurious finish to any dessert.) The effect is of a messy, warm summer fruit tart, a dazzler at dinner parties. All the parts can be made ahead and assembled at the last minute. Best of all, this approach lends itself to endless improvisations and permutations.*

At least 1 hour in advance of making the dessert, prepare and bake the pastry lids. Follow the method on page 308, using your favorite pie dough or Easy Butter Dough for Tarts, Pies, and Free-Form Pastries (page 355); or make the Brown Sugar Butter Pastry Shells and Lids for Tarts (page 305). Prepare the Warm Pie Fruit up to 2 hours ahead and leave it on the back of the stove; warm just before serving, and assemble in large shallow soup bowls.

# Boozy Prunes

- Prune and Roasted Walnut Confit
- Dried Cherries in Red Wine Syrup with or without Grappa
- Dried Apricots in Cardamom Syrup (and Roasted Dried Apricots)
- Warm Prune, Cherry, or Apricot Turnovers
- Impromptu Free-Form Prune "Napoleons"

The inspiration for these luscious prunes comes from the southwest of France, where they are traditionally steeped in Armagnac, the region's brandy. But almost any aged spirits will do, including bourbon, which turns the prunes toward the American South. After they have steeped in the vanilla-scented whiskey-spiked syrup for a week or two, the prunes mellow into an intensely flavored confection that is a cross between a candy and a confit, perfect for finishing off a meal, or as a sleep-inducing midnight snack for the anxious insomniac.

The beauty of these prunes is that they last indefinitely in the refrigerator, to be drawn upon to make an instant dessert spooned over coffee or vanilla ice cream or numerous other improvisations. I make big batches of them to use in my own entertaining or to give as gifts, packed into pretty jars, with handwritten tags listing their possibilities.

Because the traditional method of steeping dried fruits in spirits can take weeks to complete, I devised a quick version that is ready to eat in a few days and has a mellower, less assertively alcoholic flavor than the classic. Like all dried fruit, prunes–dried plums–need to be reconstituted in liquid to become soft. I plump them in a hot liquid that will accentuate their flavor: a light syrup made of sugar, water, and vanilla bean, a miraculous tool for boosting perfume and sweetness. I use pitted prunes, because the liquid can penetrate and soften them more quickly; the prunes' juices mingle with the syrup to flavor and thicken it. Heat speeds up the softening process, though too much would make the fruit fall apart, so I gently poach them in the syrup for a carefully timed 5 minutes. Because heat causes alcohol to evaporate, the booze is added when the syrup is almost cool.

Plug just about any dried fruit that has a nice balance of acidity and sweetness into the basic formula–cherries, blueberries, apricots, prunes, and raisins all work well–adjusting the quantities of water, sweetener, and alcohol accordingly. Certain fruits, dried apricots in particular, absorb a good deal of liquid, so you'll need to make more of the base syrup. Use red or white wine instead of water in the syrup to amplify the fruits' wininess and add some acidity; mildly brewed teas, such as oolong, ginger, or thyme leaf, might add interesting flavor notes.

The choice of alcohol should be determined by the fruit you are using. Vary the amount to make the fruit gently perfumed or heartily boozy (though if you plan to bake them into pastries, a mild alcohol flavor is better). Cognac and rum go with just about any dried fruits. Kirschwasser, the clear cherry brandy, complements apricots and cherries. Grappa, distilled from the pressings from wine grapes, has an earthy flavor and fiery aspect that is softened greatly by the vanilla syrup; it is fabulous with dried cherries and golden or dark raisins. I prefer to use white sugar as a sweetener for its neutral clarity of flavor, but the darker sugars, such as demerara or turbinado, would add interesting caramel undertones. To make fruits without alcohol, use fragrant honeys such as lavender or lime blossom in the syrup for both sweetening and perfume. And, of course, you can add spices or herbs to any of these concoctions.

The best way to serve these fruits in spirit-spiked syrup is as is or over premium vanilla ice cream. Because they keep indefinitely and lend themselves to quick improvisation, I always have at least one on hand in the refrigerator as a staple. Drained, they make instant fillings for tarts and pastries, as the examples that follow demonstrate. I chop them up to put in fruit salads–the cherries with ripe mango, the apricots with bananas, for example. I also like them as a fruity counterpoint to rich meats, as is, or added to wine- or broth–based sauces. Boozy Prunes are great with pork and rabbit (especially the Rabbit Rillettes on page 221); cherries in grappa love duck, rabbit, and pork.

. . . . . .

## Boozy Prunes    Makes about 3 cups, about 40 prunes

1½ cups water
3 to 4 tablespoons sugar
1 vanilla bean
12 ounces large pitted prunes
¾ to 1 cup Armagnac, Bas Armagnac, bourbon, or Cognac

**Make a light vanilla-scented syrup.** In a small nonreactive saucepan, combine the water and sugar. With a sharp paring knife, split the vanilla bean lengthwise and scrape out the seeds. Add the seeds and bean to the pan.

**Simmer the fruit over low heat.** Bring to a boil over moderately high heat, stirring until the sugar dissolves. Add the prunes and simmer—do not boil—for exactly 5 minutes. Transfer the prunes and syrup to a clean, dry jar.

**Cool and add the spirits.** Allow to cool completely, then stir in ¼ cup of the Armagnac. As the prunes age, the strength of the spirits will decrease; taste them occasionally and add more to taste. Let sit at room temperature several days to "cure." Store in the refrigerator.

## Improvisations

### Prune and Roasted Walnut Confit    Makes 1 cup

*This rich jam was inspired by a liqueur made from prunes and walnuts that a friend brought me from southwestern France many years ago. The combination of flavors was a revelation; the bitterness of the walnuts perfectly complemented the winey fruitiness of the prunes. The Boozy Prunes are jamlike when drained and mashed, and make an excellent confit when not too heartily spiked with alcohol; all you have to do is add roasted walnuts. This confit is wonderful alongside roast pork, chicken, and rabbit; with aged Cheddar or blue cheese and slabs of pâté campagne; or as a spoon sweet, right out of the jar.*

Using a slotted spoon, drain 1 cup Boozy Prunes well and place on a cutting board (I often use the prunes that are too broken or fallen apart to pack into gift jars or serve); coarsely chop them or pass them through a food mill. Transfer to a bowl and stir in about 3 tablespoons coarsely chopped roasted walnuts per cup, or to taste. Pack into clean, dry jars and refrigerate.

### Dried Cherries in Red Wine Syrup with or without Grappa    Makes about 5 cups

*In this play on Boozy Prunes, I steeped dried cherries in a syrup made with red wine instead of water, to punch up the red-fruit flavor and add a bit of acidity. Since the wine's alcohol gets cooked off, it's a great nonalcoholic alternative, especially splashed on vanilla ice cream to make instant cherry-vanilla. It is also a great base for further improvisations. Spiking the cherries-in-syrup revealed two intoxicating combinations, one made with grappa, distilled from grape pressings, earthy and primal; another made with dark aged rum, mild and caramelly. Both these combinations become a great deal more than the sum of their parts and are addictive, the perfect gift for those friends who have everything. To make* **Pickled Cherries**, *stir in balsamic and/or sherry vinegar to taste.*

In a medium nonreactive saucepan, combine 2 cups fruity full-bodied red wine, 1 cup water, 6 tablespoons sugar, and 1 vanilla bean, split lengthwise, seeds scraped out and added with the bean. Bring to a boil over moderate heat, stirring to dissolve the sugar. Stir in 8 ounces dried cherries; turn off the heat, and cover 5 minutes. Uncover and set aside to cool.

Transfer the cherries and their liquid to a clean, dry jar. If desired, add 1 to 1¼ cups grappa or dark rum. Cover and set aside to mellow at least 1 week. Taste the cherries periodically and add more alcohol as necessary.

### Dried Apricots in Cardamom Syrup (and Roasted Dried Apricots)

**Makes about 1 quart**

*Instead of alcohol, I perfumed dried apricots with a fragrant cardamom-scented syrup, which imparts a singularly Middle Eastern savor. Keep a batch on hand in the fridge for making instant desserts. Serve as a simple compote with drained whole-milk yogurt or use as a filling for tarts and turnovers. I prefer California apricots rather than Turkish apricots for their intense flavor and good texture.*

Make a light vanilla-scented syrup using 2 cups water, ½ cup sugar, 1 tablespoon fresh lemon juice, 5 whole cardamom pods, and 1 vanilla bean, split lengthwise, seeds scraped out and added with the bean. Crush 5 additional cardamom pods and add the black seeds to the pan. Add 12 ounces dried apricots and simmer—do not boil—for exactly 5 minutes. Cool, then transfer to a clean, dry jar. Refrigerate.

Apricots in Cardamom Syrup are a revelation roasted and served with crème fraîche; they become slightly caramelized, with the vivid flavor of roasted fresh apricots. Preheat the oven to 350°F. (The oven temperature is not critical; you can roast them along with other dishes at higher temperatures.) Drain the apricots and arrange them in a single layer in a buttered dish, dot with butter, and sprinkle with sugar. Roast until the bottoms of the apricots are caramelized and the bottom of the pan looks as if it is beginning to burn, about 30 minutes. Cool the pan slightly and place right on the table for your guests to serve themselves (they will delight in peeling the apricots out of the pan with their fingers). Pass crème fraîche on the side.

### Warm Prune, Cherry, or Apricot Turnovers    Serves 4

*Turnovers—flaky pastry triangles filled with fruit—make a dramatic dessert for little effort when you use prepared all-butter puff pastry and any of the fruits-in-syrup above. Puff pastry is available in the frozen food section of most markets. Be sure to thaw it slowly in the refrigerator, about 3 hours, before using.*

Position a strainer over a bowl and spoon Boozy Prunes, Cherries in Red Wine Syrup, or Apricots in Cardamom Syrup into it to drain (pour the liquid back in the jar); measure 1 cup fruit.

Unfold the pastry sheet (s) on a lightly floured surface. With a chef's knife, cut four 5-inch squares. With a thin metal spatula, transfer each one to a cookie sheet. Mix together 1 tablespoon all-purpose flour and 1½ teaspoons sugar. Spread ½ teaspoon of the flour/sugar mixture on each square, leaving a ¼-inch edge uncovered.

Imagining one of the puff pastry squares folded on a diagonal, arrange ¼ cup of the drained fruit over half the pastry, leaving a ¼-inch edge uncovered. Sprinkle the fruit with 2 teaspoons sugar and ¼ teaspoon fresh lemon juice. Brush the edges of the square with water. Fold the pastry on the diagonal so that the empty half covers the fruit to form a triangle-shaped turnover. Crimp the edges together with a fork. Repeat with the remaining pastry squares, fruit, and additional sugar and lemon juice. Chill the turnovers in the freezer while you preheat the oven to 375°F. (You can also make them ahead and freeze them, well wrapped, for up to 2 months; bake frozen.)

Bake the turnover until they are puffed and golden brown, 20 to 25 minutes. Allow to cool to warm before serving. Sift confectioners' sugar over each one.

### Impromptu Free-Form Prune "Napoleons"

*When I am really pressed for time and need a dramatic dessert, I use Boozy Prunes that I keep on hand in my fridge as a base for free-form napoleons (a play on the Free-Form Fruit Tart in a Bowl, page 311). Before guests arrive, I bake rectangles cut from a sheet of store-bought all-butter puff pastry until they are puffed and brown (just unfold the pastry on a floured surface, cut it into 4 × 2-inch rectangles, and bake according to package instructions). Just before serving, I split them horizontally through the center and sandwich the halves with drained Boozy Prunes and whipped crème fraîche or whipped cream, then sift confectioners' sugar over the top.*

# Brown Sugar Lightning Cake

I must have watched my friend Kathy Mailloux in her kitchen in the West Virginia Appalachians whip up the batter she pours over peaches for a cobbler a thousand times before it dawned on me that she produced a tender fragrant cake without an electric mixer or long beating of butter and sugar. When Kathy told me the recipe, I realized that it is a version of the simple two-egg cake modestly listed in old American cookbooks as "lightning cake," because it takes no time to make.

Back home in New York, I fooled around with the batter part of Kathy's cobbler: I plugged in brown sugar for white, flavored it with both vanilla and bourbon (a flavoring common to old-fashioned pound cakes), and baked it in a 9-inch cake pan. It is the cake that has made me a cake baker at last: eggy, tender, fragrant, and truly fast (I can mix one up by hand in just 15 minutes). Its deliciousness and fine texture belie its ease. Turned out onto a pretty plate and dusted with confectioners' sugar, it looks like the lovely plain cakes you'd be served in someone's home years ago, a perfect dessert for an impromptu dinner party, with a bowl of fresh berries. It also takes well to jazzing up, as in some of the improvisations here.

When improvising, substitute one ingredient for another in the essential formula—that is, the fat, sugar, liquid, and flour—but it's best not to monkey with the quantities too much. You can use up to ½ cup more flour; the more you use, the denser and sturdier the cake will be. If you want to add fruit to the batter, a slightly drier batter is necessary; use 2 tablespoons less butter and 1 tablespoon more flour, as in the Raspberry Cake improvisation.

Replace the melted butter with olive oil or another flavorful fat, say, roasted hazelnut oil. Sugar can be an equal amount of any dry sugar, such as white sugar, brown sugar, maple sugar, demerara, or muscovado, with its strong molasses flavor, for example. Buttermilk ensures an extraordinarily tender crumb, though you can replace it with whole milk and/or yogurt; unsweetened applesauce, in league with sweet spices such as cinnamon, clove, and nutmeg, yields a classic applesauce cake.

Flavorings offer the simplest opportunities for improvising. Replace the vanilla and bourbon with any extracts or flavorful alcohols you like, including rum, almond extract, rose water, orange flower water, and so on. Grated fruit zests—lemon, orange, tangerine, Meyer lemon—can be used alone or in tandem with other flavorings to make citrus-scented cakes. Lace the cake with a bit of sweet spices—nutmeg, mace, allspice, cinnamon, clove, coriander, fennel seed, cardamom, even black pepper—or herbs; any of the thymes and rosemary, used sparingly, can add a lovely counterpoint of flavor. Pecans and walnuts, coarsely chopped with brown or maple sugar, can be sprinkled on top before baking to create a crunchy streusel, as in the Maple Sugar Pecan Cornmeal Cake on page 263.

To make individual cakelets, pour the batter into buttered floured cupcake tins or ramekins. Serve with some caramelized pineapple slices for a deconstructed pineapple upside-down cake, or with any of the warm fruit combinations—cherries, blackberries, figs, plums—on pages 309 to 311.

Finally, this simple brown sugar cake can be split horizontally and filled with various creamy fillings/icings to make a 2-layer cake: whipped crème fraîche and coconut, or dulce de leche with toasted pecans, or a nice tart lemon curd (page 305)—all available commercially—are some of my favorites. Figure about 1 cup filling/icing for a 9-inch layer cake.

. . . . . .

# Brown Sugar Lightning Cake   Serves 8

½ cup (1 stick) unsalted butter, melted

1½ cups all-purpose flour

2 teaspoons baking powder

¼ plus ⅛ teaspoon kosher salt

2 large eggs, at room temperature

1 cup packed light brown sugar

½ cup buttermilk or ¼ cup whole milk mixed with ¼ cup plain yogurt

1 teaspoon vanilla extract

1 teaspoon bourbon

Confectioners' sugar for dusting

**Prepare the pan.** Preheat the oven to 350°F. Brush the inside of a 9-inch straight-sided round cake pan with a little of the melted butter. Spoon a teaspoon or two of the flour into the pan and tilt the pan until it is completely coated. Invert and tap to release the excess flour.

**Sift together the dry ingredients.** Place a sifter or a strainer over a bowl and sift together the remaining flour, baking powder, and salt. Stir again with a fork and set aside.

**Beat the eggs with the sugar.** Crack the eggs into a medium bowl and whisk until blended and frothy. Whisk in the sugar and beat until well blended, 1 minute.

**Mix in the dry and wet ingredients and flavorings.** Whisk in the flour mixture using as few strokes as possible, until mostly incorporated. Then whisk in the milk, the remaining melted butter, and the flavorings. Pour the batter into the prepared pan.

**Bake.** Bake the cake 35 to 40 minutes, or until a tester inserted in the center comes out clean. Cool the cake on a rack 5 minutes, then invert onto the rack. Cool completely.

**Invert the cake** onto a platter. Sift some confectioners' sugar over the top.

### Fragrant Olive Oil Cake with Fresh Thyme    Serves 8

*The idea of an olive oil cake always sounded better than any I ever tasted in restaurants. Intrigued, I decided to try my hand using the lightning cake formula as a guide, figuring the olive oil should substitute just fine for melted butter. I perked up the batter with orange and lemon zest and some fresh thyme leaves—the flavors of southern France. The result was a lovely cake yet without an overtly olive oil flavor; rather, the oil contributes to its unique floral-herbal fragrance and delicate texture. I serve slices with fresh berries, or warm fruit sauces or "stews," such as Warm Fresh Cherries (page 309), Warm "Wild" Blackberries (page 310), or Warm Raspberry Plums (page 310).*

Preheat the oven to 350°F. Butter and flour a 9-inch round cake pan. Sift together 1½ cups all-purpose flour, 2 teaspoons baking powder, and ¼ plus ⅛ teaspoon salt. Beat 2 large eggs with 1 teaspoon each grated orange and lemon zests, 1 to 1½ teaspoons chopped fresh thyme (optional), and 1 cup granulated sugar until light and frothy. Whisk in the flour mixture until almost incorporated, then whisk in ½ cup buttermilk and ½ cup fruity extra virgin olive oil. Pour the batter into the prepared pan and bake until a skewer inserted in the center comes out clean, about 45 minutes. Cool the cake on a rack 5 minutes, then invert to cool completely.

Transfer to a platter and sift confectioners' sugar over the top.

### Raspberry Cake    Serves 8

*When raspberries are baked into this butter cake, their perfume and flavor are magnified.*

*This batter, which has slightly less butter and buttermilk than the lightning cake, is perfect for incorporating raspberries, black raspberries, or blackberries into the batter—or, for upside-down cakes, poured over pineapple or peach slices, or apricot or plum halves, that you've cooked in a brown-sugar-and-butter caramel.*

Preheat the oven to 350°F. Butter and flour a 9-inch round cake pan. Sift together 1½ cups all-purpose flour, 2 teaspoons baking powder, and ½ teaspoon salt. Beat 2 large eggs with 1 cup packed light brown sugar until light and frothy. Whisk in the flour mixture until almost incorporated, then whisk in ¼ cup plus 3 tablespoons buttermilk mixed with 2 teaspoons vanilla extract and 6 tablespoons (¾ stick) unsalted butter, melted. Carefully fold in ½ pint fresh raspberries. Pour the batter into the prepared pan and bake until a skewer inserted in the center comes out clean, 45 to 50 minutes. Cool the cake on a rack 5 minutes, then invert to cool completely.

Transfer to a platter and sift confectioners' sugar over the top.

## Orange Flower and Other Citrus Cakes   Serves 8

*The grated zests of lemons, clementines, tangerines, Meyer lemons, and oranges—1 tablespoon's worth—are potent flavorings that turn Brown Sugar Lightning Cake into a citrus-scented one. (Orange flower water amplifies the citrus flavors.) I've even approximated the haunting flavor of yuzu, the fragrant Japanese citrus fruit, by blending lemon and tangerine zests in equal parts. Use this Orange Flower Cake as a blueprint for other citrus cakes. Serve it plain, with a dusting of confectioners' sugar, or poke the top with holes and saturate it with a tart glaze, as below. To make a* **Filled Citrus Cake***: Use a serrated knife to cut the plain cooled cake in half horizontally to make two layers. Spread one layer with Tangelo Jam (page 78) or Meyer Lemon Dessert Sauce and Filling (page 79) and carefully place the second layer on top. Dust with confectioners' sugar and serve with whipped cream.*

Preheat the oven to 350°F. Butter and flour a 9-inch cake pan. Sift together 1½ cups all-purpose flour, 2 teaspoons baking powder, and ¼ plus ⅛ teaspoon salt. Beat 2 large eggs with 1 tablespoon finely grated orange zest and 1 cup packed light brown or granulated sugar until light and frothy. Whisk in the flour mixture until almost incorporated, then whisk in ½ cup buttermilk mixed with 1 teaspoon orange flower water or vanilla extract and ¼ cup (1 stick) unsalted butter, melted. Pour into the prepared pan and bake until a skewer inserted in the center comes out clean, 35 to 40 minutes.

Cool the cake on a rack 5 minutes, then invert to cool completely. Transfer to a platter and sift confectioners' sugar over the top.

Or, to glaze and soak the cake, cool the cake in the pan 5 minutes while you make this **citrus glaze**: Combine a scant ¼ cup orange juice and 1 cup plus 2 tablespoons confectioners' sugar in a saucepan. Stir over low heat until the sugar is dissolved. Invert the cake onto a cooling rack; with a toothpick, poke holes into the top of the cake. Spoon the glaze over the cake, letting it soak in before adding more.

## Coconut Cake   Serves 8

*On a whim, I split a big slice of leftover Brown Sugar Lightning Cake, spread the layers with whipped crème fraîche and shredded coconut, and polished off the entire wedge. An instant, old-fashioned coconut cake was invented.*

Prepare a Brown Sugar Lightning Cake or Orange Flower Cake. When cool, invert onto a platter or cookie sheet. Use a long thin knife to split the cake in half horizontally. Carefully lift off the top layer. Spread the bottom layer with about 1 cup of whipped cream, into which you've folded a little sour cream. Then scatter sweetened shredded coconut evenly over the cream. Replace the top. Ice with more whipped cream and coconut if you wish, or simply sift confectioners' sugar over the top.

## Dulce de Leche Cake   Serves 8

*Prepared dulce de leche, goat's-milk caramel of Mexican origin, makes an excellent frosting for instant layer cakes (as does caramel sauce for parfaits). I keep a jar in my fridge for just such emergencies. Dulce de leche is available at many supermarkets.*

Prepare a Brown Sugar Lightning Cake. When cool, invert onto a platter or cookie sheet. Use a long thin knife to slice the cake in half horizontally. Carefully lift off the top layer. Spread with dulce de leche and, if you like, a layer of whipped cream. Replace the top layer. Spread with more dulce de leche and sprinkle with coarsely chopped roasted pecans.

# Rosy Baked Apples

I never really loved baked apples until I ate the ones my friend Bob Silver served at a dinner party one evening. His apples are charmingly homey with an intense apple flavor brought out by modest ingredients: red currant jelly, lemon juice, and a little butter. Because Bob cores the apples all the way through and covers them during the cooking, the apples are tender to the point of collapsing. The addition of crème fraîche just before serving brings the simple elements together to make a memorable dessert.

I often make a double batch of these baked apples to serve for dessert and as a base for improvisation.

Successful baked apples require an apple variety that will cook to a tender-though-not-falling-apart flesh with nice acidity and intense apple flavor. I find that Rome Beauties, the designated baking apple, have a lackluster flavor and rather wooden texture. Instead, look for Granny Smith, Golden Delicious, Ida Red, Northern Spy, Baldwin, Cortland, Pippin, or other cooking apples local to your area. The age of the apple is important too. Apples are a fall fruit; by summer, they will have languished in cold storage for nine months and can be woody. Bake apples in the cooler months, when they are fresh.

There is a wide range of sweeteners to choose from, each contributing its subtle flavor: sugar (granulated, light or dark brown, demerara, or muscovado); honey with its infinite range of flavors; maple syrup or maple sugar; jams, jellies, or marmalades, which add their own fruit flavors. Sprinkling the apples with lemon juice is essential to bring out their true flavor. Baking apples need some moisture in the pan to become tender. This can be water; wine, from white and dessert wines to fortified wines such as sherry and Marsala (diluted with water); apple, orange, or other fruit juices; or an herb tea.

Although the usual flavorings for baked apples are sweet spices such as cinnamon, nutmeg, and allspice, the spice drawer holds many other possibilities: cracked coriander, white pepper, juniper berries, pink peppercorns, bay leaf, fennel seed. Used sparingly, fresh herbs such as rosemary, thyme, and basil and seasonal fragrant leaves such as lemon verbena, lavender, and rose geranium complement apples. Slivered citrus zests—from orange to Meyer lemon—also contribute bright flavor notes. The hollowed-out center of the apple invites all kinds of fillings: chopped dried cherries or apricots; raisins; nuts such as walnuts, pecans, or pistachios; crystallized ginger, marzipan, and so on.

Baked apples are traditionally eaten as a dessert. Tone down the sweet elements, and they make great accompaniments for savory dishes such as roast pork, chicken, or game. They can be roasted whole, halved, or sliced, as in Roasted Apples with Cheddar Crisps (page 86). Chilled, served with heavy cream or yogurt, they make a fortifying breakfast. Leftovers can be peeled and chopped or mashed to turn into delectable applesauces and confits, flavored further, if desired, with minced herbs or spices. Freeze the pulp and puree in a food processor for an appealing sorbet or, with the addition of crème fraîche, ice cream.

· · · · · ·

## Rosy Baked Apples   Serves 6

6 large Granny Smith or other good cooking apples
Juice of 1½ lemons (about 4½ tablespoons)
½ cup red currant jelly
1 to 2 tablespoons unsalted butter
⅓ cup water
3 tablespoons sugar
6 tablespoons crème fraîche or heavy cream, lightly whipped

**Prepare the apples.** Preheat the oven to 350°F. Starting at the stem end, peel the apples halfway down. With the tip of a paring knife, score the remaining skin vertically (in the direction of the stem) with 8 equidistant cuts. Using an apple corer or melon baller, scoop out the core to form a tunnel that goes from stem to blossom end. Arrange the apples in a baking dish.

**Dress the apples with the sweetener and flavorings.** Drizzle the apples with half the lemon juice. Spoon about 1 tablespoon of the currant jelly into the cavity of each apple, followed by some of the butter and a little of the remaining lemon juice.

**Add the basting liquid to the pan.** Pour the water around the apples and stir in the remaining 2 tablespoons currant jelly. Sprinkle the apples with the sugar. Cover with aluminum foil.

**Bake.** Bake, basting occasionally with the pan juices, until the apples are very tender, about 1 hour 15 minutes. Uncover, increase the heat to 475°F, and bake 10 or 15 minutes longer until the apples are glazed and golden. Serve warm with some of their syrup and crème fraîche.

### Baked Apples with Rosemary and Pine Nuts    Serves 4

*Since I envisioned serving rosemary-scented apples both as dessert and as an accompaniment for roasted meats and poultry, I wanted to slice them in a way that would work for either. So I halved the apples crosswise through the equator to reveal the pretty flowerlike pattern of seeds. They are especially good with pork roasts and chops, instead of applesauce.*

Cut a ¼-inch slice off the stem and flower ends of 4 medium to large Granny Smith apples or other good baking apples, and discard. Cut the apples in half crosswise though the circumference. Butter a baking dish just large enough to hold the apples in one layer; arrange the apple halves seed side up in the dish. Drizzle 4½ tablespoons fresh lemon juice (from 1½ lemons) over the apples, followed by ¼ cup wildflower honey. Dot with 2 teaspoons unsalted butter. Pour ¼ cup each dry white wine and water around the apples. Nestle three 2-inch fresh rosemary sprigs and a 2-inch strip of orange zest, finely slivered, among the apples. Cover loosely with aluminum foil and bake 35 minutes. Turn the apples over, cover, and bake, basting occasionally, 30 minutes longer.

Uncover the apples, turn them again, baste, and bake 20 to 25 minutes, until very tender and nicely glazed. If the wine is evaporating too quickly, add a little warm water.

Serve as is or as a savory accompaniment. To serve as a dessert, place 2 halves and some syrup in each of 4 shallow soup bowls. Scatter 1 to 2 tablespoons roasted pine nuts over each serving. If desired, spoon some crème fraîche or ice cream alongside.

### Baked Apple Sorbet    Serves 4

*This surprising sorbet requires no ice cream maker. Baked apples are simply peeled, chopped, and frozen, then pureed in a food processor; the apples' abundance of pectin makes them creamy. It's worth making a double batch of baked apples, one to eat warm and one to turn into sorbet a few days later.*

Prepare Rosy Baked Apples. Cool the apples, then remove the peels. Place on a cutting board and coarsely chop and remove any seeds. Spread the apples on a cookie sheet, cover with plastic wrap, and freeze. Up to an hour before serving, puree the apples in a food processor, scraping down the sides occasionally, until you have a creamy sorbet. Add fresh lemon juice and superfine sugar or honey to taste, if necessary, to brighten the flavor and process briefly. Serve at once, or pack into a container and freeze. To make a **Baked Apple Soft Ice Cream**, blend in crème fraîche to taste.

### Smashed Baked Apples with Brûléed Marshmallows

*One evening I skinned and crushed the flesh of some leftover baked apples and made this gratin with the chunky roasted pulp; just-this-side-of-burned marshmallows make a molten caramelized topping. It works fine with just about any baked apple recipe, such as Rosy Baked Apples or the Roasted Apples on page 86.*

Use this formula for as many apples as you have: For each apple, you'll need 3 large marshmallows and about 1 tablespoon chopped fresh lemon segments (½ lemon's worth, see Peeling and Sectioning Citrus Fruit, page 353).

Remove the skin from the baked apples and coarsely mash the flesh, removing any seeds. Transfer to a flameproof casserole and warm over a medium flame. Toss with the lemon segments.

Slice each marshmallow crosswise into thirds and arrange on top of the apples. Just before serving, place under a preheated broiler, 3 to 4 inches from the heat source, and broil until the marshmallows are dark brown with tinges of black.

### Baked Applesauce

*Leftover baked apples make fine applesauce. Remove the peels and seeds and coarsely mash with a fork for a chunky applesauce, or puree in a food processor for a smooth sauce. Adjust the flavor by adding additional sugar, a pinch of salt, a squeeze of lemon juice, or a few drops of apple cider vinegar. Serve warm or cool.*

# Chocolate Wonders

I learned to make these huge, over-the-top chocolate cookies twenty-five years ago when I worked at the Soho Charcuterie in New York City, an early, innovative pioneer of New American cooking. Rich chocolate batter was so laced with nuts and chocolate chips that the cookies (adapted from a Maida Heatter recipe) looked like hockey puck–sized lava flows, and became something completely other: at once chunky cookie, brownie, and candy. They were so popular we couldn't make enough of them.

The Chocolate Wonders are an example of a truly great recipe: affording huge pleasures, memorable, and enduring over time. They elicit the same comment over and over: "These are the best cookies I've ever had." Like most great recipes, this one had excellent "bones," that is, a great basic structure that you can refine in a variety of ways, all using a very simple method.

Chocolate Wonders are at heart a brownie batter: butter, eggs, sugar, flour, chocolate. What makes them different from a brownie is the *proportion* of ingredients, a massive amount of nuts and chocolate chips, and the fact that they are dropped free-form like a cookie, rather than baked in a pan. Making them with the best chocolate you can find—one with at least 70 percent cacao (also called "cocoa mass")—ensures an utterly luxurious, profoundly chocolate flavor. Choose a reliable brand of chocolate, such as Valrhona, favored by chefs; Lindt Excellence; or Scharffen Berger.

For improvising, imagine this recipe as having two parts: the batter, which is a rich, tender chocolate cake, and the chunky additions in the form of nuts and chocolate chips, 3 cups worth. Substitute different nuts, chunks of chocolate, dried fruit, even chopped-up candy bars. Combining these splendid ingredients yields great, fun improvisations.

Because the chunky additions play such a big role in taste and texture, I like to use flavorings that will help amplify the chocolate flavor and perfume without adding an overt presence. Vanilla extract is essential. Cognac or Armagnac in place of some of the vanilla gives a sophisticated note. Instant espresso also amplifies the chocolate flavor, adding mocha overtones and a pleasing bitterness.

That being said, there are a great number of other flavorings, such as almond or peppermint extract or grated orange or tangerine zest; liqueurs such as Kahlúa and Fra Angelico; orange flower or rose water; spices, from cinnamon and coriander to garam masala; chile peppers; lavender; Earl Grey tea; and so on. I find these work best in the Chocolate Planets, thin, elegant cookies with an intense chocolate flavor made from the Wonder batter alone.

Taking the batter one step further, I discovered that if you bake it in a round pan (with a slight manipulation of the formula), it transmutes easily into an intensely rich chocolate cake, along the lines of a dense, single-layer, flourless French chocolate cake. Bake in individual ramekins or muffin tins to make individual cakelets. Underbake them enough that the outside is set but the center is barely thickened and saucelike, and you have molten chocolate cake.

One caveat: In all these brownielike creations, timing and oven temperature are key to perfect texture. Underbaking slightly ensures a moist, dense, truffley interior. It's worth investing in an inexpensive oven thermometer so you can make sure your oven temperature is perfect for the times given.

• • • • • •

## Chocolate Wonders    Makes about 20 big cookies

8 ounces bittersweet or semisweet chocolate (preferably at least 70%
cacao) or 6 ounces semisweet chocolate and 2 ounces unsweetened
chocolate, coarsely chopped
6 tablespoons (¾ stick) unsalted butter
⅓ cup all-purpose flour
½ teaspoon baking powder
¼ teaspoon kosher salt
2 large eggs, at room temperature
2 teaspoons instant espresso powder (optional)
2 teaspoons vanilla extract
¾ cup sugar
1 cup *each* semisweet chocolate chips, coarsely chopped pecans,
and coarsely chopped walnuts or 3 cups other chunky ingredients

**Prepare the oven and pans.** Adjust two oven racks spaced equally from top and bottom (if you only have one rack, position it in the middle of the oven). Preheat the oven to 325°F. Line two large cookie sheets with parchment paper or aluminum foil (shiny side up) and set aside.

**Melt the chocolate with the butter.** Combine the chocolate and butter in the top of a double boiler over simmering water. (Or, alternatively, combine them in a small, heavy saucepan set on a Flame Tamer over very low heat.) Stir occasionally until the chocolate is melted. Set aside to cool to barely warm.

**Sift the dry ingredients.** Meanwhile, sift together the flour, baking powder, and salt into a medium bowl; set aside.

**Mix the batter.** Combine the eggs, espresso powder, and vanilla in a large bowl. With a whisk or an electric hand mixer, beat until combined; add the sugar and beat until thick, a minute or two. Use a rubber spatula to scrape the chocolate mixture into the eggs and stir until just combined. Add the flour and stir with the spatula until just blended.

**Add the chunky embellishments.** Fold the chunky embellishments into the batter with the spatula until evenly incorporated.

**Drop the batter onto the prepared pans.** Drop the batter by heaping tablespoons onto the prepared pans, or use a ¼-cup measure, leaving 1½ inches between the cookies.

**Bake.** Bake the cookies until the tops look set and slightly cracked and dry, 16 to 17 minutes. If you are baking two sheets at a time, halfway through the cooking time, reverse them in the oven, top to bottom and front to back. To test for doneness, gently lift a cookie; it should barely hold together and the inside should be soft but not molten or runny. (It's better to err on the side of underbaking; the cookies will firm up somewhat as they cool.) Let the cookies cool to warm on the baking sheet before removing them with a metal spatula to a wire cooling rack.

**To store the cookies**, wrap them individually in plastic wrap. They will stay moist about 1 week and can be frozen up to 1 month. Allow to defrost in the refrigerator several hours, then bring to room temperature, about 1 hour, before serving.

## Improvisations

### The Wonder Variations

*In the Chocolate Wonders recipe, the possible combinations of chunky additions are infinite and can be blended to indulge specific cravings. I've included my core list below, though I keep coming across things that I'd like to try, from candied chestnuts to malted milk balls. Figure 3 cups total, in any combination. Including a proportion of some sort of chocolate chips or chunks in the mix deepens the chocolate blast. Some of my favorites are* **Chocolate Wonders with Roasted Hazelnuts, Currants, and Milk Chocolate Chips; Chocolate Wonders with Coarsely Chopped Heath Bars and Pecans;** *and the simple, elegant* **Chocolate Wonders with Roasted Pistachios.**

Semisweet, milk, or white chocolate chips or chunks
Mint chocolate chips or peanut butter chips
Nuts: walnuts, pecans, almonds, hazelnuts, pistachios, cashews, macadamia nuts, or peanuts (they are all best roasted; see page 352), coarsely chopped
Dried fruit: raisins, currants, cherries, cranberries, or chopped apricots or prunes, or peaches
Candied or crystallized ginger or orange peel, chopped or diced (these are potent and should be used sparingly)
Candy bars, such as peanut butter cups, M&Ms, Pay Day bars, Heath bars, peppermint patties, and any kind of nut brittle, diced or coarsely chopped

## Chocolate Planets    Make about forty 2-inch cookies

*On a hunch, I tried baking the Wonder batter without any chunky additions. Here less is also great: ¼-inch-thick cookies with a tender, slightly chewy, melt-in-your-mouth texture, and a resonant, intensely chocolate flavor. They are really perfect as is, although you can add interesting flavors. Taking inspiration from some of the unusual, subtly perfumed artisanal chocolates that have come on the market of late, try adding ground Mexican cinnamon, ground pink peppercorns or black pepper (about ¼ teaspoon); lavender (½ teaspoon); even Earl Grey tea (about 2 teaspoons ground tea). I sometimes serve the cookies with a bowl of whipped cream or crème fraîche, as a "dip."*

Preheat the oven to 325°F. Prepare the oven and cookie sheets, and mix up a batch of the Chocolate Wonder batter without chocolate morsels and nuts. Drop the batter by slightly heaping teaspoons onto the prepared pans. Bake 12 to 14 minutes until the tops look set and slightly cracked and dry; if you are baking two sheets at a time, halfway through the cooking time, be sure to reverse them in the oven, top to bottom and front to back. If you gently lift a cookie, it will barely hold together; the inside will be soft but not molten or runny. Let the cookies cool to warm on the baking sheet before removing them with a metal spatula to a wire cooling rack.

## Bittersweet Black Pepper Brownie Cake    Serves 8

*This moist, rich, intensely chocolate cake is another permutation of the Chocolate Wonders' basic brownie formula (with a bit more flour to make it cakelike and a bit less sugar to make it more adult), baked in a round cake pan and sliced into wedges. Inspired by the ancient and once-again popular addition of hot chiles to chocolate desserts, I often add freshly ground black pepper for subtle aromatic spiciness. Serve with whipped cream or crème fraîche, or coffee, vanilla, or pistachio ice cream—or gianduja (hazelnut-chocolate) gelato. (For a dramatic 10-inch cake, double the recipe and use a 10-inch cake pan or springform; bake the cake 30 to 33 minutes.)*

Position a rack in the middle of the oven. Preheat the oven to 350°F. Rub the inside of an 8-inch cake pan or a springform pan with unsalted butter. Swirl a few teaspoons of flour around to coat the inside of the pan completely. Invert and tap out the excess.

Combine 8 ounces coarsely chopped bittersweet chocolate (preferably 70% cocoa solids) and 6 tablespoons (¾ stick) unsalted butter in the top of a double boiler over simmering water. (Or, alternatively, combine them in a medium and heavy saucepan and set on a Flame Tamer over very low heat.) Stir occasionally until the chocolate is melted. Set aside to cool to room temperature.

Meanwhile, sift ⅔ cup all-purpose flour, ½ teaspoon baking powder, ¼ teaspoon salt, and a scant ¼ teaspoon freshly ground black pepper (optional) into a medium bowl; whisk well and set aside.

Combine 2 large room-temperature eggs, 2 teaspoons vanilla extract, and 2 teaspoons espresso powder (optional) in a large bowl. Whisk until foamy. Add ½ cup sugar and whisk until light and frothy, about 1 minute. Scrape the chocolate mixture into the eggs and blend. Add the flour mixture in two batches, whisking to blend completely each time.

Pour the batter into the prepared pan. Bake 22 to 25 minutes, until a skewer inserted 1 inch from the edge comes out clean. When inserted in the center of the cake, a bit of moist batter will cling to it.

Cool the cake on a rack 10 minutes, then invert onto a plate. Invert back onto the rack so the shiny side is up. Cool the cake completely before sliding it onto a serving plate. Sift 1 or 2 teaspoons cocoa powder over the top.

# Guava Banana "Jell-O"

- Simple, Surprising "Jell-Os"
- Blackberry, Blueberry, Black Currant, and Other Berry "Jell-Os"
- Sour Cream Panna Cotta
- Herb-Infused Wine "Jell-O"

For most of my life, I never questioned Jell-O, the garish, jiggly gelatin dessert that is the linchpin of every American childhood, never wondered what the imitation flavors were an imitation of, that there might be origins to Jell-O. So it was a revelation when I tried making a homemade "Jell-O." It was so simple to make I wondered why there was instant Jell-O—it's little more than fruit juice jelled with unflavored gelatin. This recipe is one of my favorites, made with guava nectar—with the complex pineapple-banana-citrus-mango flavor and coral color of tropical guavas—available in bottles at my supermarket. It makes a surprising, somehow grown-up "Jell-O" with great charm and vivid, true flavors.

Just about any liquid can be jelled, including fruit juices and purees, from apples to rhubarb; wines, from dry white wine and champagne to sherry (simmered 5 minutes to cook off the alcohol); broths, from poultry to seafood; vegetable juices such as tomato or cucumber; cream; even exotic teas and coffee. A basic formula is the starting point for improvising: One ¼-ounce package of unflavored gelatin (a tad over 2¼ teaspoons), available at any supermarket, will jell 2 cups of liquid. Use Guava Banana "Jell-O" as a template for sweet gelatin desserts that hold universal appeal.

The easy way to make real "Jell-O" is to buy some good-quality fruit juice: apple cider or fresh grapefruit or tangerine juice, say, or bottled nectars in exotic flavors such as passion fruit, pear, or white peach. Heighten the flavor of the juice with sugar or honey and a good dose of lemon juice, then jell according to the formula. Better still, make your own juice by passing fresh fruits through an electric juicer and sweetening the juice to taste. (If the juice tastes a bit watery, boil it to concentrate its flavor before jelling.)

To extract the juice from difficult-to-juice fruits, such as berries, peaches, black currants, and cherries, simmer them in a syrup of white wine or water and honey or sugar until they turn to a mush, then strain. Or use fruit purees for a thicker, opaque "Jell-O." This works well with ripe or thawed frozen berries. Pass them through a food mill or puree them in a food processor, strain out any seeds, and jell as you would juice. For less firm "Jell-O," use less gelatin, as, for example, in panna cotta, a barely jelled cream that uses half the amount of gelatin.

When improvising, bear in mind that flavors get muted in the process of jelling. Adding lemon juice—at least 1 tablespoon per cup—and enough sugar is essential to making flavors bright and vivid.

There are endless possibilities for layering different flavors of homemade "Jell-O" into a glass container, say white peach "Jell-O" with alternating stripes of black currant and wine-infused "Jell-O." Pour one color "Jell-O" into the container to the desired depth and refrigerate until it is completely set. Then pour another color on top and let it set. Repeat, using as many kinds of "Jell-O" as you wish. Stud "Jell-O" with fresh fruit, stirring it in gently when it is half-jelled.

Raw pineapple, mango, kiwi, and ginger have an enzyme that will prevent gelatin from setting; they must all be cooked for 5 minutes before using.

. . . . . . .

## Guava Banana "Jell-O" Serves 4

3 cups guava nectar, such as Goya

3¼ teaspoons unflavored gelatin (1 packet plus 1 teaspoon)

2 tablespoons sugar, or to taste

Pinch of kosher salt

2 tablespoons fresh lime or lemon juice, or to taste

1 ripe medium banana

**Soften the gelatin in the juice or water.** Pour ½ cup of the guava nectar into a medium glass bowl or measuring cup and sprinkle the gelatin over it. Let stand 1 minute.

**Heat the juice with the sweetener.** In a medium saucepan over moderate heat, bring the remaining 2½ cups guava nectar to a simmer. Add the sugar and salt and stir until dissolved.

**Add the softened gelatin.** Turn off the heat, add the gelatin mixture to the hot juice, and stir until dissolved.

**Add the lime or lemon juice to sharpen the flavors.** Stir in the lime juice, and set the mixture aside to cool slightly. Cut the banana into ⅛-inch slices. Place 4 or 5 slices in each of four 1-cup glasses, or all in a 1-quart serving dish. Pour the guava mixture over the top. The banana slices will rise to the top; gently push them into a nice arrangement.

**Refrigerate to set the "Jell-O."** Let cool, then refrigerate the "Jell-O" for several hours, until set. Prepare "Jell-O" up to 3 days ahead for the best flavor.


## Improvisations

### Simple, Surprising "Jell-Os"

*Over the years, I've made many "Jell-Os" using the basic formula of 1 packet unflavored gelatin to 2 cups sweetened juice, with a couple of tablespoons of lemon juice to heighten the flavors. Most are surprising because they are so rarely served. They include:*

*· **Pink Grapefruit "Jell-O":** a refreshing, sophisticated, surprising dessert I first tasted in a Korean barbecue restaurant in New York*

- **Real Grape "Jell-O":** *a play on the kids' favorite, made from frozen Concord grape juice or fresh-squeezed muscat grape juice, sometimes available in summer and fall at farmers' markets*
- **Apple Cider "Jell-O":** *made with fresh fall cider*
- **Tangerine or Tangelo "Jell-O":** *made from strained fresh juice*
- **Meyer Lemon "Jell-O":** *sweeten fresh Meyer lemon juice (diluted with water) and infuse for a few minutes with a few strips of zest*

## Blackberry, Blueberry, Black Currant, and Other Berry "Jell-Os"   Serves 4

*Rather than trying to juice blackberries, strawberries, blueberries, raspberries, or black currants, I simmer them in my standard faux dessert-wine mixture of dry white wine and honey until they release their juices; then I jell the strained syrup for fragrant, intensely flavored "Jell-O." Unjelled, the syrup can be used to make interesting cocktails. Black currants, briefly available in farmers' markets in summer, make an unusual tart, sophisticated "Jell-O." In winter, use this method with inexpensive frozen berries. (See page 345, using this method to make Rhubarb "Jell-O.")*

In a large saucepan, combine 1 cup dry white wine, ¼ cup wildflower honey, ¼ cup sugar, ½ cup water, and one 2-inch strip each orange and lemon zests; bring to a simmer over moderate heat. Simmer 5 minutes, until the alcohol is cooked off. Add 3 to 4 cups berries and 2 fresh thyme sprigs, if desired, and simmer until the berries are falling apart, about 5 minutes. Strain the fruit, pressing to extract all the syrup; discard the pulp. Meanwhile, sprinkle one ¼-ounce packet unflavored gelatin over 2 tablespoons water in a small bowl and let soften several minutes.

Return the berry syrup to the saucepan. Over very low heat, stir the gelatin into the berry syrup until dissolved. Add 1 to 2 tablespoons fresh lemon juice and more sugar to taste. Pour the mixture into a serving dish and chill several hours, or overnight, until the gelatin is set.

## Sour Cream Panna Cotta   Serves 8

*Although panna cotta is Italian for "cooked cream," it is really a cream that is barely thickened with gelatin until it sets into a rich custard. Thinking it would be lovely to have the slightly sour, intense cream flavor of crème fraîche in a panna cotta, I devised this one made with heavy and sour cream. It is astonishingly rich* and silky, the perfect dinner party dessert: easy to make (ahead) and luxurious. It stands on its own, but it would be an over-the-top accompaniment to just about any fruit, from Rhubarb Confit (page 343) to simple sugared raspberries.

Pour ¼ cup milk into a small bowl, sprinkle evenly with one ¼-ounce packet unflavored gelatin (2⅜ teaspoons), and let stand 10 minutes to soften. Meanwhile, in a medium heavy saucepan, combine an additional ¾ cup milk, 1 cup heavy cream, ½ cup sugar, and a pinch of salt; bring to a simmer over medium heat, stirring until the sugar is dissolved. Remove from the heat and whisk in the gelatin mixture until it is dissolved. Transfer to a medium bowl and cool 15 minutes.

Whisk in 2 cups sour cream. Spoon the mixture into eight 4-ounce ramekins; chill several hours, or overnight. Serve as is, or unmold by running a warm knife around the edges of each and inverting onto a plate.

### Herb-Infused Wine "Jell-O"    Serves 4

*This wine "Jell-O" tastes as if it were made from dessert wine, though in reality it is a combination of white wine, honey, and lemon and orange zests. While it is simmering, I often add sprigs of fresh herbs, removing them when they've imparted a subtle herbal flavor. Serve it alone, with crème fraîche, or alongside just about any kind of fresh fruit—sliced fresh white peaches, for example—that you've marinated with sugar and a little lemon juice.*

In a medium saucepan, combine 3 cups dry white wine, ½ cup wildflower honey, ¼ cup sugar, 1 cup water, and one 3-inch strip each orange and lemon zests; bring to a simmer over moderate heat. Simmer 5 minutes, until the alcohol is cooked off. Meanwhile, sprinkle 1 packet unflavored gelatin over 2 tablespoons water in a medium metal bowl and let soften several minutes.

Remove the wine from the heat and add 8 or 9 fresh herbs sprigs, such as thyme, lavender, lemon verbena, basil, or mint, in any combination (for example, 2 sprigs each thyme, lemon verbena, basil, and peppermint); infuse a minute or two, until the wine takes on a subtle herbal flavor. Strain the wine into the gelatin and stir until dissolved. Add 2 tablespoons fresh lemon juice. Pour the mixture into a serving dish and chill several hours, or overnight, until the gelatin is set.

Just before serving, gently scramble the gelatin with a fork to break it into small jewel-like pieces.

# Rhubarb Confit and Rhubarb Syrup
# for Improvising

- Rhubarb Tart
- Rhubarb Lemonade
- Strawberry-Rhubarb Milk Shake
- Rhubarb "Jell-O" with Sugared Berries

Sometimes a single experiment unleashes a flood of unexpected improvisations. So my attempt at making a rhubarb "Jell-O" led inadvertently to this thick, velvety rhubarb confit; it is a by-product of simmering rhubarb in a white wine syrup to release its flavor and make a "juice" I could jell. When I strained it, I discovered that not only had I made rhubarb syrup, but the leftover solids were in fact a delectable cross between a sauce and a compote—a confit. And each inspired other improvisations.

Refining it further, I infused the wine-honey syrup with strawberries before adding the rhubarb, to give the rhubarb a deeper pink color and an undertone of strawberry flavor.

The confit is extremely versatile. Serve warm or chilled for dessert in tandem with Sour Cream Panna Cotta (page 339) or with heavy cream, ice cream, or crème fraîche. It makes a splendid breakfast with yogurt or on French toast. The confit also complements many savory foods, such as roasted pork, chicken, duck, and game, in the way applesauce does. It makes an unusual accompaniment to dried-cured hams, such as serrano, prosciutto, and duck hams, and smoked chicken, turkey, and duck.

Simmering just about any fruit in a syrup breaks down its structure so that it releases its juices and flavors into the syrup to make a concentrated essence.

The strained cooked pulp of sturdy fruit such as rhubarb, apples, and peaches retains a lot of flavor and can be used as a confit. With berries, little flavor remains in the strained fruit, but the syrup inspires improvisations (see Blackberry, Blueberry, Black Currant, and Other Berry "Jell-Os," page 339). Rather than the usual water and sugar to make a syrup, I combine white wine with honey, which mimics a dessert wine and seems to intensify and broaden the fruits' flavors. Further flavorings include lemon, orange, or tangerine zests; a split vanilla bean; spices, such as cinnamon, allspice, or white peppercorns; or sprigs of herbs; or lemongrass.

The rhubarb confit makes an instant filling for tarts, turnovers, pies, and other pastrylike creations. Sandwiched in a split buttermilk biscuit with some whipped cream, it would make a marvelous shortcake. It's a natural with cream; add it to churning vanilla ice cream for rhubarb ice cream, or blend with strawberry ice cream and milk for a milk shake; layer it into a tall glass with vanilla or strawberry ice cream for a parfait. If you simmer the confit in a heavy pan over low heat, it will become a thick, old-fashioned jam.

The rhubarb syrup does in fact make a splendid "Jell-O," and inspires all kinds of drinks and cocktails. Since rhubarb is a delicate flavor, care must be taken not to overpower it; milder alcohols such as vodka and white rum work best. It makes a great sauce for sliced fresh strawberries or peaches.

. . . . . .

# Rhubarb Confit and Rhubarb Syrup for Improvising

**Makes about 2 cups confit and 3 cups syrup**

2½ cups dry white wine

¾ to 1 cup sugar

6 tablespoons wildflower honey

2 to 3 cups strawberries, hulled and halved

2 pounds rhubarb, preferably red stalks, trimmed and sliced ¼ inch thick
   (8 to 10 cups)

2 to 4 tablespoons fresh lemon juice

**Simmer the wine to cook off the alcohol and add any flavorings.** In a large saucepan, combine the wine, ¾ cup sugar, the honey, and strawberries. Bring to a low boil over moderate heat, stirring occasionally; cook until the strawberries are flabby and pale, 10 to 12 minutes. With a slotted spoon, transfer the strawberries to a bowl. As they stand, occasionally pour the juices that collect around them back into the pot. (If the strawberries still have some flavor, save them to eat with yogurt.)

**Add the fruit and simmer to release the juices.** Add the rhubarb and return to a low boil. Cover until the rhubarb has released its juices, 3 minutes. Uncover and simmer until the rhubarb is falling apart, 6 to 8 minutes.

**Strain.** Working in batches if necessary, pour the rhubarb mixture through a fine strainer set over a bowl; let sit several minutes, stirring frequently with a rubber spatula or a spoon to extract most of the liquid. Transfer the thick confit to a bowl.

**Balance the flavors of the confit and the syrup.** Stir 1 to 2 tablespoons lemon juice and additional sugar into the confit, if desired. Refrigerate. Transfer the syrup to a jar and add a pinch of salt, 1 to 2 tablespoons lemon juice, and additional sugar, if desired; refrigerate until ready to use.

### Rhubarb Tart   **Serves 6 to 8**

*The texture of the Rhubarb Confit is creamy and thick enough to be used as an instant tart filling.*

Prepare Rhubarb Confit and 1 recipe Ethereal Brown Sugar Butter Cookies dough (page 302). Rather than rolling the dough into a log, press it into a 10-inch tart tin with a removable bottom, building up the edge slightly to make a ¼-inch rim. Chill for 30 minutes. Bake in a preheated 325°F oven until the edges are just beginning to brown, 30 to 35 minutes; cool before filling.

Within 1 hour of serving, spread the Rhubarb Confit evenly in the tart shell. Smooth 2 cups unsweetened whipped cream over the top; garnish with some slivered lemon or orange zest. Refrigerate until ready to serve.

### Rhubarb Lemonade

*With a rosy color and a tart undercurrent of rhubarb, this is "beyond lemonade."*

For each serving, combine ½ cup Rhubarb Syrup, 2 tablespoons fresh lemon juice, and 2 teaspoons superfine sugar; add 2 tablespoons cold water or plain seltzer. If you're using lemonade that's already made, figure about ½ cup Rhubarb Syrup to ¼ cup lemonade and omit the sugar. Serve over ice.

### Strawberry-Rhubarb Milk Shake   **Serves 4**

*I like to serve this unusual milk shake as an unexpected and charming dessert for dinner parties, but it is perfect anytime you are in the mood for a shake.*

In a blender container, combine 2 cups strawberry ice cream, 2 cups chilled Rhubarb Confit, 2 teaspoons vanilla extract, and 2 ice cubes. Blend on low speed, dribbling in enough cold milk, up to ¼ cup, to get the mixture moving. Blend on high speed until thick and creamy, adding 1 or 2 teaspoons fresh lime or lemon juice and additional sugar to taste, if desired, to lift the flavors. Discard the ice cubes and pour the mixture into four 8-ounce glasses or goblets.

## Rhubarb "Jell-O" with Sugared Berries    Serves 4

*Serve Rhubarb "Jell-O" with the fragrant farm stand blackberries, blueberries, raspberries, or strawberries that are in season at the same time.*

Pour 2 to 2½ cups Rhubarb Syrup into a medium saucepan and sprinkle one ¼-ounce packet unflavored gelatin over it. Let stand several minutes until the gelatin has swelled and softened. Place the saucepan over medium heat and bring to a bare simmer, stirring until the gelatin is dissolved. Add fresh lemon juice and additional sugar if necessary to sharpen the flavors. Pour into a serving dish, cool to room temperature, then chill several hours, until set.

Meanwhile, hull 2 pints of berries in any combination (cut strawberries in halves, quarters, or slices). Place in a bowl and toss with sugar and a few teaspoons of fresh lemon juice. Set aside at room temperature several hours, until the juices have formed a syrup; chill.

To serve, spoon some of the "Jell-O" in each of 4 shallow bowls; spoon some of the berries alongside.

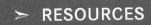 RESOURCES

# A Guide to Classic Flavor Affinities

This guide outlines classic flavor palettes of different countries and regions around the world. Use it as a place to start learning about flavor affinities or as an inspiration in your own improvisations.

Each grouping is roughly broken down into essential categories that comprise its unique vocabulary of flavor.

**Categories**

fats

aromatics (base flavorings)

dried spices

fresh herbs

acid/tart flavorings

salty/savory or sweet flavorings

textural flavor elements

some classic flavor combinations

**The Mediterranean (Southern France, Italy, Spain)**

olive oil

garlic, onion, tomato, hot or sweet peppers

saffron, fennel seed

thyme, basil, oregano, parsley, savory, rosemary

lemon, orange, wine vinegar, wine

olives, pine nuts

herbes de Provence: rosemary, thyme, summer savory, lavender

Provençal flavorings for seafood: tomato, saffron, fennel, orange zest, garlic, white wine, garlic and olive oil plus:

> peperoncino
> anchovies
> tomatoes and herbs
> basil and pine nuts

## France

butter, olive oil, smoked bacon, cream, crème fraîche, walnut oil, hazelnut oil
onion, leek, shallot, garlic, tomato
nutmeg, vanilla, saffron
basil, parsley, sage, tarragon, thyme, bay leaf, sorrel, chives
wine vinegar, capers, mustard
wine, Cognac, Armagnac

bouquet garni (basic flavorings for broths and stews): bay leaf, thyme, parsley
    fines herbes: tarragon, chives, parsley

## Italy

olive oil, pancetta, guanciale, butter
garlic, onions, tomato
peperoncino
sage, rosemary, basil, oregano, parsley
balsamic vinegar, wine vinegar, lemon juice
Parmigiano, anchovies
pine nuts, walnuts

garlic and olive oil plus sage and/or rosemary
olive oil, garlic, tomato

## Eastern Mediterranean/Greece

olive oil
garlic, onion, tomato
cinnamon, cumin
dill, mint, parsley, oregano
lemon, wine vinegar, yogurt
honey, orange flower water
olives, pistachios, pine nuts, walnuts

garlic, olive oil, lemon plus oregano, mint, parsley
tomatoes, sautéed onions with cinnamon or cumin

**Middle East/North Africa/Morocco**

olive oil

garlic, onion, tomato, peppers

saffron, cardamom, cinnamon, coriander, cloves, cumin, ground ginger, paprika, fennel

cilantro, mint, parsley, oregano, wild thyme, dill

preserved (salted) lemon, pomegranate molasses, orange flower water, rose water, honey

ras el hanout: cinnamon, nutmeg, ginger, cloves, peppers, rosebuds

**Southeast Asia/Vietnam/Thailand**

roasted sesame oil, peanut oil

onions, garlic, shallot, chiles, ginger

star anise

lemongrass, kaffir lime leaf, cilantro, mint, basil

lime, rice vinegar, tamarind

fish sauce, shrimp paste, coconut milk

sesame seeds, peanuts, coconut

**China**

roasted sesame oil, peanut oil

garlic, scallions, ginger, chiles

Szechuan peppercorns, star anise, five-spice powder (cinnamon, cloves, fennel seed, star anise,
    Szechuan peppercorns)

cilantro

rice vinegar

soy sauce, rice wine or sherry, honey

fermented black beans

sesame oil, garlic or scallions, ginger

**Japan and Korea**

roasted sesame oil

garlic, scallion, ginger

hot pepper, wasabi

shiso (herb with a bright basil-mint flavor)

rice vinegar, yuzu (fragrant lemon/tangerine citrus)

soy sauce, miso, sake, mirin (sweetened rice wine)

toasted sesame seeds

**India**

ghee (clarified butter)

garlic, caramelized onions, ginger, chile peppers

cardamom, cinnamon, cloves, coriander, cumin, black pepper, fennel seed, mustard seed, saffron, turmeric, coriander, cilantro

limes, yogurt

coconut, coconut milk

garam masala: cardamom, cinnamon, cumin, cloves, black pepper, nutmeg

curry powder: coriander, cumin, black pepper, fennel, turmeric, mustard, ginger, cinnamon

**Eastern/Northern Europe**

bacon, chicken fat, pumpkin seed oil

onion, garlic

paprika, caraway, black pepper, allspice, fennel

dill, sorrel

yogurt, sour cream, mustard

walnuts

**Mexico**

vegetable oil, lard

garlic, onions, chile peppers, tomato

cinnamon, oregano, cumin, achiote, black pepper

cilantro, oregano, marjoram, bay leaf

lime, cider vinegar, orange

coconut, tomatillos, pumpkin seeds, peanuts, avocado

**United States**

smoked ham and bacon

butter

onions

sweet spices (cinnamon, nutmeg, clove, allspice), vanilla

sage

cider and cider vinegar

maple syrup, molasses, brown sugar, bourbon

pecans

# Basic Techniques and Preparations

### Toasting and Crushing Spices

Toasting dried spices in a skillet heightens their flavor and revives those that are faded. Scatter the spices into a small skillet. Toast over moderately low heat, shaking the pan frequently, until you just get a whiff of their fragrance.

To coarsely crush spices like coriander seed or peppercorns, transfer to a mortar and coarsely crush the seeds with a pestle. Or, place a sheet of paper towel on the work surface and pour the seeds onto it. Use the side of a chef's knife or the flat bottom of a heavy glass to press down on the spices to crush them. Carefully lift the sides of the towel and tilt the crushed spices into a small bowl. Alternatively, coarsely grind them in a spice grinder or clean coffee grinder for a less rustic effect.

### Roasting Nuts

Roasting nuts intensifies and sweetens their flavor. You can roast nuts and store them in a sealed plastic bag or container in the refrigerator for up to 2 months.

I use two methods for roasting nuts, depending on how quickly I need them and if I want to heat the oven. The oven method produces a more uniform, nonoily result.

**Oven method**. Preheat the oven to 375°F. Scatter the nuts onto a baking sheet. Roast *walnuts, pecans, and pine nuts* until they are very fragrant and deep golden brown, 6 to 7 minutes, watching carefully toward the end to be sure they don't burn.

*Hazelnuts* have a papery brown skin that you need to remove. Roast the hazelnuts for 2 minutes. With a water sprayer, mist the nuts with water several times. Continue roasting until the nuts are brown and very fragrant, 10 to 12 minutes. Rub the nuts between kitchen towels to remove the skins.

Roast *pistachios* in a 300°F oven until fragrant but not brown, to preserve their green color.

**Quick stovetop method for skinned nuts.** Place the nuts in a small heavy skillet with a teaspoon of grapeseed or olive oil. Cook, stirring constantly, over moderately low heat until the nuts are fragrant and golden. Drain on paper towels.

### Slivering Citrus Zest

Using a vegetable peeler, remove the zest, leaving behind as much of the white pith as possible. Place the strips flat on a cutting board; using a sharp paring knife or a chef's knife, cut crosswise or on a diagonal into the thinnest possible strips.

### Peeling and Sectioning Citrus Fruit

With a thin sharp knife, cut the stem and flower ends off the fruit. Place the fruit with one cut side down on the work surface. Working from top to bottom, carefully cut the skin and white pith in strips off the flesh, leaving the flesh intact. Then, holding the peeled fruit over a bowl to catch the juices, cut along each side of the membranes to release the sections. Place the sections in a small bowl. Squeeze the membranes to extract any juice, and discard.

### Splitting and Scraping a Vanilla Bean

Vanilla beans are thin, pliable pods from an orchid plant that are an essential ingredient in baking. They give a deeper, more complex vanilla flavor to foods, bringing out their inherent sweetness and perfume. You'll find vanilla beans folded into jars in the spice section of your supermarket; look for plump, pliable beans, not ones that are dry or brittle.

Place the bean on the work surface. With a sharp paring knife, split the bean in half lengthwise. With the tip of the knife, scrape out the black paste in the center of each half. These are the seeds. Mix the seeds into the food you wish to flavor, or into the sugar that will be used in the recipe. Add the pods if possible and remove after cooking. You can also add the pods to a canister of confectioners' sugar to make vanilla-scented sugar to sprinkle over pastries and cakes.

### Pitting Olives

Place the olives on a work surface and tap each one lightly with a heavy can or meat pounder or the side of a chef's knife. The olives will split open, revealing the pit. Remove the pits with your fingers.

To pit a lot of olives, sandwich them between two pieces of cheesecloth or paper towels to keep them from sliding around the counter.

1 pound olives = 2 cups pitted = about 1½ cups paste

### Pitting Cherries

When caught without a cherry pitter, pit cherries the same way as olives, by smashing them lightly with a can or jar. Place the cherries in a metal baking dish with at least 2-inch sides when you are doing this to prevent the juice from squirting on your clothes. Alternatively, you can cover them with a paper towel to catch the spray.

### Rendering Bacon or Pancetta Fat

To render means to cook a fatty meat like bacon slowly until the fat liquefies and separates from the flesh; it is then strained and used for cooking. You can store rendered fat in a clean, dry jar in the refrigerator for 3 months or more; you can scale up the following formula to make bigger batches.

For 2 tablespoons rendered fat, you'll need:

- About 2 ounces regular bacon or pancetta, thinly sliced or finely diced (½ cup)

- About 3 ounces double-smoked bacon, thinly sliced or finely diced (¾ cup)

Cook the bacon or pancetta (or duck, ham, or goose fat) covered in a heavy skillet over low heat, stirring occasionally, until the fat is liquid and the remaining bits are crisp and brown. Strain into a clean, dry jar and refrigerate when cool. Use the crisp bits in recipes or as a garnish.

### Cleaning a Soft-Shell Crab

With kitchen shears, using a single cut across the body, cut off the eyes and mouth. Turn the crab over and cut off the apron, the thin tail flap that opens out from the body. Fold back one pointed side of the top shell to expose the gills; pull out the gills and discard. Repeat with the other side. Rinse the crab and pat dry.

### Seasoning Cast-Iron Pans

Cast-iron pans offer an excellent alternative to nonstick pans but must be seasoned to prevent foods from sticking. Seasoning is the process by which the surface of the skillet is cleaned of impurities and then heated with a small amount of oil, which seals the iron and creates a smooth, black, virtually nonstick surface. If your skillet is new, scrub it with soapy water to remove factory oil and dry completely. To season the pan, place it over medium heat. Cover the bottom of the pan completely with a thin layer of salt and heat several minutes, until the salt begins to darken. Remove the pan from the heat and, using paper towels, scrub the pan with the salt; discard. Rub the inside of the pan liberally with vegetable oil and set aside to cool and absorb the oil; wipe out any excess.

Never use soaps or abrasives with cast iron. Simply use warm water and a brush, and pat dry to prevent rusting; then rub with a thin coat of oil. Gradually a patina will begin to build up in the pan, becoming a smooth, black surface. If food ever begins to stick, reseason as directed.

### Essential Vinaigrette

This all-purpose vinaigrette complements just about any salad. Two teaspoons will dress 2 cups greens. Makes ½ cup.

In a small bowl or jar, combine 3 tablespoons balsamic vinegar, 1 tablespoon sherry vinegar, and a good pinch of kosher salt. Cover the jar and shake vigorously, or stir to dissolve the salt. Add ¼ cup extra virgin olive oil and 2 teaspoons hot water, and shake or stir until uniform.

Store for up to 2 weeks in the refrigerator. If the vinaigrette separates upon standing, mix again.

To make a **Nut Oil Vinaigrette**, use 1 tablespoon sherry vinegar and 2 teaspoons balsamic and replace the olive oil with a fragrant walnut or hazelnut oil.

### Easy Butter Dough for Tarts, Pies, and Free-Form Pastries

This is an easy way to make crust that is flaky, tender, and buttery. I replaced some of the usual butter with sour cream, which makes the dough easier to work and increases the tenderness and richness of the crust. The flour/butter mixture is chilled midway through the process so that when the dough is rolled, the hard butter will form flat sheets, increasing the flakiness of the dough. The recipe can be doubled or tripled, and the unused dough may be frozen, well wrapped in plastic wrap, for up to 1 month. To defrost, thaw in the refrigerator several hours before using. Makes 8 ounces dough, enough for one 9- to 10-inch tart or pie.

**Food Processor Method**: In a food processor, combine 1 cup unbleached all-purpose flour, 1 teaspoon sugar, and ½ teaspoon each baking powder and salt. Process to mix. Add 4 tablespoons (½ stick) cold unsalted butter, cut into ½-inch bits, and process to a coarse meal. Put the work bowl with the butter-flour meal in the refrigerator to chill for 15 minutes. Add 3½ tablespoons sour cream. Process until the mixture gathers together in the bowl. Gather the dough into a ball, knead several times on a lightly floured surface, and form it into a flat disk; or for cutouts, shape into a 4 × 5-inch rectangle. Wrap in plastic. Chill at least ½ hour before rolling.

**By Hand**: In a medium bowl, combine 1 cup unbleached all-purpose flour, 1 teaspoon sugar, and ½ teaspoon each baking powder and salt. Add 4 tablespoons (½ stick) cold unsalted butter, cut into ½-inch bits, and cut it into the flour with a pastry cutter or two knives until it makes a very coarse meal. Alternatively, using a pinching motion with your fingers, mix the butter into the flour; rub the butter and flour between the palms of both hands to further blend it until the mixture is the texture of coarse meal. Chill the dough in the refrigerator for 15 minutes. Add 3½ tablespoons sour cream and blend it in with a pastry cutter or fork. With your hands, knead and squeeze the dough 7 or 8 times to incorporate the loose bits and gather the dough together into a rough ball. Shape, wrap, and chill as directed above.

### Rolling and Cutting Pastry Dough into Shapes for Free-Form Pastries

An alternative to pressing pastry dough into a tart tin or pie plate is to cut the rolled-out dough into shapes to bake and use as lids and platforms for free-form tarts like the Warm Free-Form Tart of Caramelized Peppers, Olives, Pine Nuts, and Goat Cheese on page 90. The simplest shapes are squares, diamonds, strips, or rectangles, made by cutting the dough with a floured chef's knife in a crosshatch or parallel-line pattern. Or cut out appealing shapes like hearts, circles, or animals with cookie cutters. You can always roll and cut the dough up to several days ahead of baking it if you wrap the shapes well and freeze them; there is no need to defrost them before baking. Use Easy Butter Dough for Tarts, Pies, and Free-Form Pastries (page 355) or your favorite pastry dough.

Let the dough sit at room temperature about 15 minutes before rolling. Sprinkle the work surface lightly and evenly with a little flour. Rub the rolling pin with flour as well. Center the dough in the middle of the work surface. Beginning at one edge, press the rolling pin down onto the dough to flatten it, moving it across the dough in increments. Moving from the center of the dough and working outward, begin to roll the dough, adding more flour to keep the dough from sticking. Roll the dough gradually in each direction, flattening as you go, to form a 10-inch square; do not roll thinner than ⅛ inch. If the dough cracks or pulls apart, moisten the torn edges with a little water (using your finger or a paintbrush) and press together to secure. Dust lightly with flour if the surface of the dough is sticky. Use a knife or cookie cutters to cut the dough into the desired shapes. With a thin metal spatula, transfer the shapes to a baking sheet.

(Gather any scraps of dough, press into a ball, wrap in plastic, and refrigerate ½ hour to relax the gluten. Then roll and cut the dough.)

To bake the dough, refrigerate just-cut dough at least 10 minutes before baking. Preheat the oven to 375°F. Bake until the dough is golden brown and crisp, about 10 minutes.

## In a Pinch

### Dessert Wine for Cooking

Sweet, fragrant dessert wines, such as Sauternes, Monbazillac, Barsac, or Muscat de Beaumes-de-Venise, are wonderful to cook with. In a pinch, you can make the following substitution: 1 cup dry white wine mixed with 3 tablespoons golden honey.

### Buttermilk

This is a good substitute for buttermilk in baking recipes. Whisk together equal parts milk and plain yogurt.

## Long-Keeping Staples for Pantry, Refrigerator, and Freezer

Tailor this list of staple ingredients to suit your taste and your cooking; add ingredients you find inspiring, or subtract those that don't appeal to you.

### Refrigerator Staples

**long-keeping fruits:** lemons, limes, oranges, apples

**long-keeping vegetables:** yellow onions, shallots, garlic, carrots, parsnips, celery root, turnips, sweet potatoes, potatoes

**long-keeping fresh herbs and flavorings:** rosemary, thyme, and sage, fresh ginger

**dairy products:** sour cream (regular or reduced fat–not low fat); Parmigiano or other hard aged cheese; buttermilk and yogurt; heavy cream and/or crème fraîche

large eggs, preferably organic

green and black olives (unpitted, in brine or olive oil)

**nuts:** pine nuts, walnuts, and pecans

### Freezer Staples

unsalted butter

bacon and/or pancetta

ravioli or tortellini

**bread products:** baguettes, peasant bread, whole grain rolls; all-butter piecrust dough, either commercial or homemade

### Cabinet Staples and Dry Goods

**salt:** kosher (coarse) salt and sea salt, such as Maldon or fleur de sel

**oils:** extra virgin olive oil; neutral (flavorless) vegetable oil such as grapeseed or canola; roasted nut/seed oil(s) such as walnut, hazelnut, peanut, and sesame (store nut/seed oils in the refrigerator)

**vinegars:** balsamic and sherry; Banyuls, from southwest France, is a great all-purpose vinegar

**sweeteners:** granulated sugar, wildflower honey, brown or turbinado sugar, maple sugar

**canned goods:** plum tomatoes, unsalted or low-sodium chicken broth, canned beans

**dried beans and legumes:** flageolets, black beans, green lentils (preferably French lentilles de Puy) chickpeas, white beans such as baby lima beans, Great Northern, navy, or cannellini

**dried pastas:** linguine, penne, and a good egg tagliatelle or fettuccine

**grains:** stone-ground cornmeal, brown basmati rice, farro, wild rice, long-grain white rice, basmati or Texmati rice, short-grain rice such as Carnaroli, Arborio, or Vialone Nano

**wines and other alcohols for cooking and drinking:** inexpensive red and white wines, Rainwater or Sercial Madeira, ruby or tawny port, Cognac or Armagnac, grappa, rum

**Other Pantry Staples**

baking soda

baking powder

all-purpose flour

Wondra or white rice flour

bittersweet or semisweet chocolate

Dutch process cocoa powder

low-sodium soy sauce

**Dried Herbs and Spices**

bay leaves, preferably imported

oregano

rosemary

sage

savory

thyme

allspice, ground and whole berries

Chinese five-spice powder

cinnamon, stick and ground

cloves

coriander seeds, ground and whole

cumin seeds, ground and whole

curry powder

fennel seed

ginger

mustard

nutmeg

saffron

vanilla beans and vanilla extract

cayenne pepper

chili powder

paprika, pimentón de la Vera, or sweet mild single chili powder

pepper: black, white, Szechuan peppercorns; hot red pepper flakes or peperoncini (small dried hot chile peppers)

## (Almost) Essential Equipment

Here is my bottom-line, no-frills list of equipment with which you could cook almost anything.

**knives:** chef's knife, paring or utility knife
**knife sharpener:** either a steel, an electric knife sharpener, or a manual gadget
cutting board(s)

graduated measuring spoons
swivel-bladed vegetable peeler
timer (minutes/hours)
instant-read thermometer
dry measuring cups
paintbrush(es)
flexible metal spatula
rubber spatula
wooden spoons
a pair of metal tongs, 8 to 15 inches long
slotted spoon
multipurpose whisk
heavy-duty kitchen shears
ruler-shaped all-purpose rasp grater or a box grater

glass measuring cups, 1 cup and 2 cup
fine-mesh strainer, 6 to 8 inches in diameter
a set of nesting stainless steel bowls, 6 to 13 inches in diameter
colander

**saucepans and pots:** 1 quart, 1¾ to 2 quarts, 3 quarts, and 6 quarts
**heavy-duty skillets with lids:** 8 inch, 10 inch, or 12 inch, including at least one 10-inch or 12-inch nonstick or well-seasoned cast-iron skillet (see Seasoning Cast-Iron Pans, page 355)
2 baking sheets

salad spinner
**small appliances:** food processor, blender, electric hand mixer

## Sources

**Gourmet, Ethnic, and Exotic Ingredients**

ChefShop
877-337-2491
www.chefshop.com

**Selected Treasures: Olive Oils, Vinegars, Pastas, Honeys**

Zingerman's
888-636-8162
www.zingermans.com

**Italian Artisanal Products, Including Olive Oils, Vinegars, Dried Beans, Grains, Anchovies**

Gustiamo
718-860-2949
www.gustiamo.com

**Butter, Crème Fraîche, and Fresh Cheeses**

Vermont Butter and Cheese Company
800-884-6287
www.vtbutterandcheeseco.com

**Cheeses**

Murray's Cheese
888-692-4339
www.murrayscheese.com

**Grains, Grain Products, and Specialty Flours**

Bob's Red Mill Natural Foods
800-349-2173
www.bobsredmill.com

**J. LeBlanc Roasted Nut Oils**

Madrose Group
800-910-1990
www.madrose.com

### Spices and Herbs, Vanilla Beans, Chiles

Adriana's Caravan
800-316-0820
www.adrianascaravan.com

Penzey's Spices
800-741-7787
www.penzeys.com

### Game and Game Birds, Free-Range Chickens, Duck Breasts

D'Artagnan
800-327-8246
www.dartagnan.com

### Naturally Raised Beef, Pork, and Lamb

Niman Ranch
510-808-0340
www.nimanranch.com

### Pancetta, Guanciale, and Other Cured Meats

Salumi Artisan Cured Meats
877-223-0813
www.salumicuredmeats.com

### Sauces, Condiments, and Seasonings

#### Fragrant Herb Salt (pages 44–48)

Real Garlic Salt
Moroccan-Style Seasoning with
  Cinnamon, Coriander, and Cumin
Mole-Inspired Seasoning with Ancho,
  Cinnamon, and Cocoa
Fragrant Szechuan Pepper Seasoning
Duck, Rabbit, Game, and Charcuterie
  Seasoning
All-Purpose Aromatic Pepper

*Other herb salts:*
Rosemary, Thyme, and Lavender Salt
Rosemary-Sage Salt

#### Basil, Lemon, and Tomato Oil (pages 49–54)

Parsley, Thyme, Rosemary, and Bay Leaf
  Oil
Chinese Many-Flavor Oil
Sage and Garlic Oil with Fried Sage
  Leaves
Infused Oil for Grilled Meats (La Bagna
  Fredda)
Ramp, Garlic, and Other Oniony Confits
  with Their Flavored Olive Oils
Simple Flavored Oil Improvisations

*Other flavored oils:*
Rosemary Oil
Shallot Oil
Fragrant Fennel Oil
Thyme and Shallot Oil
Shallot Oil (with Shallots)
Ginger Oil (with Crispy Ginger)
Brown Butter
Garlic and Rosemary Oil

#### Essential Caesar Sauce (pages 55–59)

Bagna Cauda
Deconstructed Caesar Salad
Spaghetti with Garlic, Anchovy, and Hot
  Chile
Warm Vegetables with Anchovies,
  Currants, and Pine Nuts

#### Vinegar Redux (pages 60–64)

Raspberry Thyme Vinegar
Strawberry Balsamic Vinegar for Desserts
Cherry Aged Cherry Vinegar
Tarragon Chive, Shallot, and Other Salad
  Vinegars
Balsamic Caramel

#### Almost Homemade Mayonnaise (pages 65–69)

Bacon Mayonnaise with or without Ramps
Garlic Mayonnaise, after Aïoli
Saffron Garlic Sauce
Rosemary and (Meyer) Lemon Mayonnaise
Parmesan Mayonnaise

#### Sweet or Savory Quinces in White Wine and Honey (pages 70–75)

Upside-Down Quince Tart
Savory Apples with White Wine and
  Rosemary
Pears in Fragrant Dessert Wine
White Peaches in Red Wine Syrup
Sweet-and-Sour Spiced Prunes

*Other fruit simmered in wine recipes:*
Dried Cherries in Red Wine Syrup

#### Lemon Oregano Jam (pages 76–80)

Lemon Lavender Jam
Tangelo Jam

## Hors d'oeuvres, Appetizers, Soups, and Salads

Cilantro Salad with Fragrant Peanut or
  Sesame Oil
Salad of Cress, Pine Nuts, Pears, and
  Chives
Doctored Mesclun Salad

**Sugar Snaps with Extra Virgin Olive Oil
and Shaved Parmigiano (pages 115–119)**

Sugar Snaps, Asparagus, and Baby
  Artichokes with Parmigiano
Mushroom and Squash Carpaccio with
  Pine Nuts, Basil, and Parmigiano
Fennel and Parmigiano Salad with Toasted
  Pecans
Botanical Sliced Pears, Apples, Figs, or
  Persimmons with Parmigiano and
  Balsamic Caramel

*Other vegetables with Parmigiano recipes:*
"Lazy Man's Favas" with Extra Virgin Olive
  Oil and Parmigiano

**Celery Root, Parsnip, and Yellow
Beet Slaw (pages 120–124)**

Creamy Cilantro Slaw
Warm Smoky Cabbage Slaw with
  Cracklings and Croutons
Dandelion, Pea Shoot, and Herb Slaw
Impromptu Cabbage Slaws

*For more hors d'oeuvres, appetizer, soup, and
salad recipes, see:*
Bagna Cauda
Real Onion Dip
Cauliflower Crostini on Shallot Toasts
Cauliflower Soup with Many Garnishes
Porcini-Onion Soup with Grilled Cheese
  Toasts
Onion Tartines
"Lazy Man's Favas" with Extra Virgin Olive
  Oil and Parmigiano

Simple Bruschetta and Crostini
  Improvisations
Smoke-Grilled Bread
Fried Mac-and-Cheese
Sage-and-Garlic Popcorn
Brown Butter Popcorn
Caramelized Shallot Popcorn
Smoky Bacon Popcorn
White Truffle Popcorn
Rosemary Popcorn
Brick-Fried Birds over Salad Greens
Warm Salad of Duck Breasts, Walnuts, Figs,
  and Caramelized Shallots
Tuscan Island–Style Shellfish Stew
Lobster Demitasse with Crème Fraiche and
  Chives
Lobster Essence with Pasta and Wild
  Mushrooms
Shrimp in Olive Oil, Garlic, and Smoked
  Paprika
Curry-Fried Fish or Shrimp
Rabbit Rillettes
Impromptu Rillettes
Faux Pâté Campagne with Pistachios
Crackling Cornmeal Cakes with Sour
  Cream and Shredded Close-Roasted
  Meat
Corn Bread Crostini
French-Fried Cheese Toast
Chive French Toast
Pancetta Tartines
Manchego Crisps
Panfried Ravioli

## Vegetables and Beans

**Post-Modern Fries (pages 126–130)**

Smoky Fries
Rosemary Fries
Parsnip Fries
Parmesan Fries
Pasta "Fries"

Fennel and Parmigiano with Toasted
  Pecans
"Lazy Man's Favas" with Extra Virgin Olive
  Oil and Parmigiano
Dandelion, Pea Shoot, and Herb Slaw
Impromptu Cabbage Slaws
Warm Vegetables with Anchovies,
  Currants, and Pine Nuts
Crispy Shallots
Ramp, Garlic, and Other Oniony Confits
  with Their Flavored Olive Oils

## Fish and Shellfish

### Tuscan Island–Style Shellfish Stew
### (pages 172–177)

Mussels and Fries
Fish Fillets with Fennel Seed, Saffron, and
  Orange Zest
Linguine with (Soft-Shell) Crab Sauce
Clams, Mussels, or Fish Fillets in Green
  Curry and Coconut Milk

### Slow-Roasted Fish with Fragrant
### Fennel Oil (pages 178–184)

Slow-Roasted Fish with Crisp Pancetta and
  Balsamic
Cool Meyer Lemon, Basil, and Olive Oil
  Sauce for Slow-Roasted Fish
Slow-Roasted Cherry Tomato, Olive, and
  Lemon Zest Sauce for Slow-Roasted Fish
Brown Butter and Vinegar Sauce for
  Slow-Roasted Fish
Cold Slow-Roasted Salmon with Creamy
  Curry, Lime, and Basil Sauce

### Salt-Roasted Trout and Other Whole Fish
### (pages 185–190)

Center-Cut Salt-Roasted Salmon and
  Other Large Fish
Salt-Roasted Lobster

Salt-Roasted New Potatoes with Crème
  Fraîche and Cracked Coriander

### Lobster Essence (Rich Lobster Shell Broth)
### (pages 191–195)

Lobster Demitasse with Crème Fraîche
  and Chives
Lobster Essence with Pasta and Wild
  Mushrooms
Striped Bass or Snapper Fillets in Creamy
  Lobster and Wild Mushroom Broth
Lobster Noodles

*Other recipes made with Lobster Essence:*
Lobster Paella

### Shrimp in Olive Oil, Garlic, and Smoked
### Paprika (pages 196–201)

Shrimp with Confited Baby Artichokes
Swordfish Poached in Thyme and
  Shallot Oil
Shrimp in Coconut Milk with Ginger,
  Basil, and Crispy Shallots
Squid Pasta

### Crisp Pan-Fried Fish Fillets
### (pages 202–207)

Tuna or Swordfish with Sesame Seeds,
  Cracked Coriander, and Crispy Ginger
Curry-Fried Fish or Shrimp
Trout Panfried in Dry-Cured Ham Fat or
  Pancetta
Panfried Fish Sandwich with Bacon
  Mayonnaise

*For more fish and shellfish recipes, see:*
Deconstructed Caesar Salad
Lobster Paella
Spaghetti with Garlic, Anchovy,
  and Hot Chile
Squid Pasta
Crab, Shrimp, or Lobster and Corn Bread
  Sandwich

Corn Bread Crostini
Maple Sugar Pecan Cornmeal Cake
Sweet or Savory Crackling Cornmeal
    Cakes
Crab, Shrimp, or Lobster and Corn Bread
    Sandwich

### French-Fried Cheese Toast (pages 266–271)

Chive French Toast
Bittersweet Chocolate French Toast
Jill's Sea-Salted French Toast
French Toast Gratin

### Shallot (or Garlic) Toasts (pages 272–276)

Simple Bruschetta and Crostini
    Improvisations
Pancetta Tartines
Smoke-Grilled Bread
Manchego Toasts


*Other toasted bread-based recipes:*
Onion Tartines
Grilled Cheese Toasts
Cauliflower Crostini on Shallot Toasts
Pepper Bruschetta

### Risotto with Dry Sherry and Lemon (pages 277–282)

Warm Dessert Risotto with Bay Leaf and
    Vanilla
Crispy Panfried Risotto Cakes
Farro Risotto with Red Wine and
    Rosemary
Lobster Paella


*Other risotto-method recipes:*
Lobster Noodles

### Sage-and-Garlic Popcorn (pages 283–287)

Brown Butter Popcorn
Caramelized Shallot Popcorn
Rosemary Popcorn
Smoky Bacon Popcorn
White Truffle Popcorn

### Macaroni and Cheese with Extra Top (pages 288–292)

Saffron Pasta Gratin
Fried Mac-and-Cheese
Unbelievably Rich Manchego Gratin
Frittata di Pasta

### Pasta with Pancetta or Guanciale and Sherry Vinegar (pages 293–298)

Simple Pasta Improvisations
Ravioli with a Handful of Herbs
Panfried Ravioli
Pasta with Baby Artichokes


*Other emulsified pasta sauce recipes:*
Jumbo Shells with Peppers, Pine Nuts, and
    Molten Mozzarella
Linguine with (Soft Shell) Crab Sauce
Squid Pasta


*For more bread, grain, and pasta recipes, see:*
Crackling Cornmeal Cakes with Sour
    Cream and Shredded Close-Roasted
    Meat
Spaghetti with Garlic, Anchovy, and Hot
    Chile
Elemental Carbonara
Linguine with (Soft Shell) Crab Sauce
Jumbo Shells with Peppers, Pine Nuts,
    and Molten Mozzarella
Lobster Noodles
Squid Pasta
Lobster Essence with Pasta and Wild
    Mushrooms
Herb Soup with Tortellini

Sweet or Savory Quinces in White Wine
and Honey
Upside-Down Quince Tart
White Peaches in Red Wine Syrup
Roasted Pears with Parmesan Crisps
Roasted Apples with Cheddar Crisps
Hazelnut-Scented Whipped Cream

Botanical Sliced Pears, Apples, Figs, or
Persimmons with Parmigiano and
Balsamic Caramel
Warm Dessert Risotto with Bay Leaf and
Vanilla
Bittersweet Chocolate French Toast
French Toast Gratin

## Acknowledgments

Woven through *The Improvisational Cook* are the talent and generosity of the many people who helped bring it into being. They make up the community I live in, my great blessing.

The team at HarperCollins made this work a pleasure. Harriet Bell is a dream editor who listened to what the book needed every step of the way and found a way to make it happen. Designer Leah Carlson-Stanisic rose to the many challenges the book posed, improvising solutions to forge her beautiful clear design. Roberto de Vicq de Cumptich designed a lovely jacket that says "improvisation," no mean feat. Production editor Ann Cahn, with Karen Lumley, production manager, handled the complex evolution of the rough manuscript to finished text. Thanks also to Lucy Baker who did me a thousand favors, and to the amazing Judith Sutton for her rigorous reading of the text.

My thanks to Lydia Wills, my fabulous agent, who is the best possible mix of wise and smart, and infuses the business of making books (and everything else) with heart and integrity.

An extraordinary group of women worked together to create the photography that gives a true sense of what improvisation is. Maria Robledo, with whom I have collaborated for twenty odd years, photographs life, food, and people in ways that continually surprise me; this book would not have come into being without her generosity and friendship. Anne Disrude is a truly improvisational cook who has inspired me for years with her original approach to food and life. She created the food for the photographs, foraging fields and markets for the raw ingredients to illustrate cooking's vivid reality and brought her great good sense to both the photographs and the book. Suzanne Shaker, an inspired designer, stylist, and friend, has been knocking me out for years with her vision and style. The images are infused with her magic. Thanks also to Kendra Livingstone and Kristine Foley for lending their many talents to the shoot.

Special thanks to Tom Booth, for opening his home for the photo shoot, and his heart always. And to Stevens Kasselman, who made so many things possible.

Thanks also to Jill Anton, who assisted me in the last leg of testing recipes, for being intrepid, undaunted, game, and creative. And to Christopher Deatherage who created my Web site.

Deep appreciation to Lynn Rosetto Kasper and the staff at American Public Medias The Splendid Table, Universal Press Syndicate, and Barnes and Noble University for giving my work a forum.

Thank you to my incredibly generous friends who were there with love and help of all kinds: Fern Berman and Faith Middleton; Frances Boswell; Speed and Martha Carroll; Mary Ehni and Stephen Frailey; Josh Eisen and Ellen Silverman; Tom Fallon; Carmen Garcia; Vicki Beth Lynn; Eleanor and Kathy Mailloux, Heidi Arnett; Kay Howe, and the amazing people of Helvetia, West Virginia; Peggy Markel; Patrick Rulon-Miller; Lisa Morphew; Bob Ness; Sally-Jo O'Brien and the late dear Bill Levin; The Rowers: Holton, Sofia, Isabel, Mary, Sandy, and Sandra Calder Davidson; Eric Sakas; Wendy Schantzer; Shane Verdi; and Margot Wellington and Albert Sanders.

Very, very special thanks to my mother, Nellie Schneider, whose cooking and way when I was a kid had so much to do with what I do today; and my sister, Susy, who knows how to listen and is so wise. Their support has been essential and nourishing.

The community I live in also includes constitutionally generous cooks, chefs, farmers, restaurateurs, and purveyors whose work is food in all its guises, who love to share their knowledge and treasures. They inspire and hearten me daily. Special thanks to Keith Stewart of Keith's farm for many growing seasons of inspiration; and to Mario Batali, for his openhearted blessing to use his wonderful recipe, all marked up, for a photograph. And to Anthony Giglio and Antonia LoPresti Giglio whose yearly Pomodorata reminds me of what I sometimes forget.

A debt of gratitude to Rose Levy Barenbaum who first used "Understanding" sections in her recipes to teach readers the science of baking. Applied to improvising, they've proven an effective way to convey the inner "logic" of a recipe and its creative possibilities.

And finally, huge, heartfelt thanks to David Saltman, who embraced the book's concepts in his cooking, giving me essential feedback all along the way, as he became an improvisational cook. And for being there, big time.

I am very grateful to the stores and artisans who loaned beautiful plates, bowls, linens, and surfaces for the photographs:

Anichini
www.anichini.com

BDDW
www.bddw.com

Clio
www.clio-home.com

Gordon Foster
www.gordonfoster.com

H. Groome
9 Main Street
Southampton, NY 11968

Joan Platt
1261 Madison Avenue
New York, NY 10028

Juliska
www.juliska.com

Libeco Linen
www.libeco.com

Moss
www.mossonline.com

Neue Galerie
www.neuegalerie.org

Takashimaya
693 Fifth Avenue
New York, NY 10019

Tudor Rose
www.tudorroseantiques.com

tuna with sesame seeds, cracked coriander, and
crispy ginger, 205
turkey, ever-improvisational meat loaf, 246–47
turnovers, warm prune, cherry, or apricot, 317
Tuscan island-style shellfish stew, 174; *illus. 18*


United States, flavor affinities, 351
upside-down quince tart, 72–73


vanilla (bean), 27
    Holton's coffee cookies, 304
    root vegetable puree with, 101
    splitting and scraping, 353
    warm dessert risotto with bay leaf and, 280
vanilla ice cream, warm fresh cherries with
    balsamic caramel and (warm pie fruit), 309
veal shanks:
    impromptu rillettes, 243
    with melting onions and lemon gremolata, 237
vegetable(s):
    braising, for soups, 98
    confits, 50
    with fried egg and Parmigiano, 131–35;
        basic recipe, 133
    for oven fries, 127
    root, *see* root vegetable(s)
    in salads, 116
    salt-roasted, with crème fraîche and cracked
        coriander, 189–90
    simmered in milk, 160
    slaws, *see* slaws
    warm, with anchovies, currants, and pine
        nuts, 58–59
    *see also specific vegetables*
velouté, creamy root vegetable, for chicken
    stews and potpies, 102
venison, wild, roast leg of, 256
vinaigrette, essential, 355
vinegars, 60–64
    balsamic caramel, 64

Banyuls, 24
and brown butter sauces, 183, 204–5
cherry aged cherry, 63
raspberry thyme, 62–63
redux (basic recipe), 62
sherry, and olive oil dressing, 112
sherry, pasta with pancetta or guanciale and,
    295
strawberry balsamic, for desserts, 63
tarragon chive, shallot, and other salad, 64
understanding, 61


walnut(s):
    manchego crisps with greens, figs and, 86
    roasted, and prune confit, 315
    warm salad of duck breasts, figs,
        caramelized shallots and, 230
watercress:
    salad of pine nuts, pears, and chives, 114
    salad-soup with smoked duck breast and
        ginger, 105; *illus. 40*
whipped cream, hazelnut-scented, 158
white truffle popcorn, 287
wine:
    dessert, for cooking, 357
    fruits in, 70–75; basic recipe, 72
    herb-infused "Jell-O," 340
    as poaching liquid, 71
    red, chicken with bacon, mushrooms and,
        222–23
    red, syrup, dried cherries with or without
        grappa in, 316
    in risotto, 278
    root vegetables braised in, 148; basic recipe,
        149
    in shellfish stew, 173
    short ribs Bourguignon, 238
    syrup, white peaches in, 74–75


zest, citrus, 77, 353

*The Library of Congress has cataloged the hardcover edition as follows:*

*Schneider, Sally.*
  *The improvisational cook / Sally Schneider; photographs by Maria Robledo.*
   *p. cm.*
  *ISBN-13: 978-0-06-073164-9*
  *ISBN-10: 0-06-073164-8*
  *1. Cookery. I. Title.*

*TX651.S35 2006*
*641.5—dc22*

                                                                    *2005058352*

*ISBN: 978-0-06-202536-4 (pbk.)*

*11 12 13 14 15 WBC/QG 10 9 8 7 6 5 4 3 2 1*